REGULATORY REFORM OF STOCK AND FUTURES MARKETS

A Special Issue of the Journal of Financial Services Research

edited by

Franklin R. Edwards

Reprinted from the Journal of Financial Services Research

Vol. 3, Nos. 2/3 (1989)

KLUWER ACADEMIC PUBLISHERS
BOSTON/DORDRECHT/LONDON

ISBN 0-7923-9067-9

Distributors for North America:
Kluwer Academic Publishers
101 Philip Drive
Assinippi Park
Norwell, Massachusetts 02061 USA

Distributors for all other countries:
Kluwer Academic Publishers Group
Distribution Centre
Post Office Box 322
3300 AH Dordrecht, THE NETHERLANDS

Printed in the Netherlands

JOURNAL OF FINANCIAL SERVICES RESEARCH
Vol. 3   Nos. 2/3 December   1989

REGULATORY REFORM OF STOCK AND FUTURES MARKETS
A Special Issue of The Journal of Financial Services Research

Journal of Financial Services Research, 3: 99–100 (1989)
© 1989 Kluwer Academic Publishers

Prologue to Conference on Regulatory Reform of Stock and Futures Markets

FRANKLIN R. EDWARDS
Director,
Center for the Study of Futures Markets,
Columbia University
New York, NY 10027

Almost two years after the unprecedented October 1987 crash, we are still haunted by questions about what went wrong. There is a lingering feeling that the financial system, and our securities markets in particular, may be flawed in some fundamental way, but there is no emerging consensus on what that flaw might be.

Stock market volatility has been at the center of this debate. Rising in October 1987 and in subsequent months to levels seldom seen during the history of securities markets, volatility became a lightening rod for critics, synonymous with excessive and destabilizing speculation. In response a number of proposals to reform securities and futures markets have been advanced. Although volatility has declined to more normal levels in recent months, there remains a suspicion that speculative excesses lie just beneath the surface, ready to burst out at any time and destabilize markets.

This concern has been reinforced by the failure of the public to return to equity markets. The volume of trading in equity markets, and in particular by retail customers, is only a fraction of what it was before the crash. The result has been retrenchment in the securities industry coupled with an energetic search for alternative profit opportunities.

Leveraged buyouts have been one of these. Ironically, such takeovers, which have doubled or tripled the stock prices of targeted companies in just days, have only fueled the concern about volatility and speculative excesses. What could account for such a large change in the value of a firm in so short a time, it is asked? Is it simply the trickery of "financial engineering"? The arguments in support of and against leveraged buyouts are complex and subtle. For most investors and legislators they are difficult to evaluate. Prior beliefs, and political and philosophic dispositions, unfortunately, often determine whether these activities are viewed favorably.

Volatility also is frequently seen as a consequence of the spectacular growth of trading both in securities and futures markets. On the New York Stock Exchange more shares were traded during an average *week* in 1987 than were traded during all of 1960. As active as stock trading is, however, it is dwarfed by trading in government bonds and foreign exchange: a daily value of $25 billion and nearly $300 billion, respectively.

In futures markets trading skyrocketed from less than 4 million contracts in 1960 to nearly 250 million contracts in 1988–more trading each *week* in 1988 than in all of 1960. More than half of this remarkable increase is attributable to the innovation and growth of futures trading in financial instruments—government bonds, stock indexes, eurodollar deposits, and foreign currencies.

1

Why has trading in general soared as it has? At least part of the explanation is that markets are more efficient and more liquid than they used to be. The costs of trading have been lowered substantially. Institutions, which currently account for 80 percent of trading on the New York Stock Exchange, now pay less than 5 cents a share in commissions, as opposed to 80 cents a share 20 years ago. Similarly, increased market liquidity, due to the increase in trading volume, has sharply reduced the "execution" costs associated with trading.

Futures and options exchanges, by developing active markets in equity index contracts, have permitted institutions to buy and sell entire "baskets" of stock at only a fraction of the cost of making the same trade in cash equity markets. Stock exchanges, too, are about to introduce their own "basket" instruments, as well as new mechanisms for trading these instruments, which are likely to further reduce trading costs.

Cost-saving innovations have occurred in other financial markets as well. Bond markets, for example, have benefited from active and liquid futures and options markets in bonds, both in the United States and in foreign countries, and from the development and spectacular growth of the "swap" market. Thus, cost-saving, efficiency-enhancing innovations during the last decade have been a major reason for the dramatic increase in the trading of all kinds of financial instruments.

To critics, however, much of this trading seems socially sterile—a zero-sum game played out among speculators with no redeeming social value. In their view such trading does not enhance either the capital-raising or capital allocation functions of securities markets. Indeed, they believe that "excessive" trading makes markets worse by distorting prices and increasing the risk to pure investors (via excessive volatility). Their remedy: reduce trading by eliminating unnecessary and unproductive "noise" traders, which will in turn reduce or eliminate excessive volatility. In short, expunge the speculative mentality which they feel has overwhelmed markets in the 1980s and restore to markets the sanity of the past.

This "throw-sand-in-the-gears" approach takes many forms: new transaction taxes, higher margin regulations, "circuit-breakers," and new market-making regulations to control undesirable trading. The articles in this issue examine the most significant of these proposals. Stiglitz, Summers, and Ross analyze the impact of imposing "transaction taxes" to discourage high-turnover trading strategies; Salinger, Schwert, Hardouvelis, and Kupiec examine whether raising the required margins on stock, options, and futures will discourage speculative trading and stabilize markets; and Ma, Rao, and Sears, along with Miller and Lehmann, discuss whether using "circuit-breakers" to halt trading whenever speculative excesses threaten to overwhelm existing market liquidity can stabilize markets. Finally, Roll, Nelson, and Wadhwani examine the international aspects of the crash. In particular, Roll analyzes whether the severity of the market break in a country was related to the institutional and regulatory structure in that country. While there is a considerable amount of agreement among the authors, this issue nevertheless reveals the existence of sharp disagreements, and points to areas where further research and study is needed.

By sponsoring these articles, The Center for the Study of Futures Markets at Columbia University and the *Journal of Financial Services Research* seek to encourage additional studies of important regulatory issues related to financial markets. Only by objective analyses can we hope to adopt regulatory policies that foster efficient and fair financial markets.

Journal of Financial Services Research, 3: 101–115 (1989)
© 1989 Kluwer Academic Publishers

Using Tax Policy To Curb Speculative Short-Term Trading

JOSEPH E. STIGLITZ
Professor of Economics
Stanford University

This article addresses the question of the desirability of a tax on transactions in the securities industry. Many of the other major industrialized economies impose such a tax. In Japan, for instance, the tax raises $12 billion a year (see Roll, 1989). I propose to consider the consequences of a tax at a relatively low rate, say .5 percent to 1 percent of the value of the transactions.[1]

Underlying my analysis are two presumptions. First, as an economist, I begin with a general suspicion against narrowly based taxes (as opposed to broadly based taxes, such as income taxes). Such taxes frequently introduce unnecessary distortions,[2] and they are often inequitable, since the incidence of the tax is borne by those particular individuals who happen to like the commodity being taxed, or who happen to own shares in the industry producing the commodity being taxed. There are four circumstances under which governments frequently resort to selective taxes: (1) the commodity being taxed has a highly inelastic demand, so that the tax has little distortionary effect; (2) the commodity being taxed is a luxury good, consumed largely by the very rich, and not much weight is accordingly attached to the reduction in its consumption (perfume falls into this category); (3) the commodity being taxed is associated with certain benefits provided by the government (a benefit tax)—gasoline and airport taxes fall within this category; and (4) the commodity being taxed has some socially undesirable characteristics, such as giving rise to a negative externality. Alcohol and cigarette taxes—in spite of their regressive nature—are justified on the grounds of their inelastic demand and the negative social attributes of these commodities. Where gambling is legalized, it is almost always heavily taxed. *Corrective* (or Pigovian) taxes are designed to ameliorate some externality, where there is a deviation between private and social costs and benefits.

The second premise is that well-functioning capital markets play a vital role in modern capitalist economies. It is important that firms be able to raise capital and that risks be spread

This article, prepared for the Conference on Regulatory Reform of Stocks and Futures Markets, given at Columbia University, May 1989, is based in part on earlier research on the effects of capital taxes. Financial support for this research from the Office of Tax Analysis, U.S. Treasury, the National Science Foundation, the Olin Foundation, and the Hoover Institution is gratefully acknowledged. In preparing this article, I have benefited greatly from conversations with Larry Summers, and I have drawn heavily on Summers and Summers (1989) for estimates of tax revenues and other data used in this study. I have also benefited considerably from discussions of the paper during the conference at which it was presented.

3

widely. I suspect that I do not need to preach the virtues of well-functioning capital markets to this reading audience.

One might have thought that from these two premises I would be led naturally to the conclusion that a tax on securities transactions is undesirable. The distortions introduced by such a tax would seem to be far worse than those associated with the selective tax on automobile tires, telephones, or the distortionary impact of the trade restrictions on textiles and shoes. For such a tax interferes with the functioning of the capital markets—an institution at the heart of American capitalism. Yet, I want to try to persuade you that such a tax may actually be beneficial.

The heart of the argument is simple: the turnover tax is likely to discourage short-term speculative trading. Keynes argued quite forcefully that such speculative trading was not only not socially productive but actually interfered with the efficient functioning of the economy. Firms were induced to pay excessive attention to short-term returns rather than long-term concerns. The arguments we put forward are slightly different and are cast in the language of modern welfare economics. But the conclusion is much the same.

The article is divided into three major sections. In the first, I argue that a tax on transactions will not interfere with the major economic functions served by the stock market—and may well enable the market to serve its essential functions more effectively. This argument is predicated on the assumption that a turnover tax does not increase—and may actually reduce—price volatility. Hence in the second section, I explain why a tax on transactions is likely to reduce price volatility. In the third, I take up a few practical problems associated with the implementation of such a tax.

In my description below, I shall focus my attention on stocks, but most of the arguments apply with equal force to other capital markets.

1. The consequences of a turnover tax on economic efficiency

To understand the consequences of a turnover tax on trades on the stock market, we first have to understand why individuals trade and what the economic functions are that the stock market serves.

There are, of course, a variety of reasons for trade. Individuals buy shares during phases of their life cycle when they are saving, and sell during phases of their life cycle when they are dissaving. Changes in economic circumstances may lead individuals to wish to change their portfolios, entailing selling some securities and buying others. But most of the short-term trading in the stock market is motivated by quite different considerations: individuals believe that they can beat the market, either because they are privy to insider information, or at least information that is not widely available, or because they believe that they are better able to interpret the world around them, and thus make predictions concerning the performance of various securities, than are other investors. That is, most trades are based on (the belief of) differential information.

A standard result in economics is that the market system provides incentives that ensure economic efficiency. In this view, then, the fact that private returns seem so high on Wall Street is indicative that there is an important social function being performed. A major thrust of theoretical research in economics during the past half-century has been understanding the conditions under which there is a close congruence between social and private returns. General results (Greenwald and Stiglitz, 1986) show that when informational problems, such as those with which we are concerned here, arise, the market is not in general (constrained Pareto[3]) efficient. The reason for this may be seen intuitively as follows.[4]Assume that as a result of some new information, there will be a large revaluation of some security, say from $10 to $50. Assume that that information will be announced tomorrow in the newspaper. What is the *private* versus *social* return to an individual obtaining the information today? Assume the firm will take no action on the basis of the information—certainly not as a result of knowing the information a day earlier. There is really no social return to the information; production, in every state of nature, in every contingency, is precisely what it would have been had the information not been available. But an individual can buy the stock today, at $10, and make a $40 capital gain. He or she can obtain a four-fold return on his or her investment. Of course, some one else would have obtained the return had he or she not purchased it. The information has only affected who gets to get the return. It does not affect the magnitude of the return. To use the textbook homily, it affects how the pie is divided, but it does not affect the size of the pie.

Stiglitz and Weiss (1988) have shown that not only is the social return to this kind of information gathering—getting information slightly earlier than other investors—less than the private return, but this is even true of many of the financial innovations (like more rapid recording of transactions) that have occurred in the past decade. More precisely, they show that such financial innovations—to the extent that there are any costs associated with them—actually lead the economy to a Pareto inferior equilibrium. Barring these innovations (were this possible) could actually make everyone better off. The intuition behind this result is simple. Imagine a pile of $100 bills lying on the floor, one near each individual. Assume, given the natural lethargy of most individuals, that they all wait two periods to pick up the $100 bill. Now consider what happens if one individual wakes up one morning and says to himself, "All the other people are so slow to pick up their $100 bill. While they are getting themselves organized, I can pick up the $100 bills next to their feet. The extra $100 bill(s) will surely be worth the extra effort I have to put out." But, of course, if he does this, all will respond. In the new equilibrium, all the people rush to pick up the $100 bill near their feet as quickly as they can. In the end, they have exactly the same amount of money as they did before; but now, they have had to exert energy to rush to pick it up. They are unambiguously worse off.

The large deviation between social and private returns means that there are excessive expenditures on gathering information and on financial innovation. Individuals invest to the point where their marginal private return equals the return they could obtain elsewhere, and since their private return is more than the social return, this means that the net marginal social return is negative.

A turnover tax represents a tax on this kind of activity, and thus will serve to promote economic efficiency by discouraging the excessive expenditures on this form of "rent seeking." It can thus be viewed as a special and potentially important case of a Pigovian corrective tax, a tax that improves economic efficiency at the same time that it raises revenues.

5

We now need to ask, are there other serious consequences of such a tax that would impair the ability of the stock market to perform the vital roles that it plays in capitalist economies?

There are three functions commonly ascribed to the stock market, what I shall call (for short) the exchange, the information, and the capital-raising functions. I shall now argue that the most important of these functions may actually be enhanced by a turnover tax, and that none of its important functions are likely to be impaired.

1.1. Exchange

The stock market allows individuals to trade with each other. Traditional texts in economics begin with a discussion of the importance of exchange in economics, with the gains to trade. Just as tariffs impede the exchange of goods among countries, turnover taxes impede the exchange of assets among individuals. One of the three fundamental conditions required for the (Pareto) efficiency of the economy is exchange efficiency (all individuals should have the same marginal rate of substitution); the turnover tax interferes with exchange efficiency.

There are, however, two reasons not to be concerned much about this alleged inefficiency. First, the proposed tax rates are sufficiently small that the deadweight loss from the tax (were this a standard problem in economics) is indeed negligible: the deadweight loss is proportional to the *square* of the tax rate, and hence a tax at the rate of .005 or .01 has a very small deadweight loss.[5]

Second, there are real difficulties in interpreting the welfare losses associated with impeding trades based on *incorrect* expectations. The standard analysis of exchange takes individuals' preferences as given, and does not ask, for instance, why one individual likes oranges and another likes apples. This is as it should be. But individuals do not demand shares in GM or Ford because they have an intrinsic taste for GM shares or Ford shares. Everyone likes dollars. Each wants more dollars. The demand for GM or Ford shares is based on individuals' expectations concerning the returns that these shares will yield. Exchanges are (largely) motivated by differences in judgments concerning what those yields will be. Thus, to evaluate the consequences of the impediments to trade imposed by a turnover tax, we have to take a closer look at who trades.

1.1.1. *A Taxonomy of Traders.* We can divide those who trade in these markets into several different categories. A turnover tax will affect these groups differently.

At one extreme, there is a group of individuals who are basically uninformed. The most sophisticated of these have been persuaded by the random walk (dartboard) theory of securities markets, which holds that an individual can do as well throwing darts at a dartboard as by turning his funds over to a specialist in portfolio allocation; and a fortiori, he is not likely to do better than the market spending a few hours a week gathering information from second-hand sources. These individuals buy indexed mutual funds. They do not try to beat the market; they are content to know that they will do no worse than the market.

At the other extreme are highly informed individuals. They could be insiders, for instance, who know that their oil company has struck it rich and that that information has not yet leaked out. Or it could be the manager of a research division of a drug company who has just seen a report verifying that the company's best-selling drug causes birth defects. We call these the informed traders.

There is a third group of individuals, called noise traders, who may believe that they understand how the stock market works, who may have theories about the connection between sunspots and stock prices, or between some other observable and stock market prices. These are the dentists and doctors in the Midwest and the retired individuals in the Sunbelt, for whom "following" their favorite stocks is a favorite pastime. We should probably include many of the stock market brokers who advise them (and many of the portfolio managers who manage unindexed funds) within this category.

In between are several groups of individuals who, for simplicity, I shall call partially informed. They include those who study the noise traders[6] and base their trading strategy on "leaning against the wind." They try to take out of the market the noise that the noise traders add. They also include those who try to figure out the "true market value"—the fundamentals—and make purchases and sales when there are big deviations from their calculated values. The trouble with this strategy is that even if an outsider could gather the data on the basis of which he or she could make a reliable calculation of true market value, he or she might have to wait a long time to realize a return; in the short run—which may be years—the deviations between the market price and the "true value" that he or she has calculated may increase, not decrease, and the individual may be forced to sell out at a loss before his or her greater wisdom has been recognized by the market.

It is hard to know whether the stock market was overvalued on October 1, 1987, or undervalued on October 30; but there is a consensus that no event happened during the month that wiped out a quarter of the *fundamental* value of American corporations. Whatever position one takes, the overvaluation or undervaluation was a persistent one, one that lasted not for minutes or hours, or even weeks, but months, and perhaps years.[7,8]

1.1.2. How the turnover tax would affect different groups. Now we look at how a transfer tax would affect these various groups. The first group—the uninformed—and the truly informed are hardly likely to be affected by a tax at the moderate rates being discussed—less than 1 percent. The uninformed buy securities in diversified portfolios, holding onto them as a form of savings for extended periods of time. If bonds and stocks are treated symmetrically, such a tax would have little effect on either total savings or its allocation. By the same token, the kinds of events that form the basis of insider trading are of sufficient moment that a 1 percent tax is not likely to discourage the trading. Similarly, those who based their trading on fundamentals—who buy stocks when prices differ from fundamentals and are willing to wait for the long term to realize their returns—are also unlikely to have their behavior greatly affected. The 1 percent represents a small fraction of the returns that they must expect before they undertake the risks associated with such an investment strategy.

The turnover tax primarily affects short-term speculators, those who buy and sell within the trading day, and within days or weeks. For these, such a tax may represent a significant fraction of the returns they hope to achieve on each transaction. These short-term traders

7

consist of two groups: noise traders and those who live off them.

Those who do not simply buy the market (or an index fund) are betting that they can do better than the market, and that the extra return more than compensates them for the extra risk and extra costs (for instance, in information gathering) that such a strategy entails. The kind of trade that a turnover tax would discourage is based on the mistaken belief of (all!) speculators that they could do better than average. Inevitably, some individuals will have to be disappointed: half must have done worse than average.[9] Impeding trade is (Pareto) inefficient when viewed from the perspective of their ex ante expectations; impeding trade may actually improve welfare when viewed from the perspective of their ex post realizations. The result is similar to that of the father who forces his son to go to school against his will and who later asks him, "Are you better off as a result?" From an ex ante perspective, such coercion must be welfare-reducing. The child's ex ante expected utility is lower than it otherwise would have been, say, if he had spent the day playing. Ex post, the child *agrees* that he is better off.

As a society, there is a general consensus—reflected in a variety of laws and regulations—that there may be gains, rather than losses, from taxing or prohibiting gambling. Since the *short-term* speculative activity—the activities that will bear the brunt of the tax—consist largely of noise traders and those trying to smooth out the market, to make money from the noise traders, there may actually be a welfare gain from impeding these exchanges; in any case, there is not likely to be a significant welfare loss.

One objection arises to this analysis: some might deny the existence, or at least importance, of noise traders. The contention is that such traders would lose money and therefore be weeded out by the market. But this conclusion is wrong. It forgets the famous proposition, attributed, I think, to the great G. T. Barnum: a fool is born every moment. For every fool that is weeded out, a new one enters the market. In spite of the overwhelming evidence of the difficulty of beating the market, small investors continue trying to do it.

The attempt itself is based on the basic proposition that there must be fools in the market. For if any individual does better than the market, it must mean that someone else is, as we have said, doing worse. An individual can guarantee himself the market by buying the market. Thus, to try to beat the market, one must undertake a greater risk—a chance of doing worse; and since rationality would dictate that on average the return will be average, there is no return to compensate for this risk. It is only because each individual believes that he or she is smarter than the other speculators—a proposition that cannot be "rationally" held by all—that the market survives at all.[10]

This kind of irrationality is pervasive. Three-fourths of my students believe that they are in the top half of the class. More generally, we are not good statisticians. There is the famous story of the firm that, in the days before modern medical technology made it possible to predict the sex of a child, nonetheless claimed the ability to do so and promised a money-back guarantee. It made a profit: it always predicted male, and had to return its money only half the time. Individuals are always enticed by the stories of those who have done better than the market—not recognizing that for every such story, there is a closet speculator who has done worse. Individuals who do better than the market always claim it was insight; those who do worse say it was bad luck.

Americans love to gamble, and the stock market—while it serves other important social functions—is our largest gambling casino. It is such a popular gambling casino precisely because the winners can tell stories of their insights and theories—theories which, when subjected to the test of scientific verification (can they be used in a predictive manner?)—inevitably fail. Of course, gamblers in Las Vegas and Atlantic City tell stories of their "feel for the dice," their intuition for how things were going to turn out; but somehow, those stories connecting winning with the individual's own merits have a more hollow ring than the claims put forward by the successful stock speculator.

1.2. Information

One of the alleged roles of the stock market is that the prices established on the stock market are used to signal the expected returns to different kinds of investments. The stock market provides a mechanism by which information is aggregated—the diverse information of the many different individuals in society is all brought to bear in determining the market value—and transferred, from the informed to the uninformed individuals (Grossman and Stiglitz, 1976, 1980).

The stock market does this aggregation and transferring of information far more quickly and effectively than could be done by alternative methods. Could one imagine the deliberations of a committee assigned the task of determining the value of a stock on the basis of the information each has available?[11]

Tobin and others have developed theories in which these prices play a central role in the allocation of investment. When stock prices are high, firms know to invest more. While empirical work has provided, at best, weak support to this hypothesis, more recent work (Greenwald and Stiglitz 1988a) has cast doubt about the interpretation of what empirical support has been found and has argued that prices in the stock market play no basic informational role in the economy.

The fundamental question can be put simply: does one really believe that the managers of GM or Ford base their decisions about whether or how to invest on the prices that they see on the stock market? Do they think that those prices—reflecting judgments of the dentists in Peoria and the retired insurance salesmen in Florida—have much, if anything, to add to the analysis of their own market research departments and the reports from their engineers concerning costs of various projects? Any manager who argued that *because* the price of his stock was high it was therefore a good idea to invest more would, I suspect, quickly find himself looking for another job.

Moreover, the information revealed by the stock market price is not precise enough to be of much use to most firms. It does the firm little good to know that there is *some* investment project that the market thinks of value. Most investment does not consist of a firm simply expanding its scale of production. The firm must make myriad decisions concerning which of a multitude of possible projects to undertake. Each of these projects has to be evaluated separately. The stock market price simply plays no major role in this process of project evaluation.

In addition, much of the efforts of those gathering information are directed at obtaining

9

information that cannot plausibly be of much relevance to firms in their investment decisions, even if it were perfectly reflected in stock market prices. As Summers and Summers (1989) put it,

> It is hard to believe ... that investments made with a horizon of hours reveal much socially beneficial information to the market place (p. 16).

One circumstance does exist in which the stock market price will affect the level of investment—when the firm actually decides to raise additional funds from the stock market. But relatively, little investment is financed that way. In the next subsection, we shall argue that a transfer tax may actually enhance the efficiency with which funds raised on the stock market are allocated.

Thus, while it *may* be true that prices reflect information (even all information) of the participants in the market, that fact in itself does not mean that that information plays an important role in how investment decisions get made and resources get allocated.

Let me be quite clear about what I am arguing: I am not contending that the stock market price is irrelevant. Firms worry about how their actions affect the stock market price. (Managers who own stock market options may be particularly concerned about this.[12]) But managers do not glean information about what machines to buy or where to build a new plant—the information they need for making intelligent investment decisions—from looking at market prices.[13] The fact that stock market prices and investment decisions may be correlated may simply reflect the fact that managers and the market are responding to some of the same signals concerning the firm's prospects.

1.3. Raising capital

The third function that the security markets perform I have just alluded to: they help firms raise new capital. There is an important link between this third function and the first, the exchange function. Individuals are willing to buy shares in a firm because they are marketable, because the individual can sell them, at relatively low cost, should it turn out that he or she needs the cash for any purpose. Interfering with the exchange function thus might interfere with the ability of the market to perform its capital-raising function.

Of the three functions, it is only this last function to which I attach some limited importance. I do not think it would be greatly impeded by a small transfer tax; to some extent, I think it would be enhanced, for reasons I will explain below.

In the next section, I will argue that a tax on turnover may reduce stock market volatility. I see a distinct advantage arising from a reduction in volatility. For, to the extent that volatility would be reduced, the buyer of the security bears less risk concerning the price he or she will receive when he or she sells it. Thus, reducing the volatility will make it easier for firms to raise equity capital.[14]

Reducing volatility will also increase the efficiency with which capital is allocated. The one time that firms find it attractive to issue new shares is when the market has overvalued their shares. In that case, firms do more investment than is "socially" desirable, simply because they are obtaining funds at a lower rate, because of the unreasonable expectations of noise traders. This is one of the reasons why high volatility is undesirable: it makes this kind of misallocation of investment more likely.

If one thinks, as I do, that the most important function (from the social view) of the stock market is raising new equity, one cannot but be struck by how, under current circumstances, it seems to do so little of this at such great cost. As I noted earlier, only a small fraction of investment is financed by new issues on the stock market. In spite of the huge improvements in efficiency in the financial sector, the costs of running the financial sector are huge. Summers and Summers note that these costs, which can be viewed as part of the transactions costs of running the capitalist economy, amounted in 1987 to 16 percent of the *profits* of the corporate sector; a more inclusive measure of the costs brings them up to a quarter of corporate income and half of corporate net investment—and a multiple of the value of *new* funds raised in the stock market. Of course, most of these resources are not spent in raising new funds but in rearranging ownership claims on society's resources. They are a part of the quest for rents. They affect who gets the returns to society's productive assets, not which investments get made. Resources devoted to gambling—and to short-term speculation in the stock market—could be devoted to more productive uses. (I include in these relatively unproductive use of resources not only the transactions costs but also much of the costs spent on acquiring information, including the extra costs of getting the information slightly earlier than it would otherwise become available.) As an educator, I must convey to you my sense of disappointment as some of my best students decide to devote their lives to the quest for rents rather than to trying to increase society's productive potential. Though I am not confident that a turnover tax of 1/2 or 1 percent is likely to have a significant effect in this direction, it will help at the margin.

There is another argument sometimes put forth as to why a turnover tax may enhance the efficiency of the economy. A turnover tax is largely a tax on short-term speculation. As a percentage of long-run returns, a 1 percent turnover tax becomes negligible. If an investor is contemplating making an investment for 20 years, with a 7 percent return per year, a 1 percent turnover tax will reduce his or her return over the interim by only 1/2 percent. If the proportion of investors in the market that are long term is increased, then presumably the attention of firms will be directed toward the long term. There has been a concern that the focus on short-term returns has forced managers to focus on short-term profits, possibly to the detriment of long-run profitability.[15] Thus, this reorientation of managerial focus may provide another reason why a turnover tax may have some beneficial effects.

While I have focused my attention in this section on the stock market, similar arguments apply to bond markets, with perhaps even greater force. For the main determinant of future bonds prices are future interest rates. The task of speculators is thus to forecast the policy of the Federal Reserve Board. Here, I must confess a professional weakness: I simply do not believe that the dentist in Peoria—or his stock broker—can do a better job of predicting those policy changes than the major econometric models. I cannot but believe that whatever he bases his guesses on, they can only be thought of as adding noise to the market. And if it were desirable that information about future Federal Reserve policies be made public, then wouldn't it make more sense for the Fed to announce that information, rather than having others try to second-guess the Fed?

2. Price determination and price volatility

Prices on the stock market—as in other competitive markets—are determined by the intersection of demand and supply. But the demand and supply of assets, such as stocks, differ from that for commodities like wheat because their principal determinant is individuals' expectations about what those assets can be sold for at some date in the future. They are based, in other words, on expectations, and these expectations can obviously change dramatically in short periods of time. That is why prices on stock markets can be so volatile.

Some critics of turnover taxes have expressed a concern that such taxes would result in thinner markets, leading to greater volatility and less liquidity. In this section, I explain why I am not persuaded by those objections, and indeed, it seems quite plausible that such a tax may actually reduce price volatility.

The analysis of this section is divided into three parts. First, I explain why while a turnover tax is likely to lead to thinner markets, it is not likely to lead to significantly larger spreads between buying and selling prices. It may actually lead to smaller spreads. Second, I argue that among those who find it no longer profitable to trade are a disproportionate number of individuals who contribute to market volatility; as a result, the thinner markets, instead of leading to increased price volatility, may well result in reduced volatility.

2.1. A turnover tax leads to thinner markets but not necessarily larger spreads

A tax on turnover is likely to discourage some individuals who otherwise have traded in the market from doing so. It will discourage sellers as well as buyers. If its effects were symmetric, it would simply make the market thinner.

Thinner markets have a bigger spread between buying and selling prices, and in that sense are less liquid. The usual argument for this is simple: buyers and sellers do not in general arrive in the market at the same time. With thinner markets, it may take a longer time for, say, a seller to be matched up with a buyer. Market makers make the market by buying from the seller, then holding the security in inventory until the buyer arrives. The market makers need to be compensated for performing this function (both for the capital which is tied up and the risks which are borne). Such a transfer tax thus has not only a direct effect in increasing the spread between buying and selling price but an indirect effect as well. For widely traded stocks, on both theoretical and empirical grounds, it is hard to believe that this effect would be significant. The extra "carrying" time is probably minutes, perhaps even seconds, and it is hard to see—if markets work reasonably well—how this effect could be significant.

2.2. Why a turnover tax may reduce volatility

In the previous section, we placed investors into four different categories, and argued that a turnover tax would serve to discourage primarily noise traders and those who live off them.

12

Since these traders add to the noise of the market, discouraging them will lead to less volatile markets.

One objection to this argument is that, while it may discourage noise traders (who, as their cumulative after tax losses will appear larger, will drop out of the market more rapidly, and who, aware of the tax, will engage in trades only when they are confident of larger returns), it also discourages those who live off the noise traders, the *arbitrageurs* who stabilize the market in the short term. Isn't it possible that these individuals are discouraged even more than the noise traders? And, in that case, couldn't the market be even more volatile? There is such a possibility, but theoretical arguments and empirical evidence suggest that we should not give too much weight to that possibility.

Assume, on the one hand, that these arbitrageurs were doing a good job, and that as a result, in spite of the noise traders, prices were following their "true" values. Now, there is a tax, which makes it unattractive for them to buy or sell the stock unless the price deviates more than 1 percent from its true value. Then it is possible that there may be more volatility—within this 1 percent window of true value—but relative to the magnitude of volatility that we observe, this would seem to be truly a second order effect. It is also possible that the market would be less volatile, since prices will not adjust to reflect small changes in true values.

We can establish two general propositions. First, if an individual decides to switch from one security into another, the transfer tax will not affect the timing of the switch.[16] Second, the deviations from true market value cannot be greater on average than the magnitude of the tax. Since the size of the proposed taxes is small, the maximum increase in volatility is negligible. The argument establishing the upper bound on the increase in volatility makes it clear that the normal expectation is that there will be a significant reduction in volatility, as noise traders drop out of the market.[17]

The empirical evidence supports the hypothesis that such a tax would not likely increase volatility and might well reduce it. The effect of transactions costs are similar to those of a turnover tax. They represent a wedge between the buying and selling price. The past two decades have seen marked changes in transactions costs. While many other changes have also occurred, there is little evidence to suggest that markets are *less* volatile now than they were two decades ago. Recent experience provides strong suggestions to the contrary.

Closing a market can be viewed as an extreme case of a prohibitive tax. Does closing the market for a day lead to more or less variability in stock prices? If the market was basically tracking changes in fundamentals, the difference between the opening price on Thursday morning and the closing price on Tuesday night should be unaffected by the closing the market on a Wednesday. If much of the volatility in the market is contributed by noise traders, then closing the market on Wednesday will have reduced their opportunities to add noise to the market (some of which, admittedly, will have been removed by the arbitrageurs making money off them, but they will not have fully done their job). In this view, then, the deviation of the market price on Thursday morning from the close on Tuesday will be smaller if the market is closed on Wednesday. French and Roll (1987) provide convincing evidence that during the period in 1968 when the market was closed on Wednesday (because of the inability of the back rooms to keep up with the increasing volume of trade), volatility was greatly reduced—by a factor of 1/2![18]

13

Indeed, there are other theoretical arguments to suggest that short-term trading contributes little to price stability. The objective in short-term trading is to obtain information before others do. Information obtained more quickly is likely to be noisier. Assume, for instance, that there is a weekly shift in a fundamental variable describing a security. The value of this fundamental variable becomes publicly available at 2:00 pm on Friday. Individuals speculate all week long about what that value is. As Friday approaches, their information becomes better. The rush to get information about the value on Friday will result in statistics on Monday that are quite noisy estimators of Friday's value; but, of course, Monday's price will (in a well-functioning market) fully reflect that information.

If firms had to take actions on Tuesday morning and had to rely on the stock market value for taking those actions, then there would be some value in having this "early" information, as noisy as it is. But I argued in the previous section that early information is of little or any productive value. Indeed, to the extent that it contributes to price volatility, it will have negative effects on the economy, as I suggested above.

3. Implementing a turnover tax

A turnover tax has some distinct advantages relative to other capital taxes, particularly to capital gains taxes. The capital gains tax distorts individuals' holding periods, while the fundamental result established in section 2 is that, for those who still find it profitable to trade, the turnover tax will lead them to trade at the same time that they otherwise would have traded.

Moreover, the turnover tax has the property of (on average) automatically phasing itself out for long-term investments; that is, as a proportion of returns, it becomes negligible as the holding period increases. Thus, it will not have a significant affect on long-term investors. Its major impact will be on short-term noise traders and those who live off them.

The turnover tax has two other advantages over a capital gains tax. First, it avoids the arbitrage opportunities inherent in a capital gains tax that allows even limited loss deductability (see Stiglitz, 1983). Second, since a tax with loss deductability subsidizes losers while taxing winners, it effectively subsidizes noise traders (who, it will be recalled, on average lose money), and it taxes arbitrageurs. This differential effect may accordingly lead to increased price volatility.

There is one difficult problem in implementing such a tax, which is how to treat equitably and efficiently different categories of assets. A turnover tax on the stock market would simply encourage speculation to move to the options market. A turnover tax on the options market, based on the value of the option, would have a similar effect. Buying a call option and selling a put is equivalent to buying the share; thus, to avoid distortions, this combined transaction must face the same tax. Accordingly, to avoid a distortion, the tax imposed on the options market must be based on the striking price. (A tax at half the rate imposed on the stock, imposed on each, the call option and the put, would be roughly neutral.) But the tax would then be a large proportion of the value of the transaction. Since I am not sure that much harm—and some good—could result from discouraging the kind of short-term speculation that predominates in these markets, this does not bother me too much, but I suspect that it would generate considerable opposition.

14

Let me mention briefly one other concern. The tax reduces the return on savings and, critics charge, this will reduce savings. There is little evidence of a large elasticity of supply of savings, and hence one would not have thought that a 1 percent tax would have a significant effect on funds put away for 10 or 20 years. If, however, one decided that this was a concern, one could easily allow for a phasing down of the tax rate for investments held over several years.

4. Concluding remarks

No institution in our capitalist society is as venerable as the stock market. A turnover tax might seem, at first glance, to be an attack on this foundation of our economy. I have tried to argue that such a tax is likely to increase the overall efficiency of the economy and may actually enhance the efficiency with which the stock market performs its most important roles. The fact that at the same time it raises revenues—reducing the size of the national deficit—is but one additional benefit of a tax which, on its own merits, seems desirable.

Notes

1. Other taxes, such as capital gains tax, would have quite similar effects. I argue below (section III) that a turnover tax has some distinct advantages over a capital gains tax. For most of the analysis, I shall consider a flat rate tax, with the rate of taxation not depending on the holding period. The consequences of alternative provisions are discussed briefly in section III.

2. It used to be thought that because such taxes introduce *additional* distortions, they were therefore inefficient. Since Ramsey's classic 1927 article, it has been recognized that such an argument is false: one cannot simply count the number of distortions. Two little distortions could, in principle, be preferable to one large distortion. Atkinson and Stiglitz (1976) have shown, however, that in at least one central case, the general presumption against selective commodity taxes remains valid. For a more general exposition, see Atkinson and Stiglitz (1980).

3. An economy is Pareto efficient if no one can be made better off without making someone else worse off. The term *constrained Pareto efficiency* is employed simply to remind us that in evaluating whether a government policy would constitute a Pareto improvement, we need to take into account the constraints facing the private sector in particular, the fact that information is imperfect and costly to obtain.

4. This version of the argument was set forth—considerably earlier than the general theorem—by Hirschleifer (1971) and Stiglitz (1971).

5. One might argue that a turnover tax of even .5 percent represents a substantial fraction of the expected return for a short-term investment. But this is an inappropriate way to view the distortion. The question is, how different can the marginal rates of substitution between two assets between two individuals be without trade occurring? If their relative valuations of two assets differed by more than 1 percent, it would pay them to trade.

6. These are the judges in Keynes' famous beauty contest, whose objective was not to decide who was the most beautiful contestant but who the other judges were likely to think was the most beautiful.

7. There is, in theory, the possibility of a fifth group, those who turn to the stock market to hedge against certain risks that they face. In the futures market, these hedgers are an important class of participants, but they do not appear to be important in the stock market. Workers in the automobile industry do not sell short automobile stocks to hedge against the risks of being unemployed; on the contrary, their pension funds tend to be disproportionately weighted toward risks that are correlated with their employment risks. (In some cases, there may be good institutional reasons, such as preferential tax treatment, for these portfolio decisions.) In any case, however, the market provides little information concerning the correlation of specific securities with particular categories of risk; the only

correlation that is conventionally provided is with the market as a whole. This suggests that few investors find such information of value in making their portfolio decisions.

8. It is worth noting that even the return of the fully informed depends on the existence of the noise traders; if all individuals were of the first type, and simply purchased the market, the truly informed would affect market prices but would not be able to reap returns.

9. This would only be correct if the distribution of gains and losses were symmetric. More realistically, the stock market is like a lottery: many individuals lose a little, and a few gain a lot. If this is true, then more than half of the individuals are disappointed.

10. This proposition was originally asserted in Stiglitz (1971), and more formally stated and proved in Stiglitz (1982a). More formal proofs are provided by Milgrom and Stokey and by Tirole.

11. While we showed precisely how markets perform their role of aggregating and transferring information, we also showed that as long as information was costly, capital markets would never be efficient, that is, not all the information would be conveyed from the informed to the uninformed. Gale and Stiglitz (1985) and Jordon also show that it is only under highly special conditions that markets perfectly aggregate information, that is, that one can infer from the market price, say, all the relevant information of the participants in the market.

12. Indeed, the fact that they are particularly concerned about the short-run movements in the stock market has long been a criticism of managerial compensation schemes that relate pay to performance in the near term, rather than in the more distant future.

13. Moreover, given the kinds of criteria conventionally employed in undertaking an investment project, a small revision in market value would virtually never affect whether a project was undertaken. Given that, what value can there be to having information that would revise that value one minute earlier?

14. Greenwald and Stiglitz (1987a, 1987b, 1988) have argued, in turn, that making it easier to raise equity will have important benefits in ameliorating business cycles; they attribute much of the cyclical fluctuations to the inability of firms to divest themselves of the risks they face.

15. Dramatic evidence of this is provided by firms that failed to take advantage of accelerated depreciation, LIFO accounting, and other tax provisions that reduced reported income while reducing the present discounted value of tax payments.

16. The argument is simple. Assume the expected instantaneous return on security i at time t is $r_i(t)$, and let

$$R_i(v, T) = Tr_i(\tau)d\tau.$$

Then the total return from holding security 1 from 0 to t, and security 2 from t to T is

$$(1 - \gamma)^2 \exp R_1(0,t) \exp R_2(t, T),$$

where γ is the turnover tax rate. The value of t at which this is maximized is independent of γ.

17. Consider a 1 percent tax. If, in an average period, the maximum deviation was more than 1 percent greater than it had previously been, any arbitrageur who previously found it profitable to speculate would still find it profitable to do so. Hence, the supply of arbitrage services would remain unchanged. Yet the need for arbitrage services is reduced, since the return to noise traders after tax is lower (more negative.)

18. There is a vast recent literature providing empirical support to the argument that stock prices do not track fundamental values well, and that there is the kind of noise in prices consistent with a theory that ascribes importance to noise traders. See, for instance, Shiller (1981).

References

Atkinson, A.B. and Stiglitz, J.E. "The Design of Tax Systems." *Journal of Public Economics,* 1976.
————. *Lectures in Public Economics.* New York: McGraw Hill, 1980.
Black, Fischer. "Noise." *Journal of Finance* (1986), 529–543.
DeLong, J. Bradford, Shleifer, Andrei, Summers, Lawrence H., and Robert J. Waldmann." Noise Trader Risk in Financial Markets." Mimeo, October 1988.

————. "The Size and Incidence of the Losses from Noise Trading." NBER Discussion Paper, March 1989.

Edwards, Franklin R. "Policies to Curb Stock Market Volatility." Center for the Study of Futures Markets, Columbia University, Working Paper 176, August 1988.

French, Kenneth and Roll, Richard. "Stock Return Variances: The Arrival of Information and the Reaction of Traders." *Journal of Financial Economics* (1987), 5–26.

Gale, I. and Stiglitz, J.E. "Futures Markets Are Almost Always Informationally Inefficient." Princeton University Financial Research Center Memorandum No. 57, February 1985.

Greenwald, B. and Stiglitz, J.E. "Externalities in Economies with Imperfect Information and Incomplete Markets." Quarterly Journal of Economics (May 1986), 229–264.

Greenwald, B. and Stiglitz, J.E. "Imperfect Information, Credit Markets and Unemployment." *European Economic Review* 31 (1987a), 444–456.

————. "Keynesian, New Keynesian and New Classical Economics." *Oxford Economic Papers* 39 (1987b), 119–133.

————. "Examining Alternative Macroeconomic Theories," Brookings Papers on Economic Activity No. 1, 207–270.

————. "Information, Finance Constraints and Business Fluctuations." In: Meir Kohn and S.C. Tsiang, eds., *Finance Constraints, Expectations and Macroeconomics.* Oxford: Oxford University Press, 1988b, pp. 103–140.

Grossman, S. and Stiglitz, J.E. "Information and Competitive Price Systems." *American Economic Review* 66 (May 1976), 246–253.

————. "On the Impossibility of Informationally Efficient Markets." *American Economic Review* 70 (June 1980), 393–408.

Hirschliefer, J. "The Private and Social Value of Information and the Reward to Incentive Activity." *American Economic Review* (September 1971), 561–574.

Jensen, Michael C. "Symposium on Some Anomalous Evidence Regarding Market Efficiency." *Journal of Financial Economics* 6 (June/September 1978), 95–101.

Jordan, J.S. "On the Efficient Markets Hypothesis." Econometrica 51(1983), 1325–1343.

Keynes, J.M. *The General Theory of Employment, Interest, and Money.* London: Macmillan, 1936.

Milgrom, Paul and Stokey, Nancy. "Information, Trade, and Common Knowledge." *Journal of Economic Theory* 26 (1982), 17–27.

Ramsey, F.P. "A Contribution to the theory of Taxation." *Economic Journal* (1927), 47–61.

Roll, R., [paper presented at this conference]

Shiller, Robert J. "Do Stock Prices Move Too Much To Be Justified by Subsequent Changes in Dividends?" *AER* 71 (June 1981), 421–436.

Stiglitz, J.E. "Perfect and Imperfect Capital Markets." Paper presented to Econometric Society Meetings, New Orleans, December 1971.

————. "Information and Capital Markets." In: William F. Sharpe and Cathryn Cootner, eds., *Financial Economics: Essays in Honor of Paul Cootner.* Englewood Cliffs, NJ: Prentice Hall, 1982a, pp. 118–158.

————. "Some Aspects of the Taxation of Capital Gains." *Journal of Public Economics* 21 (July 1983), 257–294.

Stiglitz, J.E. and Weiss, A. "Banks as Social Accountants and Screening Devices for the Allocation of Credit." NBER working paper no. 2710, September 1988.

————. *Economics of the Public Sector.* New York: W.W. Norton Publishers, 1986; 2d ed., 1988.

Summers, L.H. and Summers, V.P. "When Financial Markets Work Too Well: A Cautious Case for a Securities Transactions Tax." Paper presented to the Annenberg Conference on Technology and Financial Markets, Washington, D.C., February 28, 1989.

Tirole, J. "On the Possibility of Speculation Under Rational Expectations." *Econometrica* 50 (September 1982), 1163–1181.

Journal of Financial Services Research, 3: 117–120 (1989)

Commentary: *Using Tax Policy To Curb Speculative Short-Term Trading*

STEPHEN A. ROSS
Sterling Professor of Economics and Finance
Yale School of Management
Yale University
New Haven, CT 06520

Professor Stiglitz doesn't seem to have much use for stock markets. He seems to think that they are legalized casinos, and whatever uses they might have for the discovery and display of information and the allocation of ownership claims shouldn't mislead us into recognizing sin for what it is. Like cigarette smoking and other forms of substance abuse, if society doesn't have the courage to ban it outright, the least it can do is tax it. Hence the transfer tax.

If this viewpoint seems mean-spirited, it is not my intent. But, to paraphrase Joseph Bishop, Professor Stiglitz's views on these matters are to me what the buffalo were to the Sioux. Make no mistake, despite the trappings of science, this article is a political tract in the tradition of Irving Fisher writing on the war and not on interest rates. It is devoid of the usual analysis of tax incidence or of suggestions for how one might compute such a tax. Instead we are treated to the policy implications of the latest—and still warm—theories of how the stock markets, work together with a heavy dose of just plain opinion. The article is wholly theoretical—even "speculative" in nature. The only numbers I found were that the transfer tax raises $12 billion annually in Japan and that it will "probably be less than 1 percent."

The tentative conceptual underpinnings of financial markets now being proposed as financial theory groups traders into four classifications: uninformed traders, noise traders, very informed, and partially informed. The class of uninformed traders includes the multibillion dollar pension funds who, in their supposed ignorance of the financial markets, simply index their portfolios. The very informed traders are those cunning speculators who watch all the relevant information and statistics, including such esoterica as the current price, and make sophisticated and, presumably, correct investment judgements. In between these two groups we have the partially informed who, while not smart enough to make the right inferences from the information they possess, are nonetheless wary enough to recognize that they are sheep among the wolves and will flock to trade when at their least disadvantaged.

Making all of this theoretical soup possible are the noise traders whose trading is motivated by a variety of rationales, but not by the desire to reap any return. Equivalently,

I am grateful to Richard Roll and John Ingersoll and Joe Stiglitz for their helpful comments. The opinions expressed are entirely my own.

there are those who may well wish to make money but are so stupid or ill-informed that their trading might as well be just noise. I suppose we have all met examples of such folk at one time or another, but we should note in passing that we do not generally think of them as social classes in the same way as the usual dichotomy into the "haves" and the "have nots" that is the staple of most taxation analysis.

Nevertheless, these are the groups for whom Professor Stiglitz assesses the impact of a transfer tax. Apparently, such a tax will have "little" effect on the uninformed because it will be a "little" tax. This is a common analytical theme of the article, i.e., little taxes have little effects. To be specific, little taxes have little social costs. The same diminutive is seldom applied to the benefits. The tax will, however, have a big effect on short-term traders, those who buy and sell in a day. That is presumably all right, though, because these folks are, after all, the source of the excess volatility that the tax is designed to curb in the first place.

Unfortunately for this analysis, there is not any consensus on what the term *excess volatility* means or on whether it is present in the market, whatever it means, or, for that matter, on exactly what social costs volatility might have. Nor, as a counterargument, are we given any sense of what impact such a tax might have on the monopoly concentration of power in a stock market where inventory holdings become more important for providing liquidity when short-term traders are discouraged.

Whenever questions of volatility arise, advocates of excess volatility point to the crash of '87 with what I have come to regard as an unseemly fondness. The real point, however, is not whether that was a manifestation of excessive volatility, but rather what a transfer tax would have done to prevent it. After all, markets with transfer taxes also experienced the crash of '87 (see the article by Roll).

At this stage in his argument, a hint of paternalism surfaces. We are told that people are terrible statisticians and, I suppose, must be protected from themselves. Like short-term traders, three-fourths of Professor Stiglitz' students think they are in the top one-half of the class. This prepares us to view the stock market as a zero-sum game—a casino—and is used to justify the view that we should act to protect these innocents from themselves as well as to protect the rest of us from them.

This is an appealing argument, particularly for the highly intelligent people who tend to make it and variants of it, to provide the underpinning rationale for much of the rise in consumer protection legislation. Whatever its merits in the market for automobiles, the extension of such reasoning to the stock market is far too casual to be useful. For example, 100 percent of the people crossing the street think that they will make it, and, I suspect, all of them place too low a probability on the possibility that they will not. Professor Stiglitz's logic would have us tax people for crossing the street to keep them from overindulging in such activity. It is, of course, well known that wanton street-crossing leads to an excess of people in motion on our city streets, and it is equally self-evident that such activity is zero-sum and should be discouraged. After all, it makes no difference which side of the street you are on any more that it matters whether you own GM or GE stock.

All of this presumes, of course, that a transfer tax will actually lower daily volatility, but it is not at all clear that discouraging folks who trade on supposedly spurious trading rules will, in fact, lower price volatility. Suppose such traders believe in the same mean-reversion as those whose evidence for excess volatility Professor Stiglitz cites. Then it is entirely possible their trading will be a stabilizing influence and that discouraging them could increase volatility. Anticipating this point, Professor Stiglitz assures us that the impact on corrective trading will be "small," an assertion that I find to be of "small" comfort.

It is also a misreading of the empirical volatility literature to think that discouraging trading lowers volatility. What the evidence seems to suggest is that if trading is suppressed in some period, it will reappear in another period, and the same seems true of volatility. Volatility is transferred, not lost, and a transfer tax might achieve exactly that result. A tax on stock transfers would then shift activity to other markets where transfer taxes are much more difficult to impose.

As additional support for a transfer tax, Professor Stiglitz invokes the argument that there is a wedge between the social value of information and the private value. Presumably, the private value of knowing something a fraction of a second before anyone else is greater than the social benefit to having that information revealed. He argues that a transfer tax will discourage trading on such information and the wasteful rent-seeking behavior that occurs when there is such a disparity. The logic of this seems a bit shaky. It is the expected gain from information that matters, not the actual gain that can be realized on information, and the expected gain is a product of the information and the probability of acquiring it. The latter can be quite small, and the expected-value of information acquisition can be small. Nor does it seem likely that a small transfer tax will discourage insiders from trading on such information.

The net effect, then, will be only to discourage a particular type of trader, namely, traders whose activities provide liquidity for the market. But these short-term speculators can be ignored since they don't really know what is good for them. In fact, they should thank us for taxing them out of existence.

In fairness, on the cost side, Professor Stiglitz lists a set of potential costs from such a tax, but, again, most of them are "small." Exchange efficiency loss, for example, doesn't matter because the tax is "small."

On the same cost side, we should also point out a particularly pernicious aspect of a transfer tax. If the burden of the tax is shared between the buyer and the seller and if it applies on all transactions, then individuals who are saving for retirement would find a 1 percent tax resulting in a full 1 percent burden on them. (If the tax is shared equally between the buyer and the seller, it would be a 1/2 percent tax on purchase and a 1/2 percent tax on the subsequent sale.) This is a direct tax on the purchase of equities for long-term savings, and this certainly seems an odd time to change the tax code so as to discourage savings. But not to worry, the effect will surely be "small." (However, it will not be as small as Professor Stiglitz seems to think, since a 1 percent tax is a 1 percent tax, no matter how long the investment is held.)

As a penultimate benefit of a transfer tax, Professor Stiglitz argues that lower volatility lowers risk and, as a consequence, raises the efficiency of capital allocation, but he makes no distinction between systematic and unsystematic risk which would seem crucial in this context. Furthermore, even if price risk is lowered, efficiency will be improved only if the tax leads to better (more informed) prices. I've heard nothing convincing on this. That the tax might hinder the flow of information into prices is acknowledged but is not a matter of great concern. On the one hand, valuable information will not be discouraged by a "small" tax, and, if it is, it will only be slightly delayed.

On the other hand, in a truly novel argument, Professor Stiglitz takes the point of view that real investment will not be affected even if prices do not accurately reflect information because, as he asks rhetorically, "Does one really believe that the managers of GM or Ford base their decisions about whether or how to invest on the prices that they see on the stock market?" Those of us who know such managers find it difficult to imagine a topic of greater concern to them: it is simply the height of naivete to imaging otherwise.

Perhaps what troubles Professor Stiglitz most about the stock market and, presumably, the financial markets as a whole, emerges toward the end of his article when he bemoans the apparent popularity of financial careers among his better students and seems troubled that the turnover tax will only have a "small" beneficial effect on discouraging them.

But if a transfer tax is so beneficial, why stop here? Because it is difficult to define socially undesirable trading? I may not be able to define speculation, but I know it when I see it. As he points out, governments have long taxed socially undesirable activity and, presumably, the perverse behavior of trading stocks should not be any exception. (I am less certain, though, that I would look to the government and its unashamed boosterism of state lotteries for a moral anchor in this matter.)

The article ends with the big guns. In the context of the now popular search for a new industrial policy that will turn us away from our short-term emphasis, it is argued that a transfer tax will lead to a longer-term view. But now we run out of theory: to quote, " . . . this reorientation of managerial focus may provide another reason why a turnover tax may have some beneficial effects." Then again, there has also been a concern that watching TV screens is harmful to people. I want to point out that a video tax may also lead to a reorientation of trading focus that may provide another reason why a video-tax may also have some beneficial effects.

The article concludes with a shrug in the direction of the practical problems of implementing a transfer tax in the derivative markets such as those for futures and options. I am afraid that more than just a shrug will be required since it is the growth of these markets in Japan and the very problems of extending their transfer tax that have been an important motivation for their current reconsideration of their transfer tax. It certainly would be an irony of timing if, in the name of a new industrial policy, we imposed a transfer tax just as the Japanese phased theirs out.

Journal of Financial Services Research, 3: 121–138 (1989)

Stock Market Margin Requirements and Volatility: Implications for Regulation of Stock Index Futures

MICHAEL A. SALINGER
Graduate School of Business
Columbia University
New York, NY 10027

Abstract

This article reexamines the evidence on the relationship between stock market margin buying and volatility, and discusses the implications for the regulation of futures markets margin requirements. Post-war data provide no evidence of a link between the initial margin requirements set by the Federal Reserve and stock market volatility. Over the entire period in which the Federal Reserve has set margin requirements (1934–present), there is a correlation between margin requirements and margin debt on the one hand and volatility on the other. However, margin debt is not primarily associated with downside volatility and margin requirements are not primarily associated with upside volatility, as would be expected if margin buying were the cause of the volatility. Thus, the experience with stock market margin requirements provides no support for regulating futures markets margins in order to curb volatility. While this evidence does not rule out the possibility that margin buying contributed to the speculative boom of the 1920s and the 1929 crash, margin debt represented a much greater fraction of the 1929 stock market than have stock market futures in the 1980s. Even taking the experience of the 1920s into account, therefore, there is still no justification for regulating futures margins in order to curb volatility.

1. Introduction

The October 1987 market collapse has prompted arguments that security market regulation should be tightened to curb excessive volatility in the stock market. One change recommended in the Brady Commission Report[1] is an increase in margin requirements for stock index futures and other derivative instruments.

Since 1934, the Federal Reserve Board has set initial margin requirements on loans from broker/dealers and banks to individual investors.[2] No formal rationale for these requirements exists, but there seem to be two concerns about why excessive margin purchases might destabilize stock prices. The first is simply that some investors will place irrationally high values on stocks and, given the opportunity to buy unlimited quantities on margin, will bid

This article was prepared for the Columbia Center for the Study of Futures Markets Conference on Regulatory and Structural Reform of Stock and Futures Markets. I have benefited from conversations with Alberto Giovannini, Gikas Hardouvelis, David Hsieh, Jeff Miron, Merton Miller, Giulio Pontecorvo, Bill Schwert, and especially Frank Edwards. I am, of course, solely responsible for any errors.

23

prices up to excessive levels.[3] The second is that when stocks are purchased on margin, price declines cause positions to be liquidated. This selling causes further price declines, further liquidation of margin positions, and so on.[4]

This article discusses the relationship between stock market margin requirements and stock market volatility and the implications, if any, of that relationship for increased regulation of margin requirements in other markets. Section 2 contains a selective review of previous work on this and related topics. Section 3 seeks to establish some stylized facts about the relationship between margin requirements and margin debt on the one hand and stock market volatility on the other. This section draws heavily upon and extends an analysis by Hardouvelis (1988a, 1988b). It also discusses criticisms of it by Schwert (1988), Hsieh and Miller (1989), and Kupiec (1989). The Hardouvelis analysis, a version of which appeared in the *Quarterly Review* of the Federal Reserve Bank of New York, concludes that high initial margins do curb stock market volatility. The article has received considerable publicity and has been taken as support for increased regulation of margins in other markets. The section presents evidence that although the correlation between margin requirements and market volatility disappears for some specifications of the volatility equation, the correlation between stock market debt and volatility is more robust. Section 4 presents evidence that suggests, however, that this correlation should not be interpreted to mean that margin debt causes volatility. Section 5 discusses the relevance of the experience of the late 1920s for the regulation of margins in futures markets. Section 6 contains conclusions.

2. Earlier work

Moore (1966) observed that the Federal Reserve Board's margin requirements apply only to loans by banks and broker/dealers for the purpose of purchasing stock and when the shares are used as collateral. They do not, for example, prevent banks from lending the entire purchase price of a security and taking another asset as collateral. Neither do they prevent a security from fully collateralizing a loan that has a purpose other than purchasing the security. With apparently close unregulated substitutes for the types of loans that are regulated, Moore argued that it is simply implausible that the margin regulations would be effective.[5]

Moore attempted to address empirically the question of whether margin purchases are destabilizing. He argued that the relationship between margin requirements and the demand for margin credit, while statistically significant, was economically small. He also claimed to show that the demand for margin credit was negatively correlated with recent stock returns, thus suggesting that margin purchases are stabilizing rather than destabilizing.[6]

Officer (1973) analyzed stock market volatility. He found that the stochastic properties of stock returns prior to 1929 and after 1944 were similar, but they differed from those from 1929 to 1944. Stocks were more volatile from 1929 to 1944 than they were either previously or subsequently.[7] He also examined the effects of margin requirements and concluded that while stock market volatility affected margin requirements, there was no evidence that margin requirements affected volatility. However, Officer's conclusions do not follow from the results he presents.[8] Of course, his finding that pre-1929 volatility is about the same as post-1944 volatility might make one hesitant to attribute the post-war decline in volatility to increased regulation of the securities markets in general or margin requirements in particular.

3. Hardouvelis and his critics—what are the issues?

The debate about the effect of margin requirements seems to have lain dormant throughout the late 1970s and most of the 1980s. However, Hardouvelis (1988a, 1988b) recently revived the debate. Challenging the conventional wisdom, Hardouvelis (1988a, 1988b), concludes that margin requirements are inversely correlated with volatility. Hardouvelis' article has been criticized by Schwert (1988), Hsieh and Miller (1989), and Kupiec (1989).

To understand the points of dispute, it is useful to examine graphs of a few time series. The first is the level of the Federal Reserve Board's official margin requirements, which is pictured in figure 1a. The graph reveals three regimes of margin policy. From 1934 to 1945, margin requirements were generally below 50 percent and reasonably stable. From 1945 to 1974, margin requirements were typically above 50 percent; and the Federal Reserve Board changed them much more frequently. From 1974 up to the present, they have been constant at 50 percent.

The second time series of interest is stock market volatility. Let r_t be the real return on the stock maret at time t and D_i for $i=1, \ldots, 12$ be monthly dummies. Consider the regression:

$$r_t = \sum_{i=1}^{12} \alpha_i D_i + \sum_{i=1}^{12} \gamma_i \, r_{t-i} + e_t \qquad (1)$$

The absolute value of the residual from (1) is an estimate of the standard deviation of e_t and is the measure of volatility used in this article. This measure, which is the one used by Schwert (1988) and one of the two used by Hardouvelis (1989), is plotted in figure 1b.[9]Stocks are most volatile in the period before the establishment of margin requirements. As Officer (1973) found, they are also more volatile throughout the 1930s than they were afterward. The measure of volatility used in this article is not the only one possible, but any sensible measure is going to have the general characteristic that volatility was greater in the late 1920s and 1930s than it was afterward.

A third variable of interest is the level of margin debt as a fraction of the value of the market. This variable serves two purposes. First, its size affects the plausibility of interpreting a correlation between volatility and margin requirements as a causal relationship. Second, it can help distinguish between the effect of margin buying on upside and downside volatility. The Federal Reserve Board's official margin requirement is only an initial margin requirement. It affects how easy it is to buy stock on margin, but has little to do with the sale of stock previously purchased on margin. As such, it can affect upside but not downside volatility. The level of margin debt determines the potential for sales of stocks previously purchased on margin and is therefore a determinant of downside volatility.[10]

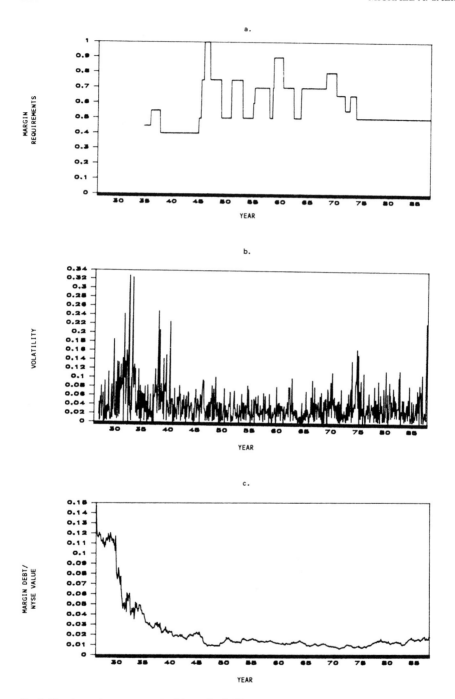

Fig. 1. Margin requirements, margin debt, and volatility

Table 1 presents data on margin credit[11] both in absolute terms and as a fraction of the value of New York Stock Exchange stocks, and figure 1c is a plot of the latter. From 1945 to 1985, margin credit never exceeded 1.5 percent of the value of NYSE stocks, and it was frequently less than 1 percent. Moreover, since margin credit can be used to purchase stocks not listed on the New York Stock Exchange, it was a still smaller fraction of the total value of stocks that could be purchased on margin. Prior to 1945, however, margin credit was a much larger fraction of the value of stocks. In the late 1920s, it was approximately 11 percent. The percentage declined dramatically after the crash and then more gradually until 1945. Even if margin buying on the order of 1 percent of the market could not affect volatility significantly, it is at least plausible that margin buying that accounted for about 10 percent of the market could.[12]

A visual examination of figure 1 suggests some stylized facts about the correlation between margin requirements, margin debt, and stock market volatility. First, if one starts in 1926 and assumes that broker-imposed margin requirements were lower than the official ones that subsequently prevailed,[13] the high volatility in the late twenties and early thirties suggests a negative correlation between margin requirements and volatility. Even if the pre-1934 data are excluded, the high volatility and relatively low margin requirements from 1934 to 1945 also indicate a negative correlation between volatility and margin requirements. The negative correlation also appears within the 1934 to 1945 period. The period in which margin requirements are 55 percent is characterized by low volatility while the beginning of the period in which the margin requirements are only 40 percent is characterized by high volatility. From 1946 to 1974, which is when margin requirements changed most frequently, the relationship is much less clear. Volatility appears roughly constant throughout the period despite substantial variation in margin requirements.[14] The correlation between volatility and margin debt is similar. From 1926 to 1945, both volatility and margin debt were higher than they were thereafter. Within the post-1945 period, no relationship is obvious.

Table 2 reports regressions of volatility on 12 monthly dummies and various other variables. The first five lines cover the entire period in which the Federal Reserve Board had minimum margin requirements.[15] In line 1, only the level of margin requirements is included, and the coefficient is negative and significant. In line 2, only DEBT is included, and the coefficient is positive and significant. When both MARGIN and DEBT are included (line 3), the coefficient on MARGIN is small and insignificant, while the coefficient on DEBT is roughly the same as in line 2.[16] In addition to the level of margin requirements, Hardouvelis includes in his regressions the percentage increases in the industrial production index and the consumer price index and the volatility of the industrial production index to reflect stock market fundamentals.[17] He also includes lagged volatility, lagged changes in the ratio of margin debt to the value of all NYSE stocks, and lagged stock returns to mitigate the endogeneity of margin requirements. As is reported in line 4, the size and significance of the coefficient on margin requirements increases when these variables are added. As in line 3, the coefficient on DEBT is positive and significant while the coefficient on MARGIN is insignificant.

The results in the first five lines of table 2 might seem to suggest that margin buying does affect volatility. As with any econometric results, four types of objections can be raised.

27

Table 1. Margin credit

Year	Margin credit	Mar. crd./ NYSE Val	Year	Margin credit	Mar. crd./ NYSE Val
1926	3668	11.9%	1957	2550	1.3%
1927	4808	11.3%	1958	3431	1.3%
1928	6815	11.6%	1959	3430	1.1%
1929	4365	7.9%	1960	3317	1.1%
1930	2269	5.5%	1961	4294	1.1%
1931	1300	6.0%	1962	4149	1.2%
1932	800	4.3%	1963	5541	1.4%
1933	1270	4.5%	1964	5101	1.1%
1934	1170	4.1%	1965	4990	1.0%
1935	1258	3.1%	1966	4910	1.0%
1936	1395	2.7%	1967	6310	1.1%
1937	985	3.0%	1968	6220	0.9%
1938	991	2.4%	1969	4970	0.8%
1939	906	2.3%	1970	5734	1.0%
1940	677	1.9%	1971	7722	1.1%
1941	600	2.0%	1972	11297	1.4%
1942	543	1.7%	1973	7221	1.1%
1943	789	2.0%	1974	5491	1.1%
1944	1041	2.2%	1975	7708	1.2%
1945	1138	1.8%	1976	11383	1.4%
1946	547	0.9%	1977	13928	1.8%
1947	578	1.0%	1978	15487	2.0%
1948	551	0.9%	1979	16373	1.8%
1949	882	1.3%	1980	20735	1.7%
1950	1358	1.6%	1981	20234	1.8%
1951	1293	1.3%	1982	18561	1.5%
1952	1365	1.2%	1983	32490	2.1%
1953	1696	1.6%	1984	32132	2.2%
1954	2429	1.5%	1985	40598	2.2%
1955	2825	1.4%	1986	52681	2.6%
1956	2856	1.3%	1987	45746	2.2%

First, some determinants of volatility that are excluded from the regression might be correlated with margin requirements and margin debt. Second, the assumptions about the error process might be inappropriate, resulting in incorrect estimates of standard errors. Third, volatility might cause changes in margin requirements and margin debt rather than the reverse. Fourth, the findings might not be robust to alternative specifications. Visual analysis of figure 1 suggests that the results might be sensitive to the sample period. Also, the hypothesis that margins affect volatility implies that changes in margins should cause changes in volatility. Thus, one should get similar results if the regression is run in first differences instead of in levels. Consider these four alternatives in reverse order.

The second five lines of table 2 contain estimates for the post-war period.[18] When no additional controls are added, the coefficients on MARGIN and DEBT are small and clearly

insignificant. With the additional controls suggested by Hardouvelis, the coefficient on MARGIN is somewhat larger but still insignificant at even the 10 percent level. Thus, Hardouvelis's findings are sensitive to the sample period. There are two possible interpretations of this result. One is that the late 1920s and 1930s were an aberration and that the failure to detect an effect of margin requirements and margin debt on volatility in the post-war period suggests that no such effect exists. Officer's (1973) finding that volatility prior to 1926 was similar to post-war volatility, even though no official margin requirements were in effect, supports such a conclusion. On the other hand, the large increase in margin debt in the late 1920s and the high levels of margin debt throughout the 1930s suggest that margin buying could have had its biggest effect on volatility during the late 1920s and 1930s. Even though margin requirements were low prior to the late 1920s, margin debt was also low. Thus, the experience prior to the 1920s cannot be used to dismiss the possibility that margin buying affected the volatility of the late 1920s and early 1930s.[19]

Now consider the argument that if high margin requirements lower volatility, one should be able to detect the effect when the regression is run in first differences. Hsieh and Miller (1989) find that changes in margin requirements have no explanatory power for changes in volatility. A glance at figure 1 makes it clear why they get this result. Most of the changes in margin requirements occurred between 1946 and 1974. Thus, when the regression is specified in first differences, more weight is given to the period when margin debt was so low that margin buying could not possibly have affected volatility significantly. Moreover, the results from the second five lines of table 2 reveal that there is no evidence for an effect of margin requirements in the post-war data. In examining the relationship between changes in volatility and changes in margin requirements, one throws out the information that margin requirements were lower and margin debt was higher from 1926 to 1945 than it was afterward. But that stylized fact is the primary reason to suspect a relationship between volatility and either margin debt or margin purchases.

The possibility that volatility affects margins rather than the reverse was first suggested by Officer (1973). Schwert (1988) also arrives at such a conclusion. Indeed, Schwert finds that margin requirements do not affect volatility even when the pre-1946 data are included. Column 1 of table 3 reports results that are similar to those in Schwert (1988). Twelve leads and lags of changes in margin requirements as well as the contemporaneous change in margin requirements are added to equation (1). The absolute value of the residual from that regression is then regressed on 12 lags of the absolute value of the residual, 12 monthly dummies, 12 lags of the change in margin requirements, the contemporaneous change in margin requirement, and 12 leads of the change in margin requirements. The sum of the coefficients on the leads and the contemporaneous change in margins is negative and significant, while the sum of the coefficients on the lags is negative but insignificant.[20]

The finding that the Federal Reserve Board increased margins in response to increases in stock prices is not controversial. It is consistent both with Hardouvelis's findings and with explanations of margin increase in the *Federal Reserve Bulletin*.[21] The key issue in interpreting Schwert's results is, however, whether it is the inclusion of the 12 leads that makes the coefficient on the sum of the 12 lags insignificant. The margin variables in Schwert's regressions are changes in margin requirements. While the dependent variable is the level of margin requirements, the regression can still be interpreted as being

Table 3. Coefficients on leads and lags of margin

Dependent variable: $|e_t^*|$		
SUM OF COEFFICIENTS ON	-0.240^+	-0.268^*
$\Delta MARGIN_{-12}$ TO $\Delta MARGIN_{+12}$	(-1.86)	(-2.05)
SUM OF COEFFICIENTS ON	-0.223^*	-0.329^*
$\Delta MARGIN_0$ TO $\Delta MARGIN_{+12}$	(-2.61)	(-3.27)
SUM OF COEFFICIENTS ON	-0.017	0.061
$\Delta MARGIN_{-12}$ TO $\Delta MARGIN_{-1}$	(-0.53)	(0.72)
MARGIN		$-0.020^\#$
		(-2.16)

Notes: Regressions include monthly dummies and 12 lags of volatility, $[|e^*_{t-i}|, i=1, 12]$. Values in parentheses are asymptotic *t*-statistics estimated with heteroskedasticity-consistent standard errors. See White (1980). +, #, and * denote significance at 10 percent, 5 percent, and 1 percent levels, respectively.

differenced because lagged volatility is one of the independent variables. Thus, Schwert's findings are, in essence, that the data do not support the proposition that changes in margins cause changes in volatility. This is what Hsieh and Miller (1989) find and it is subject to the same criticism; it discards the information that margin requirements were lower and volatility was higher from 1934 to 1945 than from 1946 to the present. The second column in table 3 reports results of a regression that is similar to Schwert's, but the level of margins is also included as an explanatory variable. The coefficient on the level of margins is negative and significant at the 5 percent level. Thus, even in a regression such as Schwert's, the level of margin requirements helps explain volatility even though changes in margin requirements do not.

There is, however, a simpler critique of Hardouvelis's results that relates to Schwert's analysis as well as to Kupiec's (1989). Hardouvelis includes only one lag of volatility in his version of equation (3), while Schwert includes 12 lags. Thus, Schwert's regressions allow for more general forms of autocorrelation than do Hardouvelis's. Kupiec (1989) estimates a GARCH-M model of stock returns,[22] which also allows for more general forms of serial correlation in volatility than single-period autocorrelation. Table 4 reports regressions that are similar to those in table 2, except that 12 lags of volatility are included in each regression.[23] For the 1934–1987 period, the coefficient on margin requirements is statistically insignificant and economically small even when DEBT is excluded from the regression. This finding suggests that the treatment of autocorrelation in volatility does affect the statistical significance of Hardouvelis's findings.

This critique does not, however, apply to the findings about the effect of margin debt. The coefficient on DEBT is significant at the 5 percent level in the second and fifth lines of table 4 and significant at the 1 percent level in the third line. If the results in table 4 are interpreted to mean that margin debt has a direct effect on volatility, then it is hard to dismiss the possibility that margin requirements have an indirect effect.

While it is certainly appropriate to examine whether Hardouvelis's results are statistically

Table 4. Volatility and margin buying—II

Dependent variable: $|e_t|$

PERIOD	MARGIN	ΔDEBT$_{t-1}$	r_{t-1}	σ_{IP}	CPI	GRIP	$|_{t-1}|$	DEBT	R²	DW
10-35— 12-87	-0.003								0.10	2.00
	(-0.13)									
								0.645#	0.12	2.00
								(2.46)		
	0.015+							0.87*	0.12	2.00
	(1.64)							(2.80)		
	-0.009	-2.4	-0.131*	0.128	0.269	-0.117+	0.011		0.17	2.00
	(-1.16)	(-1.35)	(-4.38)	(1.24)	(1.10)	(-1.91)	(0.24)			
	0.006	-2.32	-0.125*	0.059	0.304	-0.112+	0.005	0.692#	0.18	2.00
	(0.67)	(-1.33)	(-4.20)	(0.56)	(1.27)	(-1.88)	(0.11)	(2.20)		

Notes: All regressions include monthly dummies and 12 lags of volatility. Values in parentheses are asymptotic *t*-statistics estimated with heteroskedasticity-consistent standard errors. See White (1980). +, #, and * denote significance at 10 percent, 5 percent, and 1 percent levels, respectively. Coefficients on VOL$_{-1}$ to VOL$_{-12}$ are, in general, not reported. Coefficient on VOL$_{-1}$ is reported in some cases to aid comparison with results in table 2.

significant, visual examination of figure 1 makes it difficult to dismiss the possibility that volatility is correlated with margin requirements and margin debt. Indeed, if there were strong theoretical reasons to suspect that margin requirements affected volatility and the correlation between them was economically large but statistically insignificant, it would be imprudent to maintain low margin requirements until more stock market bubbles followed by crashes made the relationship statistically significant.

The primary reason to be skeptical of Hardouvelis' conclusions is not that the results may be statistically insignificant. Rather, it is that omitted variable bias is at least as plausible an explanation for his findings as a direct effect of margin requirements on volatility. The essence of the relationship uncovered by Hardouvelis is that margin requirements were low and margin debt was high in the 1930s, which is when the stock market was highly volatile. It is plausible that margin buying caused or at least contributed to the volatility. The stock market boom of the late 1920s was associated with a substantial increase in margin buying. The crash of 1929 was associated with a substantial decrease in margin debt, which is consistent with the hypothesis that margin calls forced selling that intensified the decline.

But there are other explanations. Macroeconomic variables were also unstable in this period. While Hardouvelis did try to adjust for stock market fundamentals, his controls may have been inadequate. It is unlikely that a more extensive effort to adjust for fundamentals could explain most stock market volatility.[24] It does not follow, however, that stock prices were irrationally volatile in the 1930s and that margin buying contributed to the excess volatility. The 1929 stock market crash and the Great Depression created concerns that capitalist economies were inherently unstable. It is only in retrospect that those concerns appear unfounded. An explanation for stock market volatility that is related to general macroeconomic uncertainty is that management of monetary policy was much more destabilizing in the 1920s and 1930s than it had been before the founding of the Federal Reserve Board and than it was afterward.[25] Thus, the key issue in assessing Hardouvelis's results is not whether they are statistically significant. Rather, it is whether the correlations he estimates reflect causal relationships. In particular, can the high volatility of the 1930s be attributed to margin buying?[26]

4. Does margin debt cause volatility?

It is, of course, impossible to show economic causality with econometrics. One approach in this case is to test whether the data demonstrate the asymmetries that the stories about the causal links predict. Suppose, for the sake of argument, that the empirical results were that when both MARGIN and DEBT are included in a volatility regression, the coefficient on the former is negative and significant and the coefficient on the latter is positive and significant. An interpretation of the coefficient on MARGIN is that low margin requirements facilitate margin buying and make it possible for stock prices to exceed rational levels. The positive coefficient on DEBT might suggest that a large amount of margin debt can result in sell-offs which induce larger falls either because stock prices had reached excessive levels or because of margin calls. Based on that story, the direct effect of margin requirements is only on upside volatility, while the direct effect of debt is only on downside volatility.[27] If such asymmetries are present in the data, one should be more willing to conclude that the effect is causal. On the other hand, if, for example, DEBT is just as associated with upside as with downside volatility, then it is more plausible that the volatility is driven by some other factor.

To test for these asymmetries, I create two new variables, DEBTDN and MARGUP. The first equals DEBT when the residual from the first stage regression is negative and 0 otherwise.[28] If the level of margin debt affects only downside volatility and both DEBT and DEBTDN are included in a volatility regression, the coefficient on DEBT should be 0 and the coefficient on DEBTDN should be positive. The second variable, labeled MARGUP, equals MARGIN when the residual from the first stage regression is positive and 0 otherwise. If margin requirements only affect upside volatility (once the level of margin debt is taken into account) and if both MARGIN and MARGUP are included in a volatility regression, the coefficient on MARGIN should be 0 and the coefficient on MARGUP should be negative.

Table 5 presents regressions that include these variables. The regressions were run both including and excluding 12 lags of volatility. They were run with no additional variables and with the additional variables used by Hardouvelis. Because of the insignificance of MARGIN in the 1934–1987 regressions, results of regressions in which MARGUP is excluded are also reported. In all of the regressions in which DEBTDN and MARGUP are included, the coefficients on both are insignificant. Moreover, the point estimates are generally small relative to the coefficients on DEBT and MARGIN or of the wrong sign.

When 12 lags of volatility are included in the regression, the coefficient on DEBTDN is significant at the 10 percent level. At most, that result provides weak evidence that high levels of margin debt contribute to downside volatility. However, the story that DEBT affects volatility predicts both that the coefficient on DEBTDN is positive and that the coefficient on DEBT is 0. The latter part of the hypothesis is rejected at the 1 percent level of significance.

5. Implications of the 1920s for futures market regulation

The results presented in the previous section cover the period of 1934 to 1987. No matter how strong the evidence is that margin requirements and margin debt did not affect volatility during that period, those data cannot rule out the possibility that margin buying caused the speculative boom of the late 1920s and that the sale of stocks purchased on margin exacerbated the 1929 crash. Suppose, for the sake of argument, that margin buying did affect the volatility of the 1920s. What would be the implications for proposals to regulate margins in futures markets?

As of the end of 1987, the initial margin on the Chicago Mercantile Exchange's S&P 500 futures contract was $15,000.[29] At current prices, that figure is about 10 percent of the value of the contract. Even if the variation in stock market margin requirements within the 40 percent to 100 percent range has little effect on volatility, margin requirements of 10 percent could plausibly result in more volatility than margin requirements of 40 percent or more. The current margin requirements in futures markets appear to be at least as low as broker-imposed margins in the late 1920s.

Table 5. Tests of asymmetric effects of MARGIN and DEBT

Dependent variable: $|e_t|$

PERIOD	DEBT	MARGIN	DEBTDN	MARGUP	R^2 DW	12 LAGS OF VOLATILITY
11-34—	0.893*	0.004	0.027	−0.007	0.06	No
12-87	(3.27)	(0.37)	(0.08)	(−0.88)	1.80	
	0.600#	−0.008	0.083	−0.004	0.13	No
	(2.40)	(−0.83)	(0.26)	(−0.56)	2.02	
	0.793*	0.000	0.233		0.06	No
	(3.06)	(0.05)	(1.40)		1.79	
	0.543#	−0.010	0.207		0.13	No
	(2.27)	(−1.14)	(1.27)		2.01	
10-35—	0.818*	0.017	0.204	−0.002	0.13	Yes
12-87	(2.64)	(1.60)	(0.56)	(−0.27)	2.03	
	0.630#	0.007	0.220	0.000	0.18	Yes
	(2.14)	(0.63)	(0.61)	(0.00)	2.00	
	0.783*	0.016*	0.276*		0.13	Yes
	(2.66)	(1.74)	(1.65)		2.03	
	0.629*	0.007	0.220		0.18	Yes
	(2.16)	(0.70)	(1.33)		2.00	

Notes: Each regression includes monthly dummies. In each pair of regressions, the first includes no additional variables and the second includes the other variables used by Hardouvelis. The values in parentheses are asymptotic *t*-statistics based on heteroskedasticity-consistent standard errors. See White (1980). +, #, and * indicate significance at 10 percent, 5 percent, and 1 percent levels, respectively.

Now consider the value of open interest. The stock index future with by far the largest amount of activity is the Chicago Mercantile Exchange's (CME) S&P 500 contract. Open interest on all maturities of the S&P 500 futures contracts reached a peak of about 170,000 in October 1987. Since each contract represented about $150,000, the value of New York Stock Exchange stocks exceeded $2 trillion even after the crash, the value of open interest is on the order of 1 percent of the value of New York Stock Exchange stocks. Even if all futures contracts could be considered equivalent to buying stock on margin, which they cannot, this fraction is much lower than the debt levels attained during the 1920s. Thus, even if the experience of the 1920s can be attributed to margin buying and even though current margin requirements in futures markets are comparable to stock market margin requirements of the 1920s, it is unlikely that futures markets activity had a similar effect in 1987.[30]

6. Conclusion

Over the entire period in which margin requirements have been in effect (1934–present), there is a correlation between margin requirements and margin debt on the one hand and volatility on the other. This correlation arises entirely because margin requirements were low and margin debt was high in the 1930s, a period when the stock market was extremely volatile. It is unlikely, however, that margin buying caused the volatility, since margin debt is not primarily associated with downside volatility and margin requirements are not primarily associated with upside volatility. Margin buying may or may not have contributed to the experience of the 1920s. While the current level of margin requirements in futures markets is comparable to those that prevailed in the stock market in the 1920s, margin buying represented a much larger fraction of the market in the 1920s than does futures trading at the present time. Analogies between margin buying in the 1920s and futures trading in the 1980s are not apt.

Evidence from the stock market does not, therefore, provide any justification for regulating margin requirements in futures markets.

Notes

1. The Brady Commission report is more formally known as Presidential Task Force on Market Mechanisms (1988).

2. See Sofianos (1988) for an excellent description of margin requirements that apply to different instruments.

3. Speculators might, of course, also place irrationally low values on stocks and, through short selling, bid prices down to irrationally low levels. Margin requirements apply to short sales as well as margin buying. They might, therefore, be expected to affect the possibility of overvaluation and undervaluation symmetrically. As an empirical matter, however, short sales are a much less important phenomenon than margin buying and will henceforth be ignored.

4. These last two effects are sometimes called the pyramiding–depyramiding effect. See Garbade (1982) for a discussion.

5. Insofar as people choose to use margin accounts with broker/dealers to borrow money to buy stocks (at least when margin requirements are low), that option can be presumed to be the best alternative. An increase in margin requirements that induces some people to alter the manner in which they borrow to purchase stocks is also likely to induce some marginal margin purchasers not to purchase at all.

6. When he regresses demand for margin credit on lagged stock returns, the level of stock prices, and other variables, he obtains a negative coefficient on lagged stock returns. The presence of the level of stock prices complicates the interpretation. First, the level of stock prices is nonstationary, so its inclusion as an explanatory variable alters the statistical properties of the estimates in ways not accounted for in the regressions. Second, even if the coefficients are correct, the coefficient on the level of stock prices, which is positive, should also be considered in the assessment of whether margin purchases are destabilizing.

7. Other stochastic properties that were different in 1929–1944 are the Box-Jenkins representation and the correlation with changes in industrial production.

8. Officer compares two regressions. In the first, the change in stock market volatility is regressed on the change in industrial production and the change in the margin requirement. In the second, the change in volatility is regressed on the change in industrial production and future margin changes. Officer bases his conclusion on the fact that the R^2 is much higher in the latter regression than in the former. However, the coefficient on the change in margin requirements is insignificant in both regressions. The increased explanatory power in the latter regression can be attributed entirely to the higher t-statistic on the coefficient on the change in industrial production. (To avoid serial correlation, Officer used data for every other month in each regression. The data for the second regression start one month later and thus are different from the data for the first regression. That is, the first regression begins with the change in volatility from month 1 to month 2, from month 3 to month 4, and so on. The second regression begins with the change from month 2 to month 3, from month 4 to month 5, and so on. The increased explanatory power in the second regression comes from the phase shift in the data, not the change in the relative timing of the margin requirement change.) The interpretation of Officer's results is further complicated because the standard deviation for each period is estimated with data centered around the period, so the observation for each time period includes both future and lagged volatility.

9. Hardouvelis uses the real return on the S&P 500 while Schwert uses the nominal return on the New York

Stock Exchange value weighted index. Hardouvelis multiplies the absolute value of the residual by $(\pi/2)^{1/2}$. To compare regression results in this article with his, therefore, the coefficients reported here have to be multiplied by $(\pi/2)^{1/2}$.

10. An alternative to the level of margin debt as a determinant of downside volatility is lagged values of the initial margin requirement. The level of margin debt is the better alternative because it is a more direct measure of the potential for selling and because it requires the estimation of only one additional coefficient.

11. Variable definitions and data sources are discussed in the appendix.

12. Hsieh and Miller (1989) question the conventional wisdom that margin buying contributed to the stock price increases in the late 1920s on the grounds that 10 percent is too small a number. While this judgment is subjective, some comparisons might be instructive. In 1987, foreigners owned roughly 6 percent of U.S. equities and mutual funds accounted for about the same fraction (Brady Commission Report, p. II-13). While it is possible that an exodus of foreign funds would cause only a mild correction in U.S. equity prices, it is at least plausible that it would cause a market collapse.

13. It is not entirely clear that this is true. While some investors faced margin requirements of only 10 percent, some may have faced requirements as high as 50 percent by 1929. See the Brady Commission Report, p. VIII-2.

14. I suspect that some of the difference in Hardouvelis's and Schwert's findings arise because Schwert's heteroskedasticity adjustment gives less weight to the 1934–1944 observations.

15. The federal Reserve Board's margin requirement regulations began in November 1934. Since the estimate of volatility comes from a regression of returns on 12 lagged returns, the first observation on volatility that is not based on data prior to November 1934 is November 1935.

16. The inclusion of DEBT does not cause the standard error on MARGIN to increase substantially. Thus, the insignificance of MARGIN cannot be attributed to extreme multicollinearity.

17. One may not want to adjust for fundamentals without imposing a bound on how large the response to fundamentals can be. A plausible hypothesis is that the market overreacts to news that should move the market somewhat and that the extent of overreaction is related to margin buying.

18. Kupiec (1989) also focuses on the sensitivity of the results to the sample period.

19. To pursue the argument a bit further, low margin requirements may not be sufficient to create volatility. Rather, they make it possible for there to be large volumes of margin purchases, which destabilize the market when they occur.

20. Hardouvelis reports that the initial margin requirement for the period July 1962 to November 1963 is incorrectly reported in the New York Stock Exchange *Fact Book*. Most of the difference between these results and those reported in Schwert are due to the use of the correct value. Another difference is that Schwert used nominal returns, while these results are for (ex post) real returns, which is what Hardouvelis used. The use of real instead of nominal returns does not affect the results substantially.

21. See the discussion in Hardouvelis (1988a).

22. GARCH-M stands for generalized autoregressive conditional heteroskedasticity in mean. In addition to the discussion in Kupiec (1989), see Bollerslev (1986) and Bollerslev, Engle, and Wooldridge (1988).

23. Including 12 lags of volatility greatly reduces the problem of serial correlation in the errors.

24. Attempts to explain stock market volatility based on fundamentals have, by their own admission, been unsuccessful. See, for example, French, Schwert, and Stambaugh (1987).

25. See Miron (1988).

26. The volatility measure used in this article is one of absolute volatility. Hardouvelis (1988a) makes much of the point that the policy issues turn on the relationship between margin requirements and excess volatility. While there are a number of ways to try to measure excess volatility, the most practical for detecting an affect on margins is to test for negative serial correlation in stock returns. The evidence of negative serial correlation in stock returns depends crucially, however, on the inclusion of 1926–1940 data. See Fama and French (1987) and Poterba and Summers (1987). Even with a measure of excess volatility, therefore, the question of whether margin buying contributed to the volatility of the 1920s and 1930s would emerge as the key issue.

27. Recall that I ignore short sales because they are less important empirically than margin buying. The argument that margin requirements only directly affect upside volatility is sensitive to this assumption. Because margin sales result in no margin debt, the argument that margin debt can only directly cause downside volatility is not sensitive to this assumption. Note, however, that short interest is excluded from the analysis. If short sales

and margin debt are positively correlated with each other, high levels of margin debt could be correlated with upside as well as downside volatility.

28. Since the dependent variable is $|e_t|$, one might be concerned that DEBTDN, which depends on the sign of e_t, cannot be taken as exogenous. If the distribution of e_t is symmetric, however, then its absolute value is independent of its sign.

29. See Brady Commission Report, p. VI-23.

30. The counter to this argument is that even if open interest in futures markets is small relative to the value of stocks, volume in futures markets is comparable to the volume in the stock market. Most of the increased volume due to futures markets concerns index arbitrage. Because index arbitrage entails hedged positions, it is unlikely to cause major market movements. It is, of course, quite plausible that portfolio insurance can cause or intensify market declines in particular. Even if those schemes were implemented with futures positions, it does not follow that making it more expensive to use futures markets would eliminate them. An alternative way to implement portfolio insurance is simply to sell stocks directly.

Appendix: Variable definitions and data sources

Definitions

r_t —Monthly real return on stocks, measured as the return (with dividends) on New York Stock Exchange stocks minus CPI.

CPI —Inflation, measured as the percentage change in the consumer price index.

e_t —Residual from regression of r_t on monthly dummies and 12 lags of r_t. The absolute value of e_t is an estimate of the standard deviation of r_t.

e_t^* —Residual from regression of r_t on monthly dummies, 12 lags of r_t, the contemporaneous value of ΔMARGIN, and 12 leads and lags of ΔMARGIN.

MARGIN —End-of-month initial margin requirements, measured as a fraction.

ΔMARGIN —Change in MARGIN.

DEBT —Ratio of margin debt to value of New York Stock Exchange stocks. Both values are measured as end-of-month values.

ΔDEBT —Change in margin debt divided by value of New York Stock exchange stocks. Note that ΔDEBT is not the change in DEBT.

GRIP —Growth in the industrial production index.

σ_{IP} —Size of the innovation in industrial production, measured as the absolute value of the residual from a regression of the growth of the industrial production index on monthly dummies and 12 of its own lags.

DEBTDN —Equals DEBT when e_t is negative and 0 otherwise.

MARGUP —Equals MARGIN when e_t is positive and 0 otherwise.

Data Sources: The data on the return and value of New York Stock Exchange stocks are from the Center for Research in Securities Prices (CRSP) monthly returns file. The data for initial margin requirements are from New York Stock Exchange (1987), p. 54. Hardouvelis reports that margin requirements were .50 from July 1962 to November 1963, not the .90 reported in the New York Stock Exchange *Fact Book.* I used this corrected value. Data for the growth in the Industrial Production Index were taken from Board of Governors of the

Federal Reserve System (1972), p. S-23, for 1926–1946, and from Citibase for 1947–1987. Data for the Consumer Price Index come from Ibbotson and Associates (1987), p. 128, for 1926–1986 and from the CPI-U series reported in February 1988, *Survey of Current Business*, p. S-5. Data for margin debt are Board of Governors of the Federal Reserve System (1943) for 1926 to 1941. For 1926 to October 1931, the data come from table 142 (Broker's Borrowings on Collateral in New York City). For November 1931 to 1941, they come from the series on "Customers' debit balances (net)" in table 143. A regression of brokers' borrowings on customers' debit balances for the overlap between the series yielded an intercept of 375 and a coefficient that was insignificantly different from 1. Hence, 375 was added to the brokers' borrowing series. For 1942–1969, the data come from the same series reported in Board of Governors of the Federal Reserve System (1976), table 12.23. For 1970–1987, the data come from the series "Credit Extended to Margin Customers" reported in the *Federal Reserve Bulletin*. Following Hardouvelis, I multiply the 1970–1987 data by 1.43 to make them comparable to the other series.

References

Bollerslev, Tim "Generalized Autoregressive Conditional Heteroskedasticity." *Journal of Econometrics* 31 (1986), 307–327.

Bollerslev, Tim, Engle, Robert F. and Wooldridge, Jeffrey M. "A Capital Asset Pricing Model with Time-varying Covariances." *Journal of Political Economy* 96 (1988), 116–131.

Board of Governors of the Federal Reserve System. *Banking and Monetary Statistics.* Washington, D.C.: National Capital Press, 1943.

———. *Industrial Production: 1971 Edition.* Washington, D.C.: Board of Governors of the Federal Reserve System, 1971.

———. *Banking and Monetary Statistics: 1941–1970.* Washington, D.C.: Board of Governors of the Federal Reserve System, 1976.

Fama, Eugene R. and French, Kenneth R. "Permanent and Temporary Components of Stock Prices." *Journal of Political Economy* 96 (1987), 246–273.

Garbade, Kenneth D. "Federal Reserve Margin Requirements: A Regulatory Initiative to Prevent Speculative Bubbles." In: Paul Wachtel, ed., *Crises in the Economic and Financial Structure.* Lexington, MA: Lexington Books, 1982.

Hardouvelis, Gikas A. "Margin Requirements, Volatility, and the Transitory Component of Stock Prices." First Boston Working Paper Series FB 88-38, 1988a.

———. "Margin Requirements and Stock Market Volatility." *Federal Reserve Bank of New York Quarterly Review* (Summer 1988b), 80–89.

Hseih, David A. and Miller, Merton H. "Margin Regulation and Stock Market Variability." Mimeo, 1989.

Ibbotson and Associates. *Stocks, Bonds, Bills, and Inflation Yearbook,* 1987.

Kupiec, Paul H. "Initial Margin Requirements and Stock Returns Volatility: Another Look." Federal Reserve Board, Finance and Economics Discussion Series #53, 1989.

Miron, Jeffrey A. "The Founding of the Fed and the Destabilization of the Post-1914 Economy." National Bureau of Economic Research Working Paper #2701.

Moore, Thomas G. "Stock Market Margin Requirements." *Journal of Political Economy* 74 (1966), 158–167.

Officer, Robert R. "The Variability of the Market Factor of New York Stock Exchange." *Journal of Business* 46 (1973), 434–453.

Poterba, James M. and Summers, Lawrence. "Mean Reversion in Stock Returns: Evidence and Implications." *Journal of Financial Economics* 22 (1987), 27–60.

Journal of Financial Services Research, 3: 139–151 (1989)
© 1989 Kluwer Academic Publishers

Commentary: *Stock Market Margin Requirements and Volatility*

GIKAS A. HARDOUVELIS
Department of Finance
Rutgers University
New Brunswick, NJ 08903
and Research Department
Federal Reserve Bank of New York

Michael Salinger has provided a very thoughtful and well-balanced article on margin requirements. The article builds upon and extends some of my earlier work on margin requirements and stock market volatility. Professor Salinger, however, reaches a different conclusion than I did about the influence of margin requirements on the stock market. Similarly, Richard Roll's article in this issue expresses strong doubts about the effectiveness of margin requirements. He surveys some recent work that calls into question the robustness of my results. Thus before I comment on Salinger's own work, I would like to provide a more general perspective on the issue of margin requirements and answer the basic objections of my critics. I begin in section 1 by describing the main question. Then in section 2, I give an example of the effects of margin requirements on long swings in stock prices, a key variable of interest. In section 3, I respond to the econometric criticisms of Salinger and other critics. In section 4, I comment more generally on Salinger's article. Finally, in section 5, I summarize my thoughts on the effects of margin requirements and propose possible extensions of current empirical work.

1. The key question

When I began my own research on the effectiveness of margin requirements, I was struck by the fact that despite the voluminous literature on margin requirements, no author ever examined the most interesting question: Do margin requirements in the cash market affect the behavior of destabilizing speculators, as Congress believed some 50 years ago? Or is it the case that margin requirements affect primarily the behavior of rational investors and, by restricting liquidity in the market, contribute perhaps to higher volatility? Clearly, the key variables of interest are measures of excess volatility and other speculative deviations from fundamentals, but the existing literature did not analyze such measures.

I wish to thank Richard Cantor for comments and Valerie LaPorte for editorial assistance. The views expressed here do not reflect the views of the Federal Reserve Bank of New York or the Federal Reserve System.

I found two articles that examined the effect of margin requirements on actual, as opposed to excess, volatility. Officer (1973) finds a weak negative relationship between the two variables and interprets it as evidence that volatility affects the behavior of the Federal Reserve in setting margin requirements. Douglas (1969), however, finds a very strong negative relationship (a *t*-statistic of 10), which he interprets as evidence that higher margin requirements reduce volatility. Neither article controls for the behavior of the Federal Reserve, and each one only partially controls for the variability of the economic environment. I decided to sharpen the results of the two authors and then focus on the key question of whether margin requirements affect excess volatility.

My critics concentrate exclusively on what I thought was the noncontroversial and perhaps less exciting part of my article, the relationship between margin requirements and *actual* volatility. My estimate of this relationship turned out to be stronger than Officer's but weaker than that of Douglas. Therefore, I don't see the basis for the claim by some of my critics (repeated by Roll in his article) that I am the only one in the literature reporting a negative association between margin requirements and stock price volatility, implying that my results are an aberration. But before I address criticisms of my results on actual volatility, let me discuss what I feel are some of the most interesting results on the relationship between margin requirements and long swings in stock prices.

2. Margin requirements and long swings in stock prices: an example

Recall the Fama and French (1988) result that high price-dividend ratios predict subsequent low stock returns. Fama and French propose two alternative explanations of the negative correlation. The first explanation runs as follows: a high price-dividend ratio reflects an overvalued market. Later on, stock prices decline to line up closer to fundamentals, and this movement generates a negative return. The second explanation asserts that a high price-dividend ratio reflects a low risk premium in a correctly valued market, and the low subsequent returns reflect a low reward for the small amount of risk that market participants had rationally expected. While it is difficult to discriminate between the two hypotheses, I found that the size of the negative correlation between price-dividend ratios and subsequent stock returns in excess of the risk-free rate varies systematically with the level of margin requirements: the negative correlation is weaker in periods of high margin requirements *and* in periods when margin requirements increase. Furthermore, the results are robust to the inclusion or exclusion of the depression years from the sample (see the May 1989 revision of my paper).

I interpret these findings to mean either that high (or increasing) margin requirements reduce the degree of mispricing in the market and hence the excess volatility over the long term that is generated by the presence of irrational price swings or that high (or increasing) margin requirements reduce the perceived risk in the market. Under either interpretation, higher margin requirements are effective.[1]

3. Response to the critics

Let me now address the criticisms of my results on actual volatility. The first criticism is that the negative correlation is due to the depression years and is not observed after the 1940s. This is one of Salinger's criticisms as well, although he correctly points out that even if the depression years were solely responsible for the negative correlation, the results might still be relevant for today's financial environment. The criticism is only partly correct. It is true that to exclude the depression years weakens the estimated correlation between margin requirements and volatility, yet the correlation remains statistically significant. It is also true that the size of the correlation varies across different subsamples, but such variables should be expected. At different points in time the relative effects of margin requirements on destabilizing speculators and on stabilizing rational investors may well differ. Please also note that the criticism does not apply to the relationship between margin requirements and excess volatility, which is equally strong in the post-depression sample.

   Table 1 repeats some of Salinger's tables using the S&P index and an index of small stocks but shows the results for various subperiods. The index of small stocks represents the two smallest deciles of the New York Stock Exchange stocks in terms of capitalized value; its source is Ibbotson Associates. Note that the negative association is present in *every* subperiod, although the size of the correlation varies. The coefficient of margin requirements is typically statistically significant for both the S&P Composite and the index of small stocks. Although not shown in table 1, when additional control variables are added, such as the lagged growth in stock prices or the volatility of the industrial production index, the negative coefficient of margin requirements is more significant. This evidence is quite impressive when one recalls that since November 1935, margin requirements changed only 22 times and, thus, checking for subperiod negative correlations is asking too much of the data.

   Salinger's second major criticism of my article runs as follows: if one adds 12 lags of volatility in the basic regression, the effect weakens substantially even in the 1935–1987 sample. The first row of table 2 confirms the criticism. The margin coefficient is now insignificant for both stock indices. The size of the coefficient drops substantially relative to its size in table 1, although given the estimated persistence in volatility, the size of the estimated long-run effect of margin requirements on volatility is only slightly smaller than in table 1. To assess the importance of the criticism, observe that adding 12 lags of volatility in the bivariate contemporaneous relationship between margin requirements and volatility is arbitrary and may not be innocuous. Lagged volatility may proxy for other excluded factors that affect both margin requirements and current volatility. For purposes of symmetry, the second row of table 2 adds 12 lags of each of the control variables from my earlier paper. Observe that the second row reinstates my earlier results: the margin coefficient is now statistically significant for both indices. Clearly, the results of the second row are more reliable because they control for third factors that may adversely influence the relationship between margin requirements and volatility.

   The importance of controlling for third factors in the relationship between margin requirements and volatility can be illustrated by the following example. My earlier paper shows that the Federal Reserve would increase margin requirements following a run-up in

43

Table 1. Volatility, margin requirements and margin debt

$$\sigma_{mt} = \sum_{i=1}^{12} \alpha_i SEASON_{it} + \beta_1 M_t + \beta_2 DEBT_t + u_t$$

Sample	S&P Index					Small Stocks Index				
	β_1	β_2	R^2	SEE	DW	β_1	β_2	R^2	SEE	DW
34:11-87:12	-.037* [-3.19]		.04	.040	1.78	-.090* [-4.55]		.06	.065	1.65
		1.56* [3.54]	.05	.040	1.79		3.31* [4.56]	.07	.065	1.66
	-.015 [-1.25]	1.30* [2.68]	.05	.040	1.80	-.048* [-2.39]	2.51* [3.23]	.08	.065	1.68
40:1-87:12	-.014 [-1.36]		.03	.035	1.87	-.033* [-2.09]		.03	.050	1.80
		0.54 [0.89]	.03	.035	1.87		0.56 [0.65]	.02	.051	1.78
	-.011 [-0.87]	0.26 [0.35]	.03	.035	1.87	-.038* [-2.07]	-.039 [-0.39]	.03	.051	1.80
47:1-87:12	-.027* [-2.32]		.04	.034	1.94	-.024 [-1.50]		.04	.046	1.89
		0.40 [0.60]	.03	.034	1.92		-0.42 [-0.49]	.04	.046	1.88
	-.030* [-2.07]	-0.21 [-0.27]	.04	.034	1.94	-.040* [-2.08]	-1.23 [-1.20]	.05	0.46	1.90

56:1-87:12	-.031* [-2.33]	.06	.035	1.90	-.027 [-1.43]	.06	.048	1.88
	0.47 [0.64]	.05	.035	1.88	-0.32 [-.033]	.05	.049	1.88
	-0.17 [-0.19]	.06	.035	1.90	-1.12 [-0.98]	.06	.048	1.90
34:11-55:12	-.33* [-1.98]	.07	.046	1.71	-.117* [-3.98]	.08	.083	1.61
	1.86* [3.54]	.10	.045	1.77	4.18* [4.63]	.11	.082	1.64
	1.84* [-0.07]	.10 [3.27]	.045	1.77	3.31* [-1.88]	.12 [3.39]	.082	1.66
	-.001				-.058			

Notes: $\sigma_m = \sqrt{(\pi/2)}\,|\hat{\varepsilon}_t|$, where $\hat{\varepsilon}_t$ is the estimated residual of the regression: $R_t = \sum_{i=1}^{12} \alpha_i\, SEASON_{it} + \sum_{i=1}^{12} \beta_i\, R_{t-i} + \varepsilon_t$, with R_t referring to the real monthly rate of return of a stock index including dividends. $SEASON_i$ is a monthly dummy variable. M_t is the official margin requirement. $DEBT_t$ is the ratio of broker-dealer credit to the capitalized value of the New York Stock Exchange. *t*-statistics are in brackets calculated from White (1980) heteroskedasticity-consistent standard errors. Asterisk, *, denotes statistical significance at the 5 percent level. R^2 is the coefficient of determination, *SEE* is the regression standard error, and *DW* is the Durbin-Watson statistic.

45

Table 2. Volatility and margin requirements

Sample: 35:10-87:12
Dependent variable: σ_m
Independent variable: 12 lags of σ_m, R, MCR, π, Y, $\sigma_m(Y)$, 12 monthly seasonals, and current M

Sum of 12 lags with t-statistic in brackets, and x^2 (12) for excluding all 12 lags with significance level in parentheses

Current M	σ_m	R	MCR	π	Y	$\sigma_m(Y)$	R^2	SEE
			S&P Index					
-.008	.61*						.12	.039
[-.073]	[4.46]							
	24.6*							
	(.017)							
-.030*	.50*	-.25	-.23*	-.60	-.48*	.03	.31	.036
[-2.58]	[4.53]	[-1.94]	[-2.07]	[-1.13]	[-2.32]	[0.14]		
	32.3*	58.8*	22.1*	16.4	18.3	26.9*		
	(.001)	(.000)	(.036)	(.175)	(.106)	(.008)		
			Small Stocks Index					
-.019	.74*						.21	.061
[-1.26]	[5.91]							
	48.5*							
	(.000)							
-.041*	.67*	-.19	-.29	-.54	-.06	.33	.33	.059
[-2.22]	[5.79]	[-1.50]	[-1.66]	[-0.66]	[-0.017]	[0.86]		
	61.9*	14.8	15.3	17.6	16.4	26.4*		
	(.000)	(.254)	(.225)	(.123)	(.175)	(.010)		

Notes: M = official margin requirement.
σ_m = monthly volatility of R, defined in table 1.
R = monthly real rate of return on a stock index including dividends.
MCR = monthly rate of growth of the ratio of broker-dealer credit to the capitalized value of the NYSE.
π = CPI inflation rate, monthly.
Y = growth rate of the industrial production index, monthly.
$\sigma_m(Y)$ = monthly volatility of Y.
Estimation performed with conditional-heteroskedasticity correction (White, 1980).

stock prices and would decrease margin requirements following a downward trend in stock prices. Next, recall that Christie (1982) shows that during bull markets volatility is low and during bear markets volatility is high. Christie also provides evidence consistent with the hypothesis that higher stock prices *cause* volatility to decline because they result in a lower debt-equity ratio. Hence, if an increase in margin requirements were effective in the sense that it reversed a previous speculative rise in prices, then the new lower stock prices would cause volatility to increase. Thus, in the absence of an appropriate control for the recent rate of growth in stock prices, there is a bias against finding a negative association between current margin requirements and future volatility; there is also a bias toward a negative association between current margin requirements and lagged volatility.

The previous discussion explains the counterintuitive evidence of Schwert (1988), the first of my critics. Schwert argues that volatility Granger-causes margin requirements but margin requirements do not Granger-cause volatility. Schwert regresses current volatility on 12 of its own lags and 12 lags and 12 leads of the change in margin requirements. He finds a stronger negative relationship between volatility and lead changes in margin requirements than between volatility and lagged changes in margin requirements. Salinger responds to Schwert by adding the contemporaneous level of margin requirements and shows that the contemporaneous relationship between margin requirements and volatility is still the strongest. Salinger also points out that Schwert's results are counterintuitive. Suppose for the sake of the argument that the Fed did respond to an increase in volatility because it took it as a signal of excessive speculation. Under such circumstances, the Fed would increase, not decrease, margin requirements as the Schwert estimates show. I agree with Salinger's arguments and would like to add two points. First, the Fed never mentions volatility even as a remote reason for changing margin requirements. The ordered logit results of my earlier analysis on the Fed's disposition to alter margin requirements show no relationship either. Second, Schwert's counterintuitive result that a decrease in volatility is followed by an increase in margin requirements is due to third factors such as the level of the market. In the latest revision of my paper (May 1989), I show that, indeed, Schwert's Granger-causality results are reversed when additional control variables enter the original bivariate relation between margin requirements and volatility. The control variables are stock returns, the growth in margin credit, and the volatility of the industrial production index.

Another critic, Kupiec (1989), tackles a different aspect of my paper—my measure of volatility. I use two alternative measures of volatility, one annual and the other monthly. The annual measure is a standard deviation of monthly stock returns (or unanticipated stock returns) over a horizon of one year. The monthly measure is described in the notes of table 1 and is also used by Salinger and Schwert. Kupiec argues that volatility is not constant over a year or over a month and must be allowed to vary over time. He uses a GARCH-M model and finds that the effect of margin requirements on volatility, although negative, is insignificant.

Kupiec's criticism of my measure of volatility is misplaced. Volatility per se is *not* the variable of interest. As Salinger points out, the item of interest is the pyramiding–depyramiding process that generates long swings in stock prices and that prompted Congress to establish margin use some 50 years ago. One way to capture those price swings is to use volatility measured over longer horizons such as a year. Volatility at high frequencies is not the appropriate measure. Furthermore, Kupiec's methodology limits the relevance of his results. The GARCH-M model imposes the Capital Asset Pricing Model on the data. Hence, his method assumes that the market understands the effect of margin requirements on volatility and correctly prices this risk. I interpret Kupiec's weak results as evidence that margin requirements affect excess volatility generated by irrational price swings that are unexpected and not priced in the market.

Hsieh and Miller (1989) criticize my use of overlapping data with the annual measure of volatility, but ignore my work with the monthly volatility measure or my excess volatility results. It is well known that the presence of data overlapping generates a moving average in the regression error term, which renders the OLS standard errors inconsistent. For correct inferences, the standard errors have to be adjusted. I used the correction proposed by Newey and West (1987). However, Hsieh and Miller claim that even the Newey-West correction is not enough because the residual autocorrelation is too high. Given their criticism, one would have expected them to use nonoverlapping annual data in responding to my paper, or perhaps to use monthly data with my monthly measure of volatility. Instead, they also use overlapping data, but they take the first difference to eliminate the serial correlation generated by the data overlap. But since the residual autocorrelation is substantially smaller than unity, first differencing generates negative autocorrelation. So they are forced to use Cochrane-Orcutt correction for first order serial correlation in their regressions. Yet they are still stuck with substantial residual autocorrelation at lags 12 and beyond. I am puzzled by their roundabout methodology. Indeed, they follow a very unorthodox route for reasons that are hard to understand. I have re-estimated my annual volatility equations using nonoverlapping annual data and find results that are very similar to my earlier ones (table 4A of the latest revision).

The same Hsieh-Miller criticism is echoed by Richard Roll's article in this issue. Although the Newey-West correction is very standard, Roll discards my annual volatility results on the grounds that they are based on complicated econometrics. Yet, he subsequently espouses uncritically the even more complicated econometrics of Hsieh and Miller.

Hsieh and Miller do not end up contradicting my results. They claim that one of my control variables, the lagged growth in margin credit, does not belong in my regression and suggest that a simultaneous system ought to be estimated. I agree that estimating a simultananeous system is an interesting next step, and their article would have good value added had they done it. However, as things stand, I believe I have taken care of their criticism. Using an ordered-logit model of the unobserved Fed disposition to change margin requirements, I found that the Fed responded to recent runs in stock prices *and*changes in margin credit. This is consistent with the Fed's own description of the reasons that induced it to change margin requirements. Hence, when estimating the effect of margin requirements on volatility, one has to control for changes in lagged margin credit and the lagged rates of stock returns, as I did. Note that Hsieh and Miller also compare the volatility right before and right after a margin change and, in the absence of control variables, find no evidence of a negative association. They do find strong evidence of a negative association when the control variables are present. Of course, the results that make sense are the ones that control for the Fed's actions.

4. Comments on Michael Salinger's article

Salinger's article is particularly insightful because it focuses on the central question of the effect of margin requirements on price swings generated by the pyramiding–depyramiding process. He proposes an interesting hypothesis that the direct effect of margin requirements is primarily on upside volatility, because initial margin requirements of less than 100 percent allow the market to go up but do not necessarily drive it down (recall that it is maintenance margins that force the market down). He also proposes that margin debt may have an extra effect on downside volatility because margin calls may bite more with a larger amount of margin debt when the market begins to tumble. He finds little evidence for such nonlineaer effects, but his test may have low power. One way to increase the power of his test would be to lengthen the observational interval in order to allow for the presumed unraveling of stock prices.[2]

Salinger claims that it is margin debt that matters and not margin requirements because the effect of margin requirements on volatility becomes insignificant when margin debt is included in his regressions. Of course, margin requirements cause margin debt to change, hence his regression may simply reveal that in the pre-1940 period margin requirements affected both volatility and margin debt. But note that margin requirements may have an extra effect on speculators over and above the effect revealed by margin debt. The reason is that high margins increase the cost of buying stocks even if speculators manage to get funds from alternative sources. So it is conceivable that when margin requirements increase, margin debt might not change, yet fewer speculators would enter the market, and the market would become less volatile. The regressions in table 1 bear this out. For example, in the 1947–1987 and the 1956–1987 periods margin requirements have a significant effect on volatility but margin debt has an insignificant effect on volatility.

Salinger also claims that since the 1940s margin debt never exceeded 1.5 percent the capitalized value of the NYSE, and hence it is hard to believe that margin requirements could have a substantial effect on the market. This is a powerful argument, but I would like to raise an important counterpoint: margin accounts may have a disproportionate effect on the market if they trade very actively. Surveys in the 1950s, 1960s, and 1970s by the New York Stock Exchange showed that despite the relative small size of margin accounts, margin trading constituted approximately 15 to 30 percent of trading volume.[3] My own vector autoregression results showed that trading volume is reduced following an increase in margin requirements.

5. Conclusion and possibilities for future research

Margin requirements have changed only 22 times since their establishment in October 1934. Naturally, this diminishes the power of tests to distinguish among interesting hypotheses. Despite these limitations, there is a detectable and robust negative association between official margin requirements on the one hand and volatility, excess volatility, and the transitory component of stock prices on the other. This negative association is present in

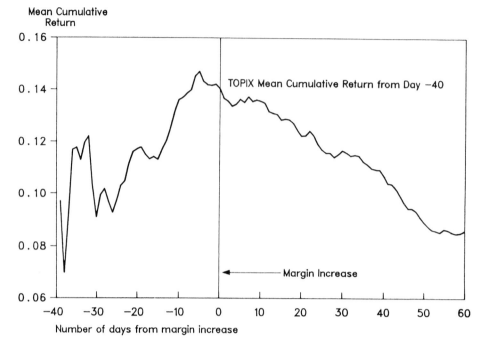

Fig. 1. The effect of an increase in margin requirements on Japanese stocks

the full sample as well as in the post-depression sample. However, the strength of the association is perhaps not of sufficient magnitude to change the strong prior beliefs held by some of my critics. Thus the question arises: Where should empirical research go from here?

Three directions for future research seem promising. First, given the small effective sample sizes (22 margin changes in the United States), it is desirable to use cross-sectional evidence of excess volatility. Kumar, Ferris, and Chance (1988) perform a cross-sectional analysis and find some evidence that the most speculative stocks are affected the most by margin requirements.

Second, it would be desirable to examine evidence from other countries that use margin requirements in a manner similar to the United States. For example, in Japan margin requirements have changed about 100 times. I am currently studying Japanese stock market data with Steve Peristiani of the New York Fed, and we have found that margin requirements have a very strong negative effect on both stock returns and volatility. Here I present two figures for the TOPIX index and comparable figures for the U.S. S&P index taken from my work with Peristiani. Figure 1 shows that in Japan margin increases occur following an upward trend in stock prices and then the market tumbles. Figure 2 shows that margin decreases occur following a downward trend in stock prices and then the market rebounds. The comparable effects in the United States are substantially weaker, as figures 3 and 4 reveal.

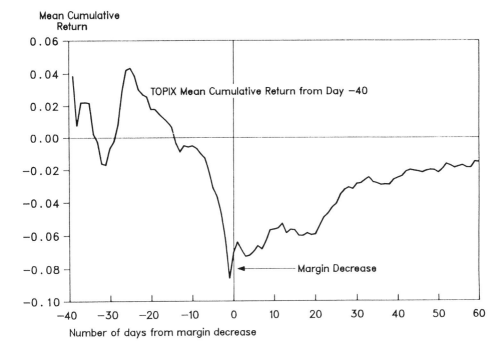

Fig. 2. The effect of a decrease in margin requirements on Japanese stocks

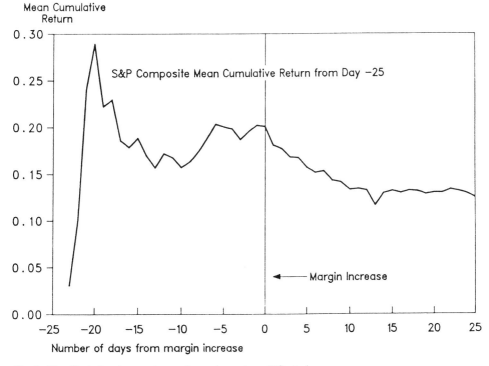

Fig. 3. The effect of an increase in margin requirements on U.S. stocks

51

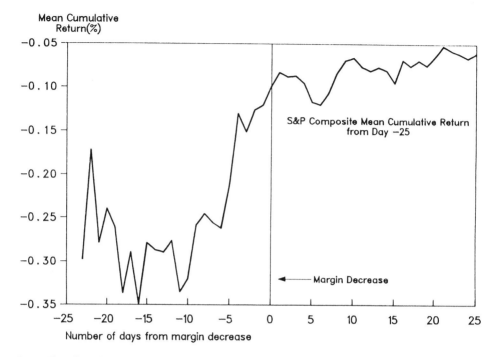

Fig. 4. The effect of a decrease in margin requirements on U.S. stocks

A third direction for future research would involve studying specific episodes of margin changes in greater detail. Salinger takes this direction when he focuses on the experience of the 1920s. Much can be learned from examining time periods characterized by unusual fluctuations in economic variables.

Notes

1. I favor the former interpretation that margin requirements affect the irrational swings of stock prices because in my earlier paper I show that regression-based tests of excess volatility reject less often during periods of high or increasing margin requirements.

2. A brief estimation over annual nonoverlapping horizons shows a significant extra effect for margin requirements in an up market (MARGUP) but no extra effect of debt in a down market (DEBTDN). I define an up market as a year that the market went up from December to December.

3. See the 1984 study of the Board of Governors of the Federal Reserve System.

References

Chrisite, Andrew A. "The Stochastic Behavior of Common Stock Variances: Value, Leverage and Interest Rate Effects." *Journal of Financial Economics* 10 (December 1982), 407–432.

Douglas, George W. "Risk in the Equity Markets: An Appraisal of Market Efficiency." *Yale Economic Essays*(Spring 1969), 3–45.

Fama, Eugene F. and French, Kenneth R. "Dividend Yields and Expected Stock Returns." *Journal of Financial Economics* 22 (October 1988), 3–25.

Federal Reserve System, Board of Governors. *A Review and Evaluation of Margin Requirements.* Staff Study, December 1984.

Hardouvelis, Gikas A. "Margin Requirements, Volatility, and the Transitory Component of Stock Prices." Federal Reserve Bank of New York Research Paper no. 89-09, May 1989; forthcoming, *American Economic Review.*

Hardouvelis, Gikas A. and Peristiani, Steve. "Do Margin Requirements Matter? Evidence from the Japanese Stock Market" Mimeo, Federal Reserve Bank of New York, October 1989.

Hsieh, David A. and Miller, Merton H. "Margin Regulation and Stock Market Volatility." Mimeo, University of Chicago, April 1989.

Kumar, Raman, Harris, Stephen P. and Chance, Don M. "The Differential Impact of Federal Reserve Margin Requirements." Mimeo, Virginia Polytechnic Institute, November 1988.

Kupiec, Paul H. "Initial Margin Requirements and Stock Returns Volatility: Another Look." Mimeo, Board of Governors of the Federal Reserve System, February 1989.

Newey, Whitney K. and West, Kenneth D. "A Simple Positive Semi-Definite, Hetero-skedasticity and Autocorrelation Consistent Covariance Matrix." *Econometrica* 55 (May 1987), 703–708.

Officer, R. R. "The Variability of the Market Factor of the New York Stock Exchange." *Journal of Business* 46 (July 1973), 434–453.

Roll, Richard. "Price Volatility, International Market Links, and their Implications for Regulatory Policies," in this issue.

Salinger, Michael A. "Stock Market Margin Requirements and Volatility: Implications for Regulation of Stock Index Futures," in this issue.

Schwert, G. William. "Business Cycles, Financial Crises and Stock Volatility." University of Rochester, William Simon Graduate School of Business Working Paper no. 88-06, October 1988.

White, Halbert. "A Heteroskedasticity-Consistent Covariance Matrix Estimator and Direct Test for Hetero-skedasticity." *Econometrica* 48 (May 1980), 817–838.

Journal of Financial Services Research, 3: 153–164 (1989)

Margin Requirements and Stock Volatility

G. WILLIAM SCHWERT
William E. Simon Graduate School of Business Administration
University of Rochester, Rochester, NY 14627
and National Bureau of Economic Research

Abstract

Since 1934 the Federal Reserve Board has had the power to set separate limits on the amount of credit that can be extended to purchasers of common stock. There has been much recent debate about the efficacy of these margin regulations. This article argues that the Fed has responded to increases in stock prices by raising margin requirements. The increase in prices has been associated with a decrease in volatility. There is no evidence that changes in margin requirements reduce subsequent stock return volatility. Also, trading halts have not had much effect on volatility in the past. Trading halts that were associated with banking panics were associated with high stock return volatility, but halts without bank panics were not associated with high levels of volatility.

1. Introduction

Since the October 1987 stock market crash there has been much discussion about the similarities and differences between the 1987 and 1929 crashes. One of the major policy issues raised by the Brady Commission Report (*Report of the Presidential Task Force on Market Mechanisms, 1988*) was whether the level of margin requirements on financial futures contracts was too low. They feared that cheap credit allowed over-enthusiastic speculators to bid up stock prices, creating the potential for a crash as prices reverted down to lower (presumably more rational) levels. Similar fears were expressed in the Congressional hearings that followed the 1929 crash. The resulting Securities and Exchange Act of 1934 not only created the Securities and Exchange Commission (SEC) but it also empowered the Federal Reserve Board (Fed) to set limits on the collateral value of stocks and bonds for loans made by banks or brokers. A 50 percent margin requirement means that an investor can borrow up to half of the cost of a new investment in stock. A 100 percent margin requirement means that an investor cannot borrow to help pay for a new investment in stock, and cannot use stocks as collateral for loans.

This article summarizes discussion that was presented at the Columbia Center for the Study of Futures Markets Conference on Regulatory Reform of Stock and Futures Markets, May 12, 1989. Support from the Bradley Policy Research Center at the University of Rochester is gratefully acknowledged.

There were two main reasons that motivated the Fed to ask for the power to set margin requirements. First was the concern that speculation was causing unnecessary volatility in securities prices (or prices that were too high.) Second, the Fed was concerned that loans by banks to stockholders would crowd out credit demands from farmers and businessmen. Some analysts, such as Friedman and Schwartz (1963), contend that the general tightening of credit by the Fed in the late 1920s and early 1930s was a major cause of the severity of the Great Depression. Miron (1986) argues that part of the reason for tightening credit was due to concern about credit to stockholders. Thus, by giving the Fed a policy instrument that could affect credit to securities markets separately from other credit markets the Fed could avoid the mistake it made before the Great Depression.

Because of the Brady Commission's interest in expanding margin regulation to the futures markets, there has been much recent interest in the effects of changes in margin regulation on the behavior of stock returns. This debate has become particularly heated since the article by Hardouvelis (1988a) appeared in the *Federal Reserve Bank of New York Quarterly Review,* accompanied by a prominent article in the October 13, 1988, *Wall Street Journal.* Hardouvelis (1988, 1989) claims to find strong evidence that the variability of stock market returns is significantly lower in periods when margin requirements are high. He presents several tests to show this effect, including measures of "excess" stock volatility. As noted by Roll (1989), many authors have come forward to challenge the methods and conclusions of Hardouvelis, including Ferris and Chance (1988), Hsieh and Miller (1989), Kupiec (1989), Salinger (1989), and Schwert (1989b). These authors take issue with different aspects of Hardouvelis's work, but they uniformly conclude that he has overstated the evidence for the efficacy of margin requirements. Previous authors, including Moore (1966), Largay and West (1973), and Officer (1973), also concluded that changes in margin requirements had little if any effect on subsequent stock returns.

Rather than rehash the arguments about the veracity of Hardouvelis's work, this article will put the question of margin regulation in perspective. It will augment the analysis in Schwert (1989b) by considering the behavior of margin credit along with margin regulations. It will also discuss the effects of "circuit breakers," or trading halts, that have been imposed in the past, since the Brady Commission also advocated the increased use of such measures if liquidity crises occur again in the future.

2. Stock return volatility and margin regulation

2.1. Estimates using monthly returns

Schwert (1989b, 1989d) uses monthly return data for a large portfolio of common stocks from 1857 through 1986 to measure the behavior of the standard deviation of stock returns through time. He uses the following procedure to estimate the conditional standard deviation of stock returns:

1. Estimate a 12th order autoregression for the returns, including dummy variables D_{jt} to allow for different monthly mean returns, using all data available for the series,

$$R_t = \sum_{j=1}^{12} \alpha_j D_{jt} + \sum_{i=1}^{12} \beta_i R_{t-i} + \varepsilon_t; \tag{1}$$

2. Estimate a 12th order autoregression for the absolute residuals from (1) $|\hat{\varepsilon}_t|$, including dummy variables to allow for different average monthly standard deviations,

$$|\hat{\varepsilon}_t| = \sum_{j=1}^{12} \gamma_j D_{jt} + \sum_{i=1}^{12} \rho_i |\hat{\varepsilon}_{t-i}| + u_t; \tag{2}$$

3. The regressand $|\hat{\varepsilon}_t|$ is an estimate of the standard deviation of the stock return for month t, σ_t (using just one observation). The fitted values from (2) estimate the conditional standard deviation of R_t, given information available before month t.[1]

This method is a generalization of the 12 month rolling standard deviation estimator used by the Officer (1973), Hardouvelis (1988, 1989), and others. It allows the conditional mean return to vary over time in (1), and it allows different weights for lagged absolute unexpected returns in (2). It is similar to the generalized autoregressive conditional heteroskedasticity (GARCH) model used by Kupiec (1989). Davidian and Carroll (1987) argue that standard deviation specifications such as (2) are more robust than variance specifications based on $\hat{\varepsilon}_t^2$. Following their suggestion, Schwert (1989b) iterates twice between (1) and (2), using the predicted values from (2) to create weighted least squares (WLS) estimates of (1). Experiments with further iteration produced only small changes in the parameter values and standard errors.

To study the relation between changes in margin requirements and stock volatility, 12 leads and lags of changes in margin requirements, $dm_t = m_t - m_{t-1}$, are added to both (1) and (2). Since Schwert (1989b, 1989d) shows that stock returns are lower and volatility is higher during recessions, two additional dummy variables are added to the regression. D_{rt} equals 1 during NBER recessions, and D_{dt} equals 1 during the recesssions that occurred between 1929–1939 (the Great Depression.) The estimates of these dummy variable coefficients are not shown in table 1, but volatility is reliably larger during recessions and especially during the Great Depression. Table 1 contains the sum of all 25 coefficients, and the sums for the leads (-12 to -1) and the lags (1 to 12.) The results strongly support Officer's interpretation that the Federal Reserve Board has increased (decreased) margin requirements after stock prices have risen (fallen). The coefficients of margin changes in the return equation are reliably positive for the leads and only about one standard error above 0 for the lags. Moreover, increases (decreases) in margin requirements seem to follow periods when stock volatility is low (high). The coefficients of margin changes in the volatility equation are reliably negative for the leads and only about one standard error below 0 for the lags. These conclusions hold for the overall 1935–1989 sample period, and for the 1935–1945 and 1946–1989 subsamples.

Margin requirements are increased after stock prices have risen and stock volatility is relatively low. There is no evidence that stock return behavior is different from normal in the 12 months following a change in margin requirements. The obvious interpretation of

Table 1. Relations of stock returns and volatility with changes in margin requirements

$$R_t = \sum_{j=1}^{12} \alpha_j D_{jt} + \sum_{i=1}^{12} \beta_i R_{t-i} + \sum_{k=1}^{12} \delta_{1k} \, dm_{t-k} + \mu_1 D_{rt} + \mu_2 D_{dt} + \varepsilon_t$$

$$|\hat{\varepsilon}_t| = \sum_{j=1}^{12} \gamma_j D_{jt} + \sum_{i=1}^{12} \rho_i |\hat{\varepsilon}_{t-i}| + \sum_{k=1}^{12} \delta_{2k} \, dm_{t-k} + \sigma_1 D_{rt} + \sigma_2 D_{dt} + u_t$$

	Sum	Std Error	T-statistic
	Tests for Returns, δ_{1k}		
October 1935–April 1989			
All leads and lags (k = – 12, . . . , 12)	.8422	.2301	3.66
Leads (k = – 12, . . . , –1)	.6591	.1529	4.31
Lags (k = 1, . . . , 12)	.1469	.1422	1.03
October 1935–December 1945			
All leads and lags (k = –12, . . . , 12)	1.207	1.169	1.03
Leads (k = –12, . . . , –1)	1.569	.4926	3.19
Lags (k = 1, . . . , 12)	–.4605	.9888	–.47
January 1946–April 1989			
All leads and lags (k = –12, . . . , 12)	1.002	.2851	3.52
Leads (k = –12, . . . , –1)	.6928	.1832	3.78
Lags (k = 1, . . . , 12)	.2884	.1712	1.68
	Tests for Volatility, δ_{2k}		
October 1935–April 1989			
All leads and lags (k = –12, . . . , 12)	–.1749	.1576	–1.10
Leads (k = –12, . . . , –1)	–.2099	.1102	–1.97
Lags (k = 1, . . . , 12)	.0404	.1033	0.39
October 1935–December 1945			
All leads and lags (k = –12, . . . , 12)	1.093	1.129	0.97
Leads (k = –12, . . . , –1)	–.2026	.4015	–.50
Lags (k = 1, . . . , 12)	1.383	.8427	1.64
January 1946–April 1989			
All leads and lags (k = –12, . . . , 12)	–.2743	.1837	–1.49
Leads (k = –12, . . . , –1)	.2746	.1241	–2.21
Lags (k = 1, . . . , 12)	.0099	.1124	0.09

Note: Asymptotic standard errors and *t*-statistics use White's (1980) correction for heteroskedasticity. Twenty-five leads and lags (–12, . . . , 12) of the change in margin requirements dm_t are added to equations (1) and (2) to estimate the relation of changes in margin requirements with stock returns or stock volatility from October 1935 through April 1989. The dummy variable D_{rt} is equal to 1 during NBER-specified recessions, and 0 during expansions. The dummy variable D_{dt} is equal to 1 during the NBER-specified recessions from 1929–1939 (the Great Depression), and 0 during expansions. Volatility is significantly higher during recessions, and particularly during the recessions from 1929–1933 and 1937–1938 (i.e., the estimates of δ_1 and δ_2 are reliably greater than 0). Average returns are insignificantly different during these periods (i.e., the estimates of μ_1 and μ_2 are within two standard errors of 0).

this result is that the Fed responds to stock market conditions. The policy actions have little or no effect on stock return behavior.

Many people, including Salinger (1989), have commented that they find it implausible that the Fed would respond to lower stock volatility by increasing margin requirements. I agree that this seems implausible. Instead, I believe that the Fed looked at the level of stock prices (i.e., high level of recent stock returns) and used that as a sign "excess speculation," causing the Fed to raise margin requirements. There is much recent literature, including Black (1976), French, Schwert, and Stambaugh (1987), Nelson (1988), Schwert (1989b, 1989c), Pagan and Schwert (1989), and Turner, Startz, and Nelson (1989), that shows that volatility falls after stock prices rise. Thus, the behavior of returns and volatility before changes in margin requirements that are shown in table 1 are typical of the behavior of stock returns. From a policy perspective, it is important that the decrease in volatility occurs along with the rise in prices *before* the Fed implements its policy change. In the language of "event studies," there is a large problem of sample selection bias here: it is the rise in prices that causes the event being studied.

Hardouvelis (1989) and Hsieh and Miller (1989) refer to tests like those in table 1 as "Granger (1969) causality tests." I have argued elsewhere (Schwert, 1979) that lead-lag regression tests such as these cannot generally be interpreted as evidence of economic causality. This is especially true when one of the variables is a financial asset price, where investors have strong pecuniary incentives to forecast its future behavior. Nevertheless, in this case it is hard to imagine a reverse causality argument that would lead investors to bid up (drive down) stock prices and reduce (increase) volatility in anticipation of an increase (decrease) in margin requirements.

2.2. The spurious regression problem

One important difference between the regression tests in table 1 and the tests performed by Hardouvelis (1988, 1989) is that I examine the response of stock volatility to *changes* in margin requirements, whereas Hardouvelis includes the level of margin requirements in his regressions. In figure 1, the time path of stock market volatility is very persistent, as is the level of margin requirements. By linking these persistent series through a fixed parameter regression relation, Hardouvelis risks the "spurious regressions" problem (see Granger and Newbold, 1977; Plosser and Schwert, 1978; and Plosser, Schwert, and White 1982). Briefly, the time-path of two random walk-like series will seem to be related, even if the increments (changes) in the series are independent of each other. In Schwert (1987), I show that stock market volatility has such unit root behavior. By using 25 leads and lags of changes in margin requirements in table 1, I allow for quite general relations between volatility and the level of margin requirements, without forcing conditional volatility to have the same value whenever margin requirements are at a given level. For example, the Fed has not changed margin requirements since 1974, yet stock volatility has certainly not been constant since that time. Hardouvelis would probably argue that the other variables in his regressions remove the unit root behavior from the errors of his regressions. While it is theoretically possible for this to occur, my experience with similar types of regression models in Schwert

Monthly Stock Market Volatility

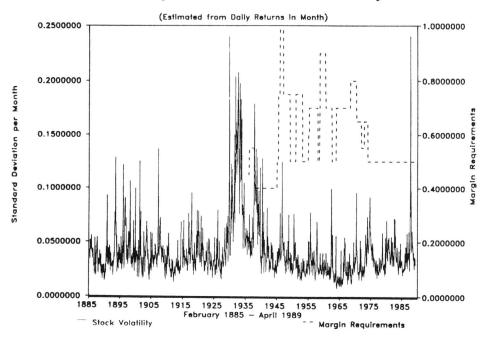

Fig. 1. Estimates of the monthly deviation of returns from daily returns to the Dow Jones and Standard & Poor's composite portfolios, February 1885–April 1989 (and margin requirements October 1934–April 1989).

(1989d) suggests that this is unlikely to result in a well-specified regression. The analysis in Hsieh and Miller (1989) also casts doubt on this contention.

2.3. Estimates of volatility using daily returns

To reinforce the evidence from the monthly returns data, look at figure 1. It shows monthly standard deviation estimates based on the daily returns within the month. I use the Dow Jones returns from 1885–1927 and the Standard & Poor's composite returns from 1928–1989 (a total of 28,884 daily returns.) There are about 21 trading days per month, so each standard deviation estimate is based on 21 times more data than the monthly estimates in table 1. I multiply the daily variance by the number of trading days to estimate the monthly variance. Note that each of these volatility estimates is based on a nonoverlapping sample. The much larger number of observations, and the use of nonoverlapping data, are both important improvements over the crude volatility estimates used by Hardouvelis (1988, 1989), Salinger (1989), and Schwert (1989b).[2] Figure 1 also shows the level of initial margin requirements since October 1934. The interoccular test[3] casts doubt on the credibility of the argument that volatility is closely related to margin requirements. As noted by Officer (1973), the level of volatility is similar from 1885–1928 to the level after 1945. This occurs even though the size and breadth of the market portfolio grew substantially over this time, which would normally cause volatility to decline. Thus, it is hard to argue that the initiation of standardized margin requirements by the Fed (or the simultaneous creation of the SEC) caused a permanent reduction in the level of stock volatility. After all, banks required collateral for loans used to purchase securities before 1934; the main effect of the regulation was to raise the minimum level of collateral required and to standardize the level across banks and customers.

2.4. Banking panics and volatility

More detailed analysis of the plot in figure 1 shows several interesting related phenomena. First, during the banking panics of 1893 and 1907, when many banks refused to convert checks into currency, stock volatility rose quickly. Friedman and Schwartz (1963) argue that the 1907 panic eventually led to the creation of the Federal Reserve System in 1913, as Congress concluded that the national banking system was incapable of dealing with simultaneous demands for liquidity by many depositors.

2.5. Circuit breakers and volatility

On July 31, 1914, at the start of World War I in Europe, the New York Stock Exchange (NYSE) closed for trading.[4] It did not reopen until December 12, 1914, and only then under the condition that prices for stocks could be no lower than they had been in late July. This was by far the longest and most serious trading halt in United States' history. Sobel (1988) argues that the NYSE closed because of fear that selling by European stockholders would drive down prices. Indeed, most of the other major world stock exchanges also closed down at the same time. As it turned out, however, European investors viewed investments in the U.S. stock market as a relatively safe haven. The restriction on price levels was quickly dropped, since prices showed no tendency to fall once trading resumed.[5] Volatiltiy around the interruption from August through November 1914 in figure 1 does not seem very high compared with earlier or later events.

There was a similar trading halt during the National Banking Holiday, from March 4–15, 1933. Stock prices were about 15 percent higher after the trading halt, but volatility remained high. Over 4,000 banks never reopened following this halt.

The 1914 trading halt differed from the 1873 and 1933 halts in several ways, but perhaps the most important difference was that there was no related interruption of the banking system. It is understandable that securities markets would stop trading if a much more fundamental part of the financial services industry (banks) was malfunctioning. The process of clearing trades requires a well-functioning banking system. In the case where NYSE trading was halted, but there was no problem with the banking system, the behavior of stock prices was not particularly unusual.

3. Margin credit and volatility

Salinger (1989) argues that borrowing by margin customers gives a more accurate reflection of the relation between stock volatility and margin regulation. Indeed, his strongest results show that margin credit relative to the value of NYSE stocks is negatively correlated with stock return volatility using data beginning in 1935. As he emphasizes, however, this result largely reflects the decline in the use of margin credit after the 1929 crash. Figure 2 plots monthly margin credit divided by the value of all NYSE stocks from October 1917 through August 1988. These data are estimated from a variety of series in the Federal Reserve Board's (1976a, 1976b) volumes on security market credit from 1914–1970, and from recent data from Citibase. The data show higher levels of credit in the early years and lower levels in the later years than those used by Hardouvelis (1989) or Salinger (1989), because I use different methods to splice adjacent and overlapping series. Nonetheless, the general character of the data is similar to those used by Hardouvelis and Salinger. The important point to note in figure 2 is that margin credit was a large percentage of NYSE value (above 12 percent) throughout the 1917–1930 period. It did not rise precipitously during 1928–1929. Margin credit moves up and down with stock value, except the factor of proportionality was around 20 percent from 1917 through 1929, and it was below 5 percent

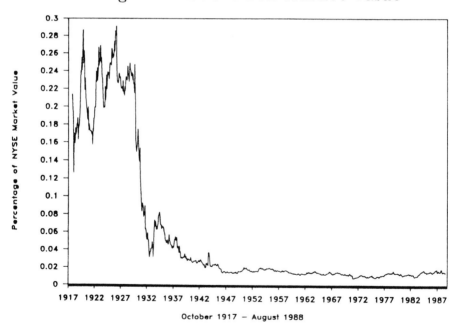

Fig. 2. Margin credit as a fraction of the total value of NYSE stocks, October 1917–August 1988.

most of the time after 1935. The period from 1929–1934, before margin requirements took effect, was a period of transition where investors and lenders apparently decided that the relatively large amount of personal leverage that was common before 1929 was not optimal. As noted by Salinger (1989), the steady proportion of margin credit in the 1917–1929 period casts doubt on the argument that high stock volatility in the 1929–1933 period was due to high levels of margin credit.

At a more basic level, I have doubts about the interpretation of margin credit as a measure of Fed policy. While it is certainly true that the Fed can stop the growth of margin credit by raising initial margin requirements to 100 percent as they did in 1946, most of the variation in margin credit reflects changes in investors' demand for credit. Figure 3 contains log-linear plots of margin credit, consumer credit, and the proceeds raised from new corporate security issues from 1910–1988. All of these curves drop after 1929, and again in 1937, during the Great Depression. If I had included a plot of the number of stock splits from Fama, Fisher, Jensen, and Roll (1969), it would exhibit the same general pattern. In fact, there are many series reflecting stock market activity that move up and down together. Since volatility and margin credit are both correlated with the level of stock prices, it is not

Margin and Consumer Credit, New Security Issues

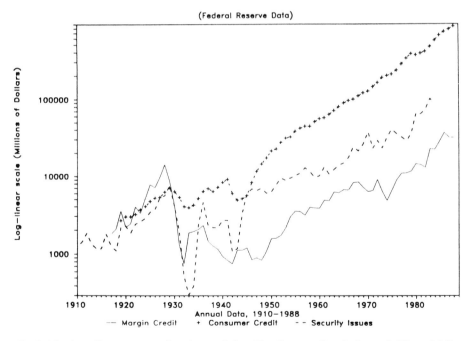

Fig. 3. Margin credit, consumer credit and proceeds from New Corporate Security Issues, (millions of dollars per year), 1910–1988 (long-linear scale).

surprising that they move together. This provides no evidence, however, for the issue of whether Fed policy actions have an effect on stock prices or volatility.

4. Conclusions

I agree with Salinger (1989) that there is no evidence from the stock market that increasing margin limits for financial futures contracts will have any effect on the behavior of stock prices. Such a change would increase transactions costs for traders in futures markets, and could cause trading to move outside the United States.

Before advocating a drastic change in margin rules for futures markets, one should try to identify the externality that this rule is trying to remedy. Given my conclusion that there are no data that show effects on stock price behavior after changes in margin requirements, the only externality I can imagine would involve bankruptcy costs that might occur if many futures traders defaulted on their positions. If this also caused defaults of banks (which are supplied with underpriced insurance by the Federal Deposit Insurance Corporation), then taxpayers would bear part of the brunt of these insolvencies. Since futures traders and clearing corporations have strong private incentives to assure the solvency of these transactions, it is not clear to me that additional regulatory oversight is necessary.

Similarly, experience with circuit breakers does not give me much confidence that they will reduce volatility. If anything, the obvious reduction in liquidity that is implied by a system that has frequent discretionary trading halts could reduce prices and trading volume and increase volatility.

Thus, empirical evidence from over 100 years of stock return data suggests that increases in margin requirements and circuit breakers are not likely to be effective policy tools. I am much more confident that I can predict the relation between the economic rents available to competing financial institutions and the positions they will take in such policy debates. If the NYSE can raise the costs of the futures exchanges, it will cause a wealth transfer from the futures industry to the stock brokerage industry. Similarly, regulators seek broader powers to increase their future employment opportunities or their enjoyment of their job. Such rent-seeking behavior is perfectly rational from the perspective of private utility, but it should not be confused with "socially optimal" public policy.

Notes

1. Since the expected value of the absolute error is less than the standard deviation from a Normal distribution, $E|\hat{\varepsilon}_t| = \sigma_t(2/\pi)^{1/2}$, all absolute errors are multiplied by the constant $(2/\pi)^{-1/2}$. Dan Nelson suggested this correction.

2. Merton (1980) shows why more frequent observations are valuable in estimating volatility, but not in estimating mean returns.

3. That is, do the data "hit you between the eyes"?

4. Trading was halted for 10 days during the banking panic of 1873, when banks also refused to convert checks into currency. This action was taken by the New York Stock Exchange because trades could not be settled when the banking system was faltering.

5. On the day of the October 19, 1987, stock market crash there was a story about previous crashes in the *Wall Street Journal* (by Cynthia Crosser, October 19, 1987, p. 15) that quoted the beginning of World War I as the largest

one-day drop in stock prices in NYSE history. This mistake occurred because Dow Jones changed the definition of their industrial portfolio during the period of the trading halt. The level of the new index number on December 12, 1914 (54.0), was indeed far below the level of the old index number on July 30, 1914 (71.42), but this was solely due to the change in composition. The level of the old index was 74.56 on December 12, 1914. Thus, stock prices rose by about 4.4 percent during the trading halt.

References

Black, Fischer. "Studies of Stock Price Volatility Changes." *Proceeding of the 1976 Meetings of the Business and Economics Statistics Section,* American Statistical Association, 1976, pp. 177–181.

Davidian, Marie and Carroll, Raymond J. "Variance Function Estimation." *Journal of the American Statistical Association* 82 (1987), 1079–1091.

Fama, Eugene F., Fisher, Lawrence, Jensen, Michael C. and Roll, Richard. "The Adjustment of Stock Prices to New Information." *International Economic Review* 10 (1969), 1–21.

Federal Reserve Board. *Banking and Monetary Statistics, 1914–1941.* Washington, D.C.: U.S. Government Printing Office, 1976a.

——————. *Banking and Monetary Statistics, 1941–1970.* Washington, D.C.: U.S. Government Printing Office, 1976b.

Ferris, S. and Chance, D. "Margin Requirements and Stock Market Volatility." *Economics Letters* 28 (1988), 251–254.

French, Kenneth R., Schwert, G. William and Stambaugh, Robert F. "Expected Stock Returns and Volatility." *Journal of Financial Economics* 19 (1987), 3–29.

Granger, C.W.J. "Investigating Causal Relations by Econometric Models and Cross-Spectral Methods." *Econometrica* 37 (1969), 424–438.

Granger, C.W.J. and Newbold, Paul. "Spurious Regressions in Econometrics." *Journal of Econometrics* 2 (1974), 111–120.

Hardouvelis, Gikas A. "Margin Requirements and Stock Market Volatility." *Federal Reserve Bank of New York Quarterly* (Summer 1988a).

——————. "Margin Requirements, Volatility, and the Transitory Component of Stock Prices." *American Economic Review,* forthcoming 1989.

Hsieh, David A. and Miller, Merton H. "Margin Regulation and Stock Market Variability." *Journal of Finance,* forthcoming 1989.

Kupiec, Paul H. "Initial Margin Requirements and Stock Returns Volatility: Another Look." Federal Reserve Board, Finance and Economics Discussion Series #53.

Largay, J. A. and West, Richard R. "Margin Changes and Stock Price Behavior." *Journal of Political Economy* 81 (1973), 328–339.

Merton, Robert C. "On Estimating the Expected Return on the Market: An Exploratory Investigation." *Journal of Financial Economics* 8 (1980), 323–361.

Miron, Jeffrey A. "Financial Panics, the Seasonality of the Nominal Interest Rate, and the Founding of the Fed." *American Economic Review* 76 (1986), 125–140.

Moore, Thomas G. "Stock Market Margin Requirements." *Journal of Political Economy* 74 (1966), 158–167.

Nelson, Daniel B. "Conditional Heteroskedasticity in Asset Returns: A New Approach." Unpublished manuscript, University of Chicago, 1988.

Officer, Robert R. "The Variability of the Market Factor of New York Stock Exchange." *Journal of Business* 46 (1973), 434–453.

Pagan, Adrian R. and Schwert, G. William "Alternative Models for Conditional Stock Volatility." *Journal of Econometrics,* forthcoming 1989.

Plosser, Charles I. and Schwert, G. William. "Money, Income and Sunspots: Measuring Economic Relationships and the Effects of Differencing." *Journal of Monetary Economics* 4 (1978), 637–660.

Plosser, Charles I., Schwert, G. William and White, Halbert. "Differencing as a Test of Specification." *International Economic Review* 23 (1982), 535–552.

Presidential Task Force on Market Mechanisms. *Report of the Presidential Task Force on Market Mechanisms.* Washington, D.C.: U.S. Government Printing Office, 1988.

Roll, Richard. "Price Volatility, International Market Links, and Their Implications for Regulatory Policies," *Journal of Financial Services Research,* this issue.

Salinger, Michael A. "Stock Market Margin Requirements and Volatility: Implications for Regulation of Stock Index Futures." *Journal of Financial Services Research,* this issue.

Schwert, G. William. "Tests of Causality: The Message in the Innovations." *Carnegie-Rochester Conference Series on Public Policy* 10 (1979), 55–96.

——————. "Effects of Model Specification on Tests for Unit Roots in Macroeconomic Data." *Journal of Monetary Economics* 20 (1987), 73–103.

——————. "Tests for Unit Roots: A Monte Carlo Investigation." *Journal of Business and Economic Statistics* 7 (1989a), 147–159.

——————. "Business Cycles, Financial Crises and Stock Volatility." *Carnegie-Rochester Conference Series on Public Policy,* forthcoming 1989b.

——————. "Stock Volatility and the Crash of '87." *Review of Financial Studies,* forthcoming.

——————. "Why Does Stock Market Volatility Change Over Time?" *Journal of Finance,* forthcoming 1989d.

Sobel, Robert. *Panic on Wall Street,* rev. ed. New York: E. P. Dutton, 1988.

Turner, Christopher M., Startz, Richard and Nelson, Charles R. "A Markov Model of Heteroskedasticity, Risk and Learning in the Stock Market." *Journal of Financial Economics,* forthcoming.

White, Halbert. "A Heteroskedasticity-consistent Covariance Matrix Estimator and a Direct Test for Heteroskedasticity." *Econometrica* 48 (1980), 817–838.

Journal of Financial Services Research, 3: 165–199 (1989)

Volatility, Price Resolution, and the Effectiveness of Price Limits

CHRISTOPHER K. MA
Associate Professor of Finance
College of Business Administration
Texas Tech University
Lubbock, TX 79409

RAMESH P. RAO
Assistant Professor of Finance
College of Business Administration
Texas Tech University
Lubbock, TX 79409

R. STEPHEN SEARS
Professor of Finance and Director of the
Institute for Banking and Financial Studies
College of Business Administration
Texas Tech University
Lubbock, TX 79409

1. Introduction and overview

Following the market crash in 1987, there has been increased interest in the usefulness of price limits as well as other forms of market controls. The purpose of this research is to investigate price limits and the empirical behavior of futures prices for a selected group of commodities around price limits. For the group of commodities examined in this research, the empirical results show that for the time periods analyzed, in general:

1. The period of time immediately preceding limit moves is characterized by major changes in the direction of the limit price while following the limit move; prices tend to either stabilize or reverse directions, thus suggesting that price limits may provide a *cooling-off* period for the market.

2. Price limits also appear to be accompanied by substantial reductions in volatility. This attenuation of volatility in the post-limit period and the maintenance of volume in the post-limit period tend to suggest that liquidity may not be severely impaired by the limit move process.

This article was presented for and at the Conference on Regulatory and Structural Reform of Stock and Futures Markets, May 12, 1989. This research has benefited greatly from the helpful comments provided by Franklin R. Edwards, Bruce N. Lehmann, and Merton H. Miller. However, the results and conclusions presented in this research do not necessarily reflect their opinions.

67

The topic of price limits and their perceived benefits and costs is a controversial issue in light of the market crash in 1987 and the subsequent reports and recommendations regarding institutional reform. To provide a better understanding of the nature and controversy surrounding price limits, the following section will briefly discuss the market crash of 1987 along with the committees' investigations of the crash and their major recommendations.

In section 3 we focus specifically on the recommendations regarding the imposition of price limits, their pros and cons, and feasibility for usage. Given the various concerns on the part of regulators, we then discuss various criteria by which the effectiveness of price limits can be judged. In sections 4 and 5 we discuss the methodology, data base, and empirical results. The article concludes with a brief summary in section 6.

2. The crash—its studies and their recommendations

Following the crash of October 1987, there was widespread concern among regulators, politicians, and investors regarding whether or not U.S. financial markets were operating *properly*. In particular, because of the events on and surrounding October 19, 1987, there was strong interest in whether institutional reform was needed in financial markets so as to avoid, in the future, the difficulties experienced by the markets during this period.

As a result of the crash and these concerns, several studies have been conducted regarding the events of October 1987. These studies include examinations by: the Brady Commission (1988), the Securities and Exchange Commission (SEC) (1988), the Chicago Mercantile Exchange (CME, referred to as the Miller Report) (1987), the Chicago Board of Trade (CBOT) (1987), the Commodity Futures Trading Commission (CFTC) (1988), the New York Stock Exchange (NYSE) (Katzenbach, 1987), and the General Accounting Office (GAO) (1988).[1] In addition to these studies, several well-known members from the academic community (e.g., Barro, 1989; Edwards, 1988a, 1988b; Fama 1989; Fischel, 1989; Meltzner, 1989; Roll, 1989; and Telser, 1989) have conducted independent analyses of these events.

Probably the most widely known and publicized study of the crash is the *Report of the Presidential Task Force on Market Mechanisms* (the Brady Report, Nicholas F. Brady, Chairman). In the Brady Report, three general factors were ascribed as contributing to the crash: (1) an unexpectedly high trade deficit that pushed interest rates higher; (2) proposed tax legislation that affected the stock prices of firms targeted as *takeover candidates;* and (3) the activities of a number of institutions that employed *portfolio insurance* strategies and a small group of mutual funds reacting to redemptions which, in turn, led to a number of aggressive, trading-oriented institutions selling in anticipation of further market declines.[3]

A general reading of the Brady Report gives one the impression that the Brady Commission felt that a factor that contributed significantly to the crash was the trading strategies (e.g., portfolio insurance, index arbitrage) of a few institutions who actively trade not only in the stock market but also in its related futures and options markets. This feeling, however, is not shared in all of the other reports: e.g., see reports to the CME (Miller, Scholes, Malkiel, and Hawke, 1987) and the CFTC (1988). On this matter, studies by Fama

(1989), Meltzner (1989), and Roll (1989) have generally concluded that the crash was attributable primarily to fundamental factors rather than because of specific trading strategies. That is, the decline in prices was due to a revaluation of equity prices, which, in turn, was related to such factors as expected earnings and risk, which is measured through required returns and discount factors. This conclusion, in part, draws from the observation that the crash was international in scope, and affected equity markets worldwide that differed systematically in terms of their institutional features and trading practices.

While there appears to be disagreement as to the influence of some of the newly created trading strategies, it would seem that most experts would agree that the market crash of 1987 was caused by a variety of factors—fundamental, political, and psychological—and it would be difficult to isolate any one factor as the culprit. Furthermore, the new trading strategies employed by investors today have necessarily linked stock, futures, and options markets both domestically as well as internationally.

In establishing recommendations for structural change, the Brady Commission reviewed several areas of market performance which they viewed as important in assessing the functioning of financial markets.[4] Based on their analysis, they made the following general recommendations.[5]

1. There should be one agency to coordinate regulatory activities across financial markets;

2. Clearing systems should be unified across markets to reduce financial risk;

3. Margin requirements should be consistent across financial markets in order to control speculation and financial leverage;

4. Circuit breakers such as price limits and coordinated trading halts should be formulated and implemented to protect the market system; and

5. Information systems should be established to monitor transactions and conditions in related markets.

The focus of this analysis is on item 4, circuit breakers. In the following section, various proposals that have been made concerning these devices are presented, in particular, with regard to price limits. Included in this discussion are the various pros and cons of price limits, along with potential problems pertaining to the feasibility of implementing such mechanisms. The section concludes with a discussion of the ways by which the effectiveness of such rules can be evaluated in light of the concerns expressed by the various reports on the crash.

3. Circuit breakers

3.1. Recommendations

Following the crash, various committees and commissions that investigated these events made specific recommendations regarding the consideration and implementation of circuit breakers. Table 1 outlines the major points presented in these reports. A reading of these proposals indicates a couple of noteworthy aspects. First, circuit breakers (sometimes

Table 1. Summary of proposals regarding circuit breakers

A. Brady Report	B. SEC
1. Implement coordinated price limits across markets.	1. No stock price limits.
2. Coordinate trading halts across markets. These should be as brief as possible and have coordinated restart procedures.	2. Brief, coordinated trading halts among markets should be analyzed.
3. Circuit breakers should be predetermined to be a part of exchanges in-place operating procedures	3. Delay the opening of options and futures markets until stock markets markets open.
4. Circuit breakers should not be at levels causing frequent triggering.	
C. CME (Miller Report)	**D. GAO**
1. Price limits need to be carefully examined. If price limits are used, there should be brief pauses in trading, rather than a complete stop until the next day.	1. Circuit breakers such as price limits must be coordinated across markets.
2. Carefully examine whether the use of price limits would aid in the problems incurred at the opening of trading.	2. Intermarket regulation is needed to implement decisions regarding price limits.
E. CFTC	**F. CBOT**
1. Any price limits placed in force must consider their effects on other related markets.	1. If the goal is limiting stock price movements, then stock price limits should be used.
	2. Trading halts should be considered.
G. NYSE	
1. An intermarket regulator is needed to coordinate any use of circuit breakers.	

referred to as trading halts) can come in a variety of forms. For example, although the Brady Commission did not make any specific recommendations, its report mentions the possibility of trading halts triggered by reaching established price limits, position limits, and circumstances arising out of a significant imbalances between buy and sell orders. However, the most commonly mentioned form is the price limit—a trading halt based upon the movement, either up or down, of prices to an established price (the limit). Second, it would appear that there is not complete agreement on whether price limits would be useful. For example, while the Brady Committee seems positive about the benefits of these tools, other reports by the SEC, the CME, and NYSE are more cautious and, in general, recommend careful examination prior to actual implementation. Because the topic of price limits is controversial, a better understanding of the issues surrounding the controversy requires discussion of their perceived benefits and costs, as well as the feasibility of introducing them.

3.2. Price limits—their benefits, costs, and feasibility

Nearly all of the commissioned studies address the issue of price limits. In particular, the Brady Report and the CFTC study outline specific benefits and costs regarding these tools. We now examine the more commonly mentioned aspects of this controversy.

3.2.1. Benefits. One potential benefit ascribed to price limits in the Brady Report and the CFTC study is that such measures may serve to limit credit risk on the part of market participants and thus aid in mitigating the loss of financial confidence by providing a period to *settle up* and ensure that everyone is solvent. That is, price limits may serve to constrain the daily financial exposure of trading by providing a ceiling on the amount of margin calls due as a result of the day's trading.[6]

Apparently, some would view established margins in futures markets as inadequate in protecting against this type of risk. Regarding the issue of solvency and protection against credit risk, Brennan (1986) notes that there may be some redundancy here in that margins in futures markets and price limits in the futures markets would, to some degree, serve the same purpose. The issue of establishing the proper level of limits in the stock index futures markets, relative to existing margin requirements, also caught the attention of Miller.[7] In any event, if one of the purposes of price limits is to provide protection against credit risks, it would seem that such measures would need to be coordinated with existing margin levels.

A second mentioned benefit from the use of price limits is that such measures can protect the market from *overreacting* to news events, particularly during periods of significant uncertainty.[8] The issue of overreaction in financial markets is an interesting one that has attracted the attention of several academic researchers (e.g., see De Bondt and Thaler, 1985; and French and Roll, 1986). The study by French and Roll (1986) asserts that the volatility in the prices of financial assets is related to the effects of trading, which in turn is motivated by public information, private information, and by traders' overreaction (*noise*). The overreaction hypothesis is consistent with the notion that prices are headed in the wrong direction and will eventually reverse themselves as traders sort through the information. In this sense, price limits may aid the market in the price discovery process by allowing the market to pause and *cool off*. As French and Roll (1986) also note, *noise* is associated with *excess volatility* and, as the noise begins to dissipate, volatility should return to its normal level. In summary, proponents of the overreaction hypothesis would seem to argue that price limits would be beneficial in controlling for excessive volatility as well as unwarranted price movements.

A third benefit mentioned in the Brady Report is that price limits counter the illusion that markets are perfectly liquid and can absorb massive one-sided volume. Thus, limits can serve to slow down certain trading strategies (e.g., portfolio insurance and index arbitrage) which can be disruptive to not only the institutions employing them but also the market.[9] Presumably, there is the belief that traders need protection against their follies and, that given ample time to review the situation they will monitor their activities more carefully. To a large extent, this argument seems related to the first two benefits.

3.2.2. Costs. A commonly mentioned disadvantage concerning the imposition of price limits is that they represent barriers to the market clearing on days in which these are in effect. Thus, some traders will be unable to liquidate their positions or establish hedging positions because the equilibrium price is outside (either higher or lower) the price limit in effect on that day. Thus, because of limits, long (short) positions in a downward (upward) moving market face liquidity problems because of the potential unwillingness of buyers (sellers) to enter the market because of further anticipated price decreases (increases). In addition, limits can disrupt spot and futures price co-movements, thus increasing the price risk for hedgers.[10]

A second (and competing view to benefit #2) argument against price limits is that they serve no purpose other than to slow down or delay the price change. This argument views price limits as impeding, rather than enhancing, the price discovery process. Rather than stabilizing price changes, price movements will continue to move in the direction of the equilibrium price as new trading limits are established in subsequent trading periods. This view has many proponents in the academic community (e.g., Fama, 1989; Meltzner, 1989; Miller et al., 1987; and Telser, 1989). In related evidence on this view, Roll (1989) did a comparative study for the *cash equity* markets of 23 countries and found that, after controlling for differences in price volatilities, price limits had no differential effect on the rate of decline in prices during the market crash.

A final argument against price limits is that they would tend to become self-fulfilling. That is, because of the fears of illiquidity and being locked in to a position (see cost #1), traders would rush to cover themselves through active trading. Consequently, volume would be very heavy and the price limit would serve as a *magnet* drawing the price closer to it. The magnet concept is discussed in the report by the CFTC (Kampuis, Kormendi, and Watson, 1989) and by Fama (1989).

3.2.3. Feasibility. One thing seems clear—there are many opinions and differences in opinion regarding the usefulness of price limits. Assuming for the moment that price limits are to be imposed, it would seem that several institutional factors need to be addressed before limits can be effectively implemented. First, and an issue mentioned in all the studies we read, is that there would need to be some intermarket regulatory agency to coordinate price limits. Because the cash, futures, and options markets are linked by the trading activities of investors, limits should be imposed in all related markets. Aside from the issue of how much and when, there is the current problem that these markets are governed in one or another by differing sets of regulatory groups, which, in turn, determine policies pertaining to their trading activities. Disentangling this network would seem to be a formidable task.

On an operational level, issues pertaining to differential opening times in related markets, margin requirements, and specific rules regarding price limits would need to be addressed. For example, the Miller Report (Miller et al., 1987), as well as others, has noted the problems associated with the different opening hours of the cash and futures markets and matters dealing with *frontrunning*. For price limits to be effective, some consideration is needed on this problem. As previously mentioned, some proponents feel that limits serve as credit risk valves. *If* this is an objective of price limits, then these breakers should be established at levels commensurate with margins. Furthermore, since margins in cash and futures markets serve different purposes, it is not clear that limits would serve the same purpose within this objective. Finally, a perplexing issue is how to place specific limits in the cash market for such securities as stock indexes, when the corresponding instrument in the futures market is the stock index futures. While the futures contract is traded, the cash commodity is only proxied through investment holdings that closely correspond to the index. Thus, do you halt trading in a specified number (or percent) of the stocks in the index when the futures has hit its limit? Or do you use some other rule?

These are only some of the issues that come to mind when addressing the feasibility of price limits. On the whole, it would seem that probably the biggest hurdle to overcome is the regulatory matter of coordinating such measures.

3.2.4. Evaluation criteria.
Given all the viewpoints regarding the benefits and costs of price limits, two important issues emerge: (1) would price limits be effective? and (2) by what criteria can price limits be examined to evaluate their effectiveness? Issue #1 is examined in the following section. Issue #2 is addressed first.

Judging from the discussion of the benefits and costs, it would seem that two empirical statistics that can provide some information about the effectiveness of price limits are the behaviors of price movements (levels) and volatility around limit movements. According to the overreaction (*noise*) hypothesis (benefit #2), *if* price limits are beneficial, then we should observe:

> H1A: the price during an up (down)-limit move should not be significantly different from the price in the following period.
> H2A: volatility in the post-limit period should be significantly less than in the pre-limit period.

Thus, the limit serves to cool down the overreaction and aids in the price resolution process.

An opposing view (cost #2) is that limit moves serve only to slow down price changes since these movements reflect movement toward the equilibrium price. Thus, trading activities reflect information, not noise, and we should observe:

> H1B: the price during an up (down)-limit move should be significantly less (greater) than the price in the following period.
> H2B: there should be no difference in volatility between pre-limit and post-limit periods.

A third issue present in the price limits controversy is the effects of such measures on *liquidity*. Proponents seem to argue that liquidity is enhanced with the imposition of price limits; opponents argue the opposite. Liquidity effects are difficult to measure. One proxy, used by Roll (1989), is the aggregate market value of securities traded. In established futures markets, trading occurs in standardized units of a given commodity. Thus, the total volume, in numbers of contracts, could be used as a proxy for total market value traded.

One problem with evaluating volume is that it is not independent of the effects of volatility. Empirical evidence seems to indicate that the two are positively correlated. Even so, it would seem that if price limits are effective in controlling for illiquidity, one should observe a leveling off of volume after the limit move as traders pause and retrench. That is, if post-limit volatility stabilizes and declines, it may indicate a lessening of concern on the part of the traders of being locked in or locked out. On the other hand, if price limits serve only to delay trading and increase the anxiety of traders, volume should be heavy on successive days around the limit moves as traders attempt to close out positions to avoid potential liquidity problems. Thus:

H3A: the volume on the day following a limit move should stabilize and decline.
H3B: the volume on the day following a limit move should maintain a high level.

Having discussed these issues, we now turn to our empirical evidence.

4. Empirical design

4.1. The data

Although the major thrust of the price limit recommendations has been aimed at stocks and their derivative products, price limits for these products have been used for only a brief time. However, price limits have been in effect for some time in futures markets for selected agricultural products, precious metals, and other financial securities. To provide a more thorough examination of the behavior of prices around limit moves, we examine futures contract prices for four commodities: corn, soybeans, silver, and Treasury bonds. Although this is a limitation of our study, it does provide a data base of commodities—agricultural, precious metal, and financial—by which to examine the behavior of prices around limit moves for a more extended period of time. The choice of these particular contracts is motivated, in part, by volume considerations as well as the need to have markets that experienced a significant number of limit moves over extended time periods. Conversation with officials of the Chicago Board of Trade (CBOT) and the Chicago Mercantile Exchange (CME) indicated that contracts on these commodities would meet both of these criteria.

Data availability varies across the four commodities examined. For this reason, the analysis of price limits is divided into two parts. The first part of the analysis includes the *daily* market data for all of the commodities. Open, high, low, and closing prices, as well as daily trading volume and open interest for the nearby futures contracts for each commodity, are collected from the *Wall Street Journal.* The sample periods for most contracts in this part of the analysis are about 10 years. Table 2, panel A, summarizes the data base for each commodity while panel B provides current limit rules and the number of limit moves analyzed during the periods for each of the four commodities.

In the second part of the analysis, *intraday* futures market price changes around limit moves will be examined from the tick prices for the four commodities. These data are obtained from the *Time and Sale File* as compiled by the CBOT. The sample periods as well as current limit rules and limit moves for the tick data sample are presented in table 3, panels A and B. The shorter time periods for the intraday data set is governed by limitations on data availability. For the intraday data sample all contracts are included in the analysis.

Table 2A. Daily futures contract sample description

Commodity	Sample Period	Number of Trading Days
Treasury Bond	July 1977–July 1988	2744
Silver	Jan. 1975–July 1987	3149
Corn	Jan. 1977–Dec. 1987	2528
Soybeans	Jan. 1977–Dec. 1987	2528

Note: The sample includes the nearby contract.

Table 2B. Current price limits and number of limit moves in the daily sample

Futures Contracts	Daily Limit	Number of Up Limits	Number of Down Limits
Treasury Bond	3 points	62	55
Silver	50 cents	222	168
Corn	10 cents	48	34
Soybeans	30 cents	41	52

Table 2C. Characteristics of daily successive price limits for down-limit moves in the daily sample

Future Contracts	Total Number of Successive Down-Limit Moves	Number Occurring in Pairs	Number Occurring in Triplets	All Others
Treasury Bond	18	8	0	10
Silver	48	40	3	5
Corn	0	0	0	0
Soybeans	15	8	3	4

Table 2D. Characteristics of daily successive price limits for up-limit moves in the daily sample

Futures Contracts	Total Number of Successive Up-Limit Moves	Number Occurring in Pairs	Number Occurring in Triplets	All Others
Treasury Bond	20	14	6	0
Silver	133	54	24	55
Corn	4	4	0	0
Soybeans	2	2	0	0

Table 3A. Intraday futures contract sample description

Commodity	Sample Period	Number of Trading Days	Number of Tick Records
Treasury Bond	1980–1983	1042	1395284
Silver	1984–1986	754	987253
Corn	1980–1985	1298	1286123
Soybeans	1984–1986	771	1004157

Table 3B. Price limits and number of limit moves in the intraday sample

Futures Contracts	Daily Limit	Number of Up Limits	Number of Down Limits
Treasury Bond	2 points**	94	60
Silver	50 cents	58	116
Corn	10 cents	89	78
Soybeans	30 cents	45	56

Table 3C. Characteristics of daily successive price limits for down-limit moves in the intraday sample

Futures Contracts	Total Number of Successive Down-Limit Moves	Number Occurring in Pairs	Number Occurring in Triplets	All Others
Treasury Bond	2	2	0	0
Silver	35	14	3	18
Corn	6	6	0	0
Soybeans	4	4	0	0

Table 3D. Characteristics of daily successive price limits for up-limit moves in the intraday sample

Futures Contracts	Total Number of Successive Up-Limit Moves	Number Occurring in Pairs	Number Occurring in Triplets	All Others
Treasury Bond	16	16	0	0
Silver	20	12	6	2
Corn	29	26	3	0
Soybeans	0	0	0	0

Table 3E. Number of trading halts and limit moves after the first limit move in intraday sample

	Treasury Bond	Silver	Corn	Soybeans
Down Limit	60	116	78	56
Halts	22	57	12	5
% Limit Moves	15%	24%	33%	36%
Up Limit	94	58	89	45
Halts	35	21	12	9
% Limit Moves	13%	26%	33%	51%

4.2. Price limit rules to identify days of limit moves

Based on Regulation 1008.01 of Chicago Board of Trade, trading is prohibited any day in futures contracts of commodities traded on the exchange at a price higher or lower than plus or minus the specified price limit of a given commodity and determined by: (1) the settlement price for such commodity on the previous day, or (2) the average of the opening range of prices or the first trade during the first day of trading in a futures contract.

Furthermore, a variable limit will be applied if three or more contracts within a contract year close on the limit bid, or on the limit sell, for three successive business days. In these cases, the limit for the following three business days will be expanded an additional 50 percent of the current level. All provisions of the limit rules do not apply to trading in the current month on and after the first notice of delivery day.

4.3. Single limit moves, successive limit moves, and trading halts

Using the above rules, we identify the cases of up and down limit moves for both the daily sample and the intraday sample.[11] As previously shown, panel B of tables 2 and 3 presents the number of up and down limit moves for the daily and intraday samples analyzed in this study. In the daily sample, each day in which a limit is reached is treated as an independent observation. However, it is instructive to note that daily limit moves often occur in clusters. In panels C and D of tables 2 and 3, the number of successive limit moves (defined as consecutive daily limit moves in the same direction for the same contract) are also reported for both the daily and intraday samples. As shown in panels C and D of these tables, consecutive daily limit moves may occur for two consecutive days (pairs), three consecutive days (triplets), or longer periods of consecutive days (all others).

It is important to recognize that, ex post, the occurrence of successive daily limit moves varies significantly across different commodities. From an analysis of the data in tables 2 and 3, it appears that successive limit moves often occurred in a trending market, as evidenced by the unequal proportion of successive limit (out of total limit moves) between up and down markets. Furthermore, there is a significantly higher proportion of successive (up) limit moves in the daily sample of silver contracts, compared with the other three commodities. A more careful examination of the silver data indicates that successive limit moves occurred predominantly during 1979 and 1980, a period of speculation during which the Hunt family attempted to corner the silver market. Opponents to price limit rules often argue that successive limit moves are a sign of ineffectiveness of price limit rules. If so, panels C and D of tables 2 and 3 would seem to suggest that price limits may prove futile to stop a market trend or to curb market manipulation.

For the intraday sample, the limit day is identified by the first limit move of the day. However, subsequent limit moves may occur after the first limit move as well as continuous trading in the opposite direction of the limit move. That is, on a given day, the market price may hit the limit more than once. Furthermore, in some cases trading may be completely halted. The distinction between limit moves and trading halts is important since the latter case (trading halts) is considered a significant cost of price limit rules, i.e., the liquidity cost.

In panel E of table 3, the frequencies of intraday trading halts (until the end of the day) after the initial limit move are presented for each of the four commodities. Also reported in panel E are the number of times (as a percent of the total number of transactions following the initial limit move) that a particular commodity re-hits its limit during the rest of the day. As can be seen from the table, for some commodities—in particular, soybeans—once a limit is reached, it is consistently re-hit throughout the rest of day.

4.4. Methodology—daily data

4.4.1. The daily price movement around limit moves. Using the daily data sample, investigation of the price movement hypothesis (H1) is done through the use of an event study methodology, where the event (t=0) is the *day* of the limit move. Let $DR_{i,t}$ represent the daily return for the ith limit move measured in event time. Using two consecutive daily closing prices at times ($t-1$) and t, the daily return is computed as:

$$DR_{i,t} = [1n(P_{i,t}/P_{i,t-j})] \tag{1}$$

Similarly, the average daily return (ADR_t) for a given day t across n limit moves is defined as:

$$ADR_t = \sum_{i=1}^{n} DR_{i,t}/n \tag{2}$$

Across different limit moves, the cumulative average daily return ($CADR_t$) over time to t days from the limit move may be defined as follows:

$$CADR_t = \sum_{k=1}^{t} ADR_k \tag{3}$$

The direction and the level of $CADR_t$ can provide information about the price movement around the limit move.

4.4.2. Volatility comparisons. The change in volatility hypothesis (H2) is examined through a comparison of the futures price variance in pre-limit and post-limit periods. One way to evaluate the market impacts of price limit rules is to examine changes in price volatility associated with limit moves. We first examine the volatility around the days of limit moves. Because volatility can change quickly around price limit moves, use of an historical daily volatility measure (e.g., variance in the prior 30 days' price changes) may not effectively capture rapid changes in price movements. For this reason, the daily volatility is estimated as follows:

$$Volatility_t = (P_{ht} - P_{lt})/4\log_e 2 \tag{4}$$

where P_{ht}, P_{lt} are high and low prices for day t. This daily volatility measure is proposed by Parkinson (1980) and further evaluated by Garman and Klass (1980). Although this estimator is sensitive to mismeasurement of the high and low prices, it does provide a more current approximation of volatility than standard historical measures.[12] Based on this daily volatility measure, the average daily volatility across different cases of limit moves for contracts on each commodity in the daily sample can be computed as follows:

$$AV_t = \sum_{i=1}^{n} Volatility_{it}/n \tag{5}$$

where AV_t is the average daily volatility measure t days from the limit move. $Volatility_{it}$ is the tth daily volatility measure for the ith limit move, and n is the number of limit moves in the sample. The average daily price volatility measures for the 10 days around up and down limit moves are computed for each commodity individually.

4.4.3. Trading volume. The third criterion in evaluating the effectiveness of price limit rules is to examine the change in trading volume (a proxy for liquidity) around limit moves. The trading volume is measured by the number of contracts traded on a given day. Across different cases of limit moves and around the time of limit moves, the average market volume is computed as follows:

$$AVOL_t = \sum_{i=1}^{n} Volume_{it}/n \tag{6}$$

where $AVOL_t$ is the average daily volume measured t days from the limit move, $volume_{it}$ is th $t$the daily volume measure for the ith limit move, and n is the number of limit moves in the sample.

Using the event study methodology described above, the clustering of successive limit moves may pose a significant problem in the empirical testing of this study. This is because successive daily limit moves probably contain common (correlated) information; thus, these event dates do not represent independent samples. An alternative approach would be to treat the cluster of limit moves as a *single* limit move. Although both methods introduce some type of biases, the alternative approach would appear to create a more serious measurement error on the changes of each variable around the limit move. If each cluster of limit moves is recorded as a single limit move, the *first* nonlimit move day immediately following the cluster would be treated as day +1. For the price resolution hypothesis, the price behavior following the cluster will arbitrarily be more stable by the selection procedure.

On the other hand, treating each limit moves as an independent case (either alone or as a member of a cluster) may also generate biases to a different direction. If the entire sample is predominantly comprised of successive limit moves, the continuance of price trends and (higher) volatility levels is expected. This tends to introduce a bias since the trading volume and the volatility level will be higher, and the price level will continue to move to the same direction in day +1, since day +1 is actually another limit day. However, for the hypotheses that each market variable will reverse in the day following the limit day, treating each limit move as a separate observation provides a stricter and more conservative test of the hypothesis that price limits are useful. Therefore, in the empirical section of the daily sample, we treat each limit move independently.

5.1. Methodology—intraday data

5.1.1. The intraday price movement around limit moves. Since the impact of limit moves on the market can be short-lived, investigation of the price movement hypothesis (H1) is also repeated through an examination of intraday data. Using the event study methodology described in the previous section, where now the event ($t=0$) is the *minute* of the limit move, let $R_{i,t}$ represent the minute-to-minute return for the ith limit move at minute t. Using two consecutive transaction prices at minute $t-j$ and at minute t, the return per minute between $t-j$ and t is computed as:

$$R_{i,t} = [1n(P_{i,t}/P_{i,t-j})] \tag{7}$$

Similarly, the average return (AR_t) at a given minute t across n limit moves is defined as:

$$AR_t = \sum_{i=1}^{n} R_{i,t}/n \tag{8}$$

Across different limit moves, the cumulative average return (CAR_t) over time at a given minute t may be defined as follows:

$$CAR_t = \sum_{k=1}^{t} AR_k \tag{9}$$

Since the intraday empirical examination begins the day before, and ends after the day after, the limit move, the entire observation period covers three calendar days. However, since the first intraday limit move may occur at any time during the trading day, the observation period for that day (of the limit move) lasts twice as long as a regular trading session. To illustrate, consider a six-hour trading session where the observation period for the day of the limit move ranges from minute -360 to minute $+360$, while minute 0 represents the minute of the first limit move for each case. If the first limit move occurs at the beginning of the trading session, there will be no observations in the pre-limit move period ($-360<t<0$), and all the price movements after the limit move are recorded in the interval $0<t<+360$. On the other hand, if the limit move occurs at the end of a trading session, all observations in that day are treated as occurring in the pre-limit move interval, $-360<t<0$. This procedure is designed to standardize the different calendar timing of each limit move in the intraday sample while ensuring that price movements are recorded for times only during the day of the limit move. As a result, because limit moves do not necessarily occur either at the beginning or the end of a trading session, this results in varying numbers of cases when averaging at each given minute between -360 and $+360$ with a higher concentration of observations around minute 0.

Statistical significance of price (dis)continuity around limit moves is tested by means of the Kruskal-Wallis nonparametric statistic. To examine if the price level has significantly moved, the distribution of the *AR* during a given time interval is compared with that in another time interval. In these tests, the pre-event observation period starts from one day prior to the day of limit moves, and the post-event observation period is the day after the limit move occurs. Since a given limit move may occur at any minute during the entire trading session, the event period for the entire sample elapses through a two-day time interval. The *AR* is computed starting from the first transaction price one day before the limit move, and ends at the closing transaction price of the day after the limit move. We repeat the same procedure on both subsamples of up-limit moves and down-limit moves.

5.1.2. The intraday volatility test. For the intraday sample, we also compare measures of return volatility in different subperiods. Measures of intraday return volatility are calculated for the entire day of the limit move (V_m), pre-limit and post-limit period on the limit day (V_b and V_a, respectively), and the day after the limit move (V_n). To test the hypothesis regarding whether the limit move is related with the reduction of the high volatility, we compare the intraday return volatility for the day of the limit move (V_m) and the day after the limit move (V_n), the pre-limit (V_b) and post-limit (V_a) volatility on the day of the limit move, and the pre-limit volatility on the day of the limit move with the volatility on the day after (V_n).

One distinction in dealing with successive limit moves between the daily sample and the intraday sample needs to be clarified here. Unlike the daily sample, whenever the limit is first hit during the day, subsequent price movements are constrained to be at or below (above) the price level limit for up (down)-limit moves. By contrast, for the daily data sample, subsequent price movements can go up or down by the established limit amount since the limit is re-established each day. Because successive limit moves occurred frequently in the intraday sample (see table 3, panel E), treating each subsequent intraday limit move in the same day as an independent case can introduce a downward (upward) bias on subsequent price trends up (down) moves. Therefore, in the intraday sample, each limit day is identified singularly by the first limit move on such day. Any subsequent limit moves in the same day are treated as occurring in the post-limit move period.

5. Discussion of results

5.1. Daily data

Tables 4A–4D provide summary data on the CAR patterns, volumes, and price volatility measures during the ten days surrounding up- and down-limit moves for the four commodities futures contracts. As the data indicate, there is a substantial increase (decrease) in prices as measured by the CAR values on the day an up (down)-limit is hit. The pattern of the CAR movements also reveals that following the day of a limit move, the price pattern tends either to stabilize or reverse. These results would seem to imply that limits do not appear to *arrest* any underlying price trend movements based on fundamental factors and that limits do not merely delay the price movement to a new equilibrium level.

With respect to the volume figures, limit-move days, not surprisingly, are associated with heavy volume (see tables 4A–4D). This is consistent with the hypothesis set forth by Fama (1989) that trading, in anticipation of an expected limit move, should be very heavy as traders attempt to clear their positions. However, there appears to be no evidence that limits affectively "shut-out" traders from the market. The volume on the first post-limit day, in virtually all cases, is of relatively the same magnitude as on the day the limit is triggered. Following the first post-limit day, the volume then shows a tendency to decline to levels comparable to the volume on pre-limit days. This tendency, in combination with the earlier observation that price tends to stabilize or even reverse on the first post limit day, would suggest that liquidity may not be severely impaired. Of course, this does not preclude the possibility that liquidity may suffer within the day of the limit move.

With respect to price volatility, we find that in the case of up-limits for Treasury bonds and silver, volatility declines on the first post-limit day. Down-limit moves reveal a similar reduction in volatility on the day after the limit move for Treasury bonds and soybeans. In all other cases volatility declines on the second or third day after the limit move.

On the whole, the descriptive statistics presented in tables 4A–4D seem to suggest that limits may play a role in monitoring the price movements and volatility levels in a volatile market. Because these characteristics may change rapidly, the analysis of intraday data may be helpful in fine-tuning these observations.

Table 4A. Daily price, volume, and volatility movements around limit moves in Treasury bond futures contracts

	Up-Limit Moves			Down-Limit Moves		
Day	CAR(%)	Average Volume	Volatility	CAR(%)	Average Volume	Volatility
−10	0.11	85730	27.94 ticks	0.03	63273	27.56 ticks
−9	−0.22	90409	31.42	−0.13	65389	28.25
−8	−0.17	89106	30.94	−0.37	66686	26.98
−7	−0.02	85179	28.08	−0.50	64225	27.86
−6	−0.14	86830	32.80	−0.57	60972	25.02
−5	0.06	98609	32.74	−0.74	62419	27.56
−4	−0.04	101339	32.74	−0.67	67265	26.97
−3	−0.12	99107	31.00	−0.91	66374	26.55
−2	0.05	88074	30.00	−1.08	65063	28.46
−1	0.46	85599	31.85	−1.10	66757	28.84
0	2.33	87335	40.76	−2.74	75974	37.40
1	2.73	95874	35.70	−2.89	77037	33.46
2	2.79	86440	33.11	−3.12	67196	33.29
3	2.72	84554	31.89	−3.10	71232	34.80
4	2.83	86912	31.76	−2.99	64763	30.80
5	2.78	79455	31.28	−2.94	63632	27.80
6	3.06	84750	31.69	−2.58	60456	29.19
7	3.20	79173	29.04	−2.51	60388	30.47
8	3.13	82598	29.28	−2.59	62272	31.26
9	3.12	82131	29.70	−2.61	57350	30.79
10	2.96	83549	29.58	−2.54	59390	28.49

Note: Day 0 represents the day of the initial limit move.

Table 4B. Daily price, volume, and volatility movements around limit moves in silver futures contracts

	Up-Limit Moves			Down-Limit Moves		
Day	CAR(%)	Average Volume	Volatility	CAR(%)	Average Volume	Volatility
−10	0.58	10926	73.90 cents	0.34	10949	61.20 cents
−9	1.35	10774	71.07	0.56	10884	64.52
−8	1.82	10811	69.07	0.65	11379	70.52
−7	2.37	11309	73.59	0.99	10707	64.45
−6	2.94	11369	82.61	1.00	10702	60.38
−5	3.11	11203	76.74	1.35	11347	63.48
−4	3.34	11499	84.21	1.71	10785	58.23
−3	3.75	11129	85.84	1.93	10484	58.83
−2	3.96	10594	88.31	2.25	10536	56.35
−1	4.59	10589	82.18	2.40	10172	65.44
0	8.10	11707	93.71	−2.04	12057	72.33
1	8.44	11864	80.20	−2.58	12007	76.54
2	8.76	10972	87.37	−2.63	10523	61.84
3	8.99	10686	86.59	−2.44	10159	59.66
4	8.92	10369	80.33	−2.19	9703	66.56
5	9.04	10143	80.87	−1.58	9995	62.64
6	9.17	9837	84.11	−1.45	9519	57.79
7	9.32	9797	83.25	−1.14	9410	54.93
8	9.48	9710	83.86	−0.92	9601	53.52
9	9.77	9207	75.18	−0.94	9354	64.89
10	10.02	8944	75.24	−1.01	9185	64.67

5.2. Intraday data

We now turn to the analysis of the results for our intraday data. figures 1A and 1B present the CAR patterns for the down (up)-limit moves for Treasury bonds. Similarly, figures 2A and 2B, 3A and 3B, and 4A and 4B present these results for silver, corn, and soybeans. Since the total trading time will vary across the four commodities, appropriate demarcating lines are placed to highlight the CAR patterns on the day before the limit (day-1), before and after the limit trigger point on the day of the limit (day 0), and the day after the limit (day +1) on each figure. Statistical tests for the significances of the price movements around the limit move are presented in tables 5, panels A and B, while tests for changes in volatility are shown in table 6, panels A and B.

5.2.1. T-Bond. The CAR pattern for Treasury bond down-limit moves is presented in figure 1A. The sharp decline in the CAR before the limit move appears to be followed by a stable pattern on the day of the limit move and, then, a reversal on day 1. Although trading appears to continue after the limit, we cannot make any strong statements of liquidity in the immediate vicinity of the limit move unless a careful examination of intraday volume and

Table 4C. Daily price, volume, and volatility movements around limit moves in corn futures contracts

	Up-Limit Moves			Down-Limit Moves		
Day	CAR(%)	Average Volume	Volatility	CAR(%)	Average Volume	Volatility
−10	0.02	224747	3.51 cents	0.40	238418	4.31 cents
−9	−0.05	226070	3.44	0.62	229425	3.95
−8	0.28	227946	3.81	0.98	227568	3.84
−7	0.29	229790	4.16	1.29	230129	3.85
−6	0.17	248892	4.39	1.21	221289	3.84
−5	0.42	232877	4.67	1.21	223076	4.01
−4	0.25	230949	4.13	1.35	238661	4.91
−3	0.29	224162	3.91	1.07	213121	4.43
−2	0.49	212624	3.84	1.28	236319	4.89
−1	0.70	203139	3.88	1.23	22850	4.75
0	3.90	230552	5.28	−2.89	252564	5.73
1	3.52	244125	5.04	−2.51	232754	4.78
2	3.73	223908	3.02	−2.61	200843	4.26
3	3.84	221728	4.71	−2.97	221231	4.31
4	3.73	206376	4.12	−2.38	215660	4.66
5	3.70	209674	3.99	−2.23	210017	4.15
6	3.97	205577	3.98	−2.08	204797	4.08
7	4.01	212879	4.07	−1.73	213065	4.83
8	4.02	199788	3.81	−1.73	210974	4.18
9	3.87	215932	3.81	−1.62	207254	4.25
10	3.99	216660	3.57	−1.91	201416	3.96

bid-ask spreads is made. However, as table 5, panel A, indicates, the average post-limit returns on day 0 ($L<t<E_0$) hover around zero (although significant), and are slightly positive, but insignificant, on day 1 ($B_1<t<E_1$). Conversely, the pre-limit day 0 returns ($B_0<t<L$) are significantly negative. The chi-square statistics, however, do not reveal any significant difference in the mean returns for the two post-limit periods.

Figure 1B is the CAR pattern for the up-limit moves in Treasury bond futures. Similar to the down-limit patterns, prices tend to stabilize in the post-limit period. Table 5, panel B, shows that the significant positive mean returns prior to the limit move are followed by average returns that are only slightly positive. As before, the chi-square values indicate insignificance between return differences in the two post-limit periods.

5.2.2. Silver. Figures 2A and 2B present the CAR patterns for silver around down-limit and up-limit moves, respectively. We note from figure 2A that there is a precipitous decline in the prices leading up to the point when the limit is activated, with subsequent trading occurring around the limit value. This evidences a stable price pattern on the post-limit day. The significance of these patterns is confirmed in table 5, panel A. We note from this table that the average return is negative and significantly different from zero on day 0 prior to the limit being hit. This confirms the sharp decline in prices just prior to the triggering of

Table 4D. Daily price, volume, and volatility movements around limit moves in soybeans futures contracts

	Up-Limit Moves			Down-Limit Moves		
Day	CAR(%)	Average Volume	Volatility	CAR(%)	Average Volume	Volatility
-10	0.57	287721	12.87 cents	0.54	276170	15.88 cents
-9	1.27	271301	12.07	0.69	290644	15.52
-8	2.14	275454	13.08	0.55	284482	13.33
-7	2.48	303473	16.17	0.84	267453	13.58
-6	2.82	293154	14.77	1.09	282972	14.84
-5	2.94	294360	16.26	1.96	265262	14.15
-4	2.87	300483	15.87	2.24	293093	15.81
-3	2.78	270238	13.71	2.50	282860	15.42
-2	3.39	279174	13.29	2.02	300328	17.96
-1	3.36	262206	12.83	1.42	277548	15.63
0	6.67	273657	17.14	-2.03	295782	18.89
1	6.87	311387	17.23	-2.07	283810	15.52
2	6.62	298373	16.69	-2.05	257757	14.40
3	6.14	303107	16.66	-1.99	275901	16.28
4	6.39	283973	16.01	-1.63	259063	15.04
5	5.84	283464	15.22	-1.10	261240	14.68
6	6.30	282924	14.90	-1.31	247353	14.25
7	6.38	286121	15.72	-1.58	253431	14.05
8	6.29	280901	16.29	-1.45	247641	14.49
9	6.61	287603	15.17	-1.68	250781	15.29
10	7.27	279208	15.60	-2.15	255192	15.56

down limit. However, average return is not significantly different from zero in the post-limit period on day 0 ($L<t<E_0$), suggesting that all trades in the post-limit period on day 0 occurred around the limit price. Table 5, panel A, also shows that the average returns between these two subperiods is significantly different from zero, but is significantly different from the average return during the post-limit period on day 0 ($L<t<E_0$). This suggests that prices stabilized on the first post-limit day. Thus, there does not appear to be evidence of the continued downward trend in prices on day +1.

Figure 2B shows the CAR pattern for up-limits for silver. Different from the case of down-limits, we note that the upward spiral in prices just before the up-limit is followed by a dramatic downward spiral in prices on day 0. This is confirmed in table 5, panel B, that shows a significantly positive return on day 0 before the limit and a significantly negative average return after the limit. Also from the plot in figure 2B, we note that the downward spiralling of prices in the post-limit period on day 0 is followed by a stable series of prices on day +1. This is confirmed in panel B of table 5 that shows the average returns on day +1 is not significantly different from zero. The chi-square statistic in table 5 also shows that the average return in day 1 is significantly different than the average return in the post-limit period on day 0.

5.2.3. Corn. Figure 3A shows the CAR pattern for corn futures around down-limit moves.

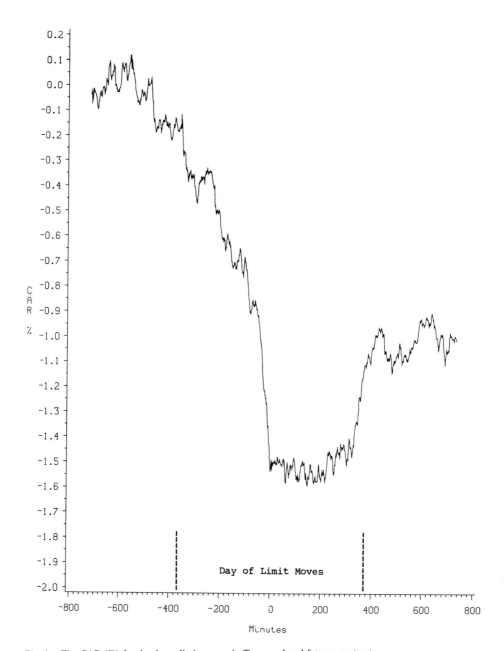

Fig. 1a. The CAR (%) for the down-limit moves in Treasury bond futures contracts

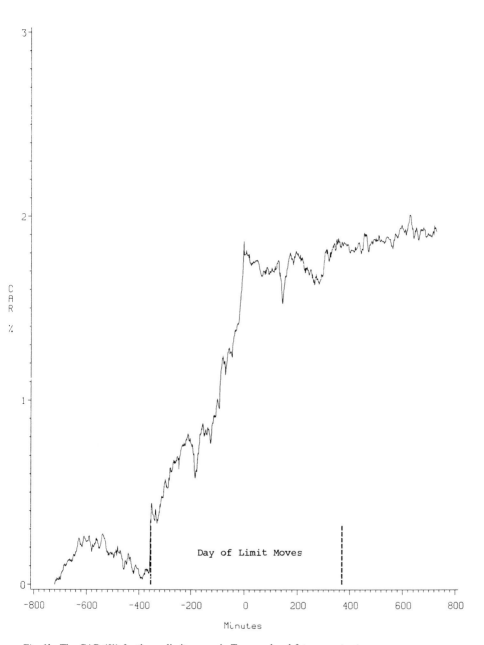

Fig. 1b. The CAR (%) for the up-limit moves in Treasury bond futures contracts

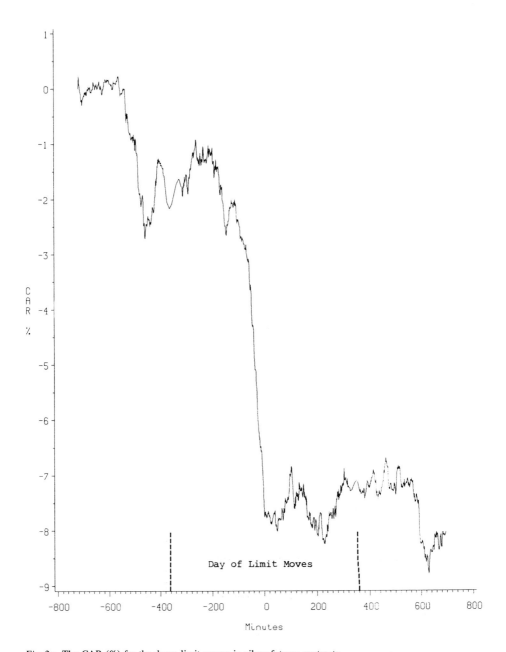

Fig. 2a. The CAR (%) for the down-limit moves in silver futures contracts

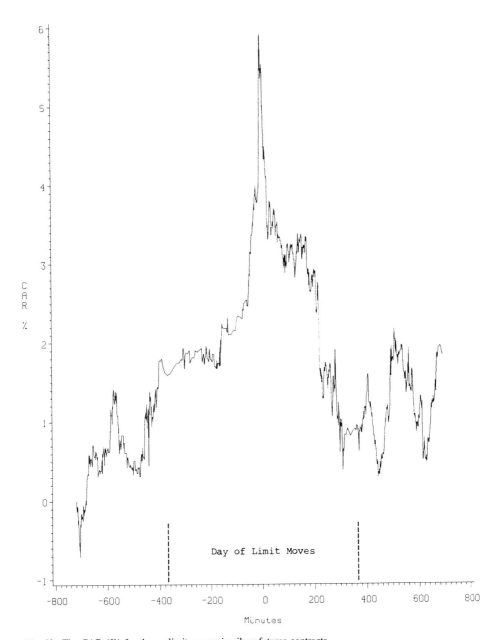

Fig. 2b. The CAR (%) for the up-limit moves in silver futures contracts

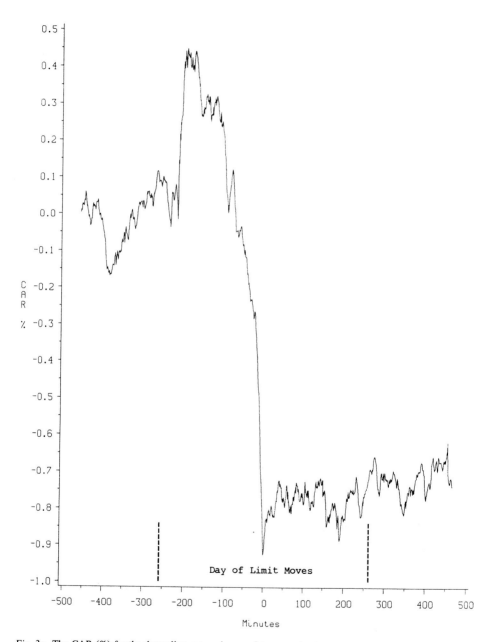

Fig. 3a. The CAR (%) for the down-limt moves in corn futures contracts

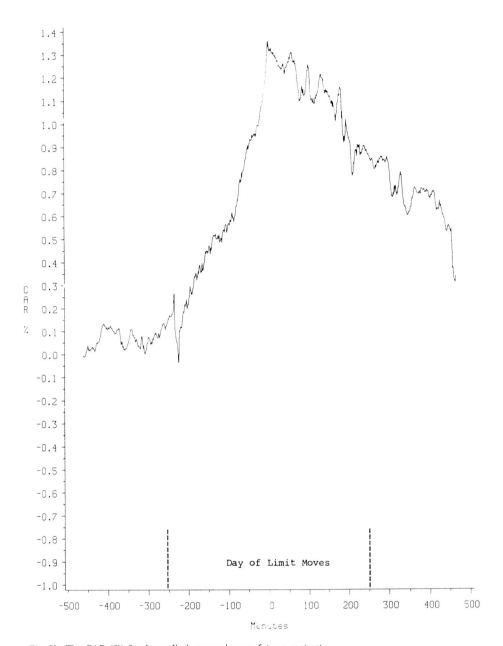

Fig. 3b. The CAR (%) for the up-limit moves in corn futures contracts

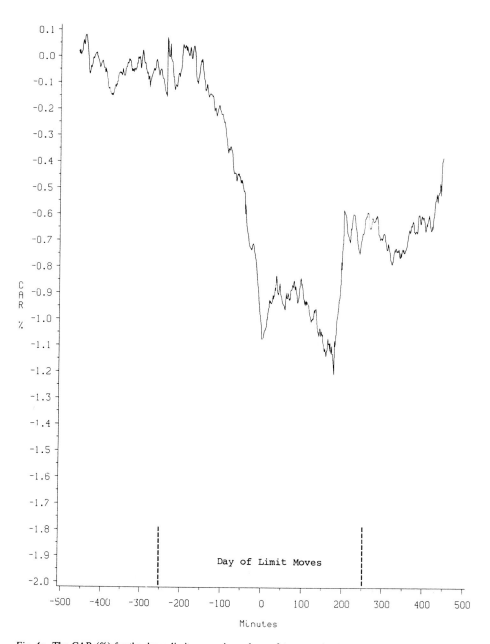

Fig. 4a. The CAR (%) for the down-limit moves in soybeans futures contracts

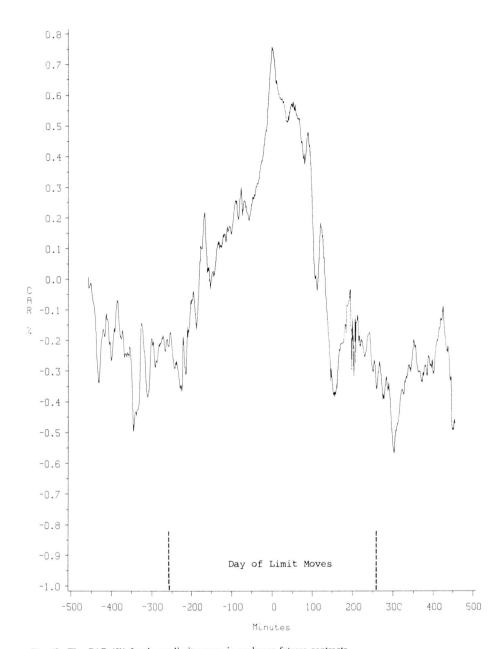

Fig. 4b. The CAR (%) for the up-limit moves in soybeans futures contracts

Table 5. Average return (AR) distributrions for the sample of limit moves
[Average returns (%) and *t*-statistic (in parentheses)]

Panel A: Down-Limit Moves

Period	Treasury Bond	Corn	Soybeans	Silver
Interval A: $B_0<t<L$	−0.007	−0.011	−0.008	−0.099
	(−7.89)*	(−9.50)*	(−8.90)*	(12.58)*
Interval B: $L<t<E_0$	0.002	0.002	0.003	−0.014
	(2.01)**	(2.34)**	(2.17)**	(−1.45)
Interval C: $B_1<t<E_1$	0.001	0.0005	0.001	0.006
	(1.71)	(0.69)	(2.28)**	(1.09)

B_0,B_1 : the beginning trading time on the limit day and the day after.
E_0,E_1 : the ending trading time on the limit day and the day after.
  L : the time of the first limit move.

Kruskal-Wallis Tests Between Return Distributions in Different Intervals Chi-Square Statistics Reported

Hypothesis	Treasury Bond	Corn	Soybeans	Silver
HO: $AR_A = AR_B$	19.73*	68.25*	61.34*	43.14*
HO: $AR_B = AR_C$	0.12	3.53	1.68	3.89**

*Significant at the 1 percent level.
**Significant at the 5 percent level.
AR_A, AR_B, AR_C: The average return in interval A, B, and C.

Panel B: Up-Limit Moves

Hypothesis	Treasury Bond	Corn	Soybeans	Silver
Interval A: $B_0<t<L$	0.011	0.0009	0.008	0.167
	(11 .22)*	(8.38)*	(7.98)*	(9.18)*
Interval B: $L<t<E_0$	−0.001	−0.003	−0.006	−0.041
	(−1.76)	(−2.60)*	(−5.29)*	(−2.62)*
Interval C: $B_1<t<E_1$	0.000	−0.002	−0.0009	0 .008
	(0.351)	(−2.93)*	(−1.16)	(0.81)

B_0,B_1 : the beginning trading time on the limit day and the day after.
E_0,E_1 : the ending trading time on the limit day and the day after.
  L : the time of the first limit move.

Kruskal-Wallis Test Between Return Distributions in Different Intervals (Chi-Square Statistics Reported)

Hypothesis	Treasury Bond	Corn	Soybeans	Silver
HO: $AR_A = AR_B$	75.95*	79.53*	74.96*	53.56*
HO: $AR_B = AR_C$	0.05	0.42	10.63*	5.38**

Table 6. Volatility comparisons

Panel A: Intraday Price Volatility (%) in Various Periods		
Period	Up-Limits	Down-Limits
Limit Day (V_m)		
Treasury Bond	11.1590	10.7708
Silver	0.0988	0.4359
Corn	1.2132	1.6439
Soybeans	2.7088	3.3409
Before Limit Moves (V_b)		
During Limit Day		
Treasury Bond	7.8710	6.9980
Silver	0.0801	0.1484
Corn	1.0300	1.0676
Soybeans	1.7855	2.4201
After Limit Moves (V_a)		
During Limit Day		
Treasury Bond	1.4648	1.7451
Silver	0.1062	0.0306
Corn	0.4496	0.1355
Soybeans	3.3869	0.8315
The Day After Limit Day (V_n)		
Treasury Bond	1.1282	1.3302
Silver	0.0454	0.0602
Corn	0.3936	0.1553
Soybeans	0.9016	0.5990

Panel B: Significance Tests of Price Volatility		
Test	Up-Limits	Down-Limits
HO: $V_m = V_n$		
Treasury Bond	9.89*	8.10*
Silver	2.18*	7.24*
Corn	3.08*	10.59*
Soybeans	3.00*	5.58*
HO: $V_b = V_n$		
Treasury Bond	6.98*	5.26*
Silver	1.76*	2.47*
Corn	2.62*	6.87*
Soybeans	1.98*	4.04*
HO: $V_b = V_a$		
Treasury Bond	5.37*	5.26*
Silver	0.75	4.85*
Corn	2.29*	7.88
Soybeans	0.53	2.91*

Notes: The test statistics (F) for volatility comparisons are computed as $F_{i,j} = V_i/V_j$ with degrees of freedom of (l,k), where l and k are the numberf of observations used in calculating V_i and V_j, respectively, where:

V_m: The intraday price variance on limit days.
V_n: The intraday price variance on the day following limit moves;
V_b: The intraday price variance before the limit moves; and
V_a: The intraday price variance after the limit moves.
*Significant at the 1 percent level.

95

The price pattern is generally similar to the one observed for silver futures. The sharp decline in prices on day 0 leading up to the limit is followed by a slight tendency to bounce back up and then remain stable into the next day. The sharp decline on day 0 in the pre-limit period is captured by the significantly negative average return noted in table 5, panel A. The table also reveals a small but significant positive average return in the post-limit period on day 0 and an average return that is not significantly different from zero on day +1. The chi-square statistic shows that the mean returns in the post-limit period between day 0 and day 1 are not significantly different from each other, suggesting that the prices become stable after the limit is activated.

In the case of up-limits, the price pattern for corn is once again generally similar to that for silver with the exception that the upward price spiral before the limit is followed by a downward trend in prices that continues into day 1. Table 5B shows that the significant positive average return prior to the limit is followed by a significant negative average return in day 0, while the chi-square statistics show that the average returns between these two intervals are significantly different. Furthermore, we note that the average returns continue to be negative in day 1, indicating a continuing decline in prices through day 1. Thus, the up-limit cases for corn are followed on average by a price reversal that continues into the post-limit day.

5.2.4. Soybeans.
Figure 4A presents the CAR pattern for soybean futures for the cases where the down-limit was triggered. The sharp decline in prices prior to the limit move is followed by a minor reversal and then continued stability, albeit with a wider dispersion than noted for corn or silver futures contracts. Table 5, panel A, confirms that the significant negative return on day 0 prior to the limit is followed by positive average returns which continue into day 1. The chi-square statistics show that the mean returns for the two post-limit periods are not significantly different from each other.

As in the case of silver and corn futures, the soybean futures are characterized by a sharp reversal of prices following an up-limit being activated. This is very clear in Figure 4-B. The substantial price reversal is further documented in tabel 5, panel B, which shows a significant negative average return on the post-limit period for day 0. The day 1 returns tend to stabilize. The chi-square statistics reveal that average downward spiralling of prices in the post-limit period is less in day 1 than day 0.

By now a general pattern appears to emerge with respect to the price behavior around limit moves. On the whole, the evidence seems to indicate that there is an asymmetry between the reaction to down-limit versus up-limit moves. Whereas the down-limit moves are characterized by prices that adjust only slightly upward and then remain stable, the up-limit moves are characterized by a much stronger price reversal that generally carries through into the post-limit day trading period.

5.2.5. Volatility.
Table 6, panel A, summarizes the findings with respect to changes in volatility around the limit move. Data are presented on the average volatility before (V_b) and after (V_a) the limit move on day 0, volatility for the entire limit day (V_m), and the volatility for day +1(V_n). Table 6, panel B, presents significance tests for differences in volatility for the various time intervals using an F-test.

A close scrutiny of table 6 reveals some fairly consistent patterns across all four commodities. From the tables, the average volatility on the limit day (V_m) is significantly higher than the volatility on the post-limit day (V_n). This follows from the dramatic changes in prices that occur on the limit day. The ratio of day 0 to day +1 volatility ranges from 5.58 (soybeans) to 10.59 (corn) in the case of down-limits and from 2.18 (silver) to 9.89 (T-bonds) in the case of up-limits. A similar phenomenon is observed when comparing volatility prior to the limit move on day 0 (V_b) with volatility on day +1 (V_n). When comparing volatility before and after the limit move on day 0, we observe a significant decline in the case of down-limits for all four contracts. This is consistent with CAR patterns for down-limits where we noted a general tendency for prices to stabilize, as reflected in the stable CAR pattern in the post-limit period. In the case of up-limits, the volatility in the post-limit interval is less than the pre-limit interval for corn and T-bond futures contracts, and is reflected in their relatively stable CAR pattern for the later interval. For soybean and silver futures the volatility in the post-limit period is greater than for the pre-limit period on the day of the limit move. This probably reflects the fact that the price declines in the post-limit period were steeper than the corresponding price increase in the pre-limit interval. Overall, these tests evidence a reduction in volatility in the post-limit period, thus rejecting the hypothesis of no change in volatility around the limit move.

In reviewing, the empirical results in the intraday sample presented above, one needs to be cautioned that since subsequent price movements are constrained not to continue in the same direction for the rest of the day, intraday post-limit price levels can only stabilize or move in the opposite direction (overreaction). This condition will also tend to reduce volatility in the post-limit intraday period. Therefore, it is not surprising to see a stabilizing market for the rest of the day. However, it is instructive to examine the stabilizing nature of the market for the day following the limit move since the same constraining level does not exist anymore. The cool off after the limit move seems to be even stronger in light of the averaging procedure that treats subsequent limit moves as part of the post-limit period.

6. Concluding comments

The results for the daily data reveal that limits are triggered by substantial price revisions on that day, accompanied by heavy volume and high volatility relative to the immediately preceding period. The price patterns reveal, in general, a substantial price reversal on the day after the limit accompanied by high volume and somewhat lower volatility. The days after the post-limit day do not appear to be any different from the corresponding pre-limit period. The price reversal on the day after the limit-move suggests that limits do not hamper the price discovery process by simply delaying the price movement to its new equilibrium level. Indeed, if anything, the triggering of limits appears to give the market *breathing room* to reassess the frenetic activity leading to the trading halt. Furthermore, the volume of trading on the day after the limit and the days immediately following does not appear to have abated. This suggests that liquidity is maintained and does not support the notion raised in some quarters that limits tend to effectively *lock out* traders from the market.

However, we feel that a better appreciation for limits is provided by examining intraday transaction-to-transaction data. Such a micro-structure view should provide greater insight into understanding of the influence of price limits on the price discovery process. Recapitulating, we observe that the markets display a reversal in prices in the hours immediately following a price limit trigger. These are especially prominent in the case of down-limits, while in the case of up-limits, prices tend to stabilize. The period immediately preceding the limit trigger is accompanied by major price changes in the direction of the limit. These results suggest that price limits provide a *cooling-off* period for the market, allowing traders the time to digest the information that caused the substantial price revisions culminating in the activation of the limit. The limits also appear to be accompanied by substantial reductions in volatility. The attenuation of volatility in the post-limit period and the maintenance of volume in the days after the limit move suggest that the liquidity is not impaired in the wake of the limit's becoming effective.

The collective evidence across the commodity futures contracts suggests that limits can have a sobering influence on the markets with no indication that the price discovery process was impacted negatively. However, this analysis has focused upon the short-run, immediate behavior of prices, volume, and volatility around the time of limit moves. Our research has not examined whether the benefits of price limits have any long-run implications for price behavior. Furthermore, these results are not without the usual caveats that accompany any empirical investigation and are not necessarily generalizable to other asset markets or other periods. We now turn to these limitations.

This study has investigated only one segment of the market—the futures markets. A more complete investigation would have to focus on the effects of limits on the underlying spot markets and other geographically separate markets to which traders could easily turn in the event that a limit is triggered. For instance, when the T-bond futures limit was activated on October 19, 1987, the trading moved to the London futures exchange which experienced a significant increase in volume. Thus, a complete assessment of the feasibility and effectiveness of limits would involve these other markets. As mentioned elsewhere, this would entail consideration not only of the price discovery process in these various markets but also the equally significant issue of coordination between the various markets—a point not lost on both sides of the reform argument fence spawned in the aftermath of the 1987 crash.

Although the period covered in the empirical portion of the study included an adequate number of limit cases, the period did not cover any instance of *substantial* price instability or one that was *systematic* across various economic sectors as was the October 1987 crash.[13] Thus, our findings may or may not hold in the event of a tumultuous period such as the 1987 crash. The results, however, do bear out the benefits of limits over less drastic market environments.

The seemingly association of limit moves and changes in volatility and price trends could be the result of sample selection bias. Since limit days are obviously periods of high volatility and directional price movements, subsequent changes in volatility and price trends around those days may reflect no more than the sample screening criterion used in the testing instead of the direct impact of triggering of price limit rules. That is, limit periods following such limit moves might be expected to be characterized by relatively lower levels of volatility and more stable price trends.

Finally, one must be cautioned that the results may not necessarily be expropriated to the equity markets that have been the focus of attention for various reforms in the wake of the 1987 crash. Because the institutional structure, nature of trading, the market clearing mechanisms, demands on liquidity from program trading, and the major players differ across markets, one needs to exercise great caution in ascribing to the equity markets the results found here.

Notes

1. Other examinations include those conducted by the Securities Industry Association, the National Securities Industry Association, the National Securities Traders Association, and the Futures Industry Association. In addition, the President's Working Group on Financial Markets (1988) made specific recommendations regarding the establishment of circuit breakers.

2. An excellent summary of the recommendations of the studies as well as others, including Congressional testimonies, can be found in Becker and Underhill (1988).

3. See the Brady Commission, 1988, p. V.

4. See the Brady Commission, 1988, pp. 45–53.

5. See the Brady Commission, 1988, p. vii, 69.

6. See the Brady Commission, 1988, p. 66(i) and Kampuis, Kormendi, and Watson, 1989, pp. 351–354.

7. See Kampuis, Kormendi, and Watson, 1989, p. 220.

8. See the Brady Commission, 1988, p. 66.

9. See the Brady Commission, 1988, p. 66. See also Hill and Jones, (1988, p. 38) for further discussion.

10. See the Brady Commission, 1988, p. 66; and Kampuis, Kormendi, and Watson, 1989, pp. 351–354.

11. Panel B of table 2 reports the current price limit rules in effect. Prior to December 1979, the price limit for silver was 20 cents. Initially, the price limit for Treasury bonds was .75 points; in 1979, it became 1 point; in 1980, it became 2 points; and in September 1986, it was changed to 3 points.

12. A third possibility would be to measure the volatility implied in options that are traded on commodity futures. While this approach would provide an instantaneous measure of changes in volatility, not all commodity futures have listed options.

13. A notable exception is the daily data for the silver market for the period 1979–1980.

References

Ball, C., Torous, W. and Tschoege, A. "The Degree of Price Resolution: The Case of the Gold Market." *The Journal of Futures Markets* 5 (1985), 29–43.

Barro, R. "The Stock Market and the Macroeconomy: Implications of the October 1987 Crash." In: R. Kampuis, R. Kormendi, and J. Watson, eds., *Black Monday and the Future of Financial Markets*. Homewood, IL: Irwin, 1989, pp. 83–100.

Becker, B. and Underhill, D. "Market Reform Proposals and Actions." *Eleventh Annual Commodities Law Institute*, September 26, 1988.

Brady Commission "Report of the Presidential Task Force on Market Mechanisms." January 1988.

Brennan, M. "A Theory of Price Limits in Futures Markets." *Journal of Financial Economics* 16 (1986), 213–233.

Brennan, M. and Schwart, E. "Evaluating Natural Resources Investments." *Journal of Business* 58 (1985), 135–157.

Brown, S. and Warner, J. "Using Daily Stock Returns." *Journal of Financial Economics* 14 (1985), 3–31.

Chicago Board of Trade. "The Report of the Chicago Board of Trade to the Presidential Task Force on Market Mechanisms." December 1987.

Commodity Futures Trading Commission (CFTC). "Final Report on Stock Index Futures and Cash Market Activity during October 1987 to the U.S. Commodity Futures Trading Commission." The Division of Economic Analysis and the Division of the Trading and Markets, January 1988.

Dann, L. "Common Stock Repurchases: An Analysis of Returns to Bondholders and Stockholders." *Journal of*

Financial Economics 9 (1981), 113–138.

DeBondt, W. and Thaler, R. "Does the Stock Market Overreact?" *Journal of Finance* 40 (1985), 793–805.

Edwards, F. "The Clearing House in Futures Markets: Guarantor and Regulator." In: Ronald W. Anderson, ed., *The Industrial Organization of Futures Markets.* Lexington, MA: D.C. Heath, 1984.

——————. "Does Futures Trading Increase Stock Market Volatility," *Financial Analyst Journal* (January/February 1988a), 63–69.

——————. "Policies to Curb Stock Market Volatility." Center for the Study of Futures Markets. Working paper #176, 1988b.

Fabozzi, F. and Ma, C. "NASD Activities During NYSE Trading Halts." *The Financial Review* (1989, forthcoming).

Fama, E. "Perspectives on October 1987, or, What Did We Learn from the Crash." In: R. Kampuis, R. Kormendi, and J. Watson, eds., *Black Monday and the Future of Financial Markets.* Homewood, IL: Irwin, 1989, pp. 71–82.

Fischel, D. "Should One Agency Regulate Financial Markets?" In: R. Kampuis, R. Kormendi, and J. Watson, eds., *Black Monday and the Future of Financial Markets.* Homewood, IL: Irwin, 1989, pp. 113–120.

French, K. and Roll, R. "Stock Return Variances: The Arrival of Information and the Reaction of Traders." *Journal of Financial Economics* 17 (1986), 5–26.

Garman, M. and Klass, M. "On the Estimation of Security Price Volatilities from Historical Data." *Journal of Business* 53 (1980), 67–78.

Gilpin, K. "Merc's Price Limit Plan Dismays Many Traders." *The New York Times,* 1987.

Hieronymus, T. *Economics of Futures Trading.* New York: Commodity Research Bureau, 1971.

Hill, J. and Jones, F. "Equity Trading, Program Trading, Portfolio Insurance, Computer Trading and All That." *Financial Analysts Journal* (July/August, 1988), 29–38.

Hopewell, M. and Schwartz, A. "Stock Price Movement Associated with Temporary Trading Suspensions: Bear Market Versus Bull Market." *Journal of Financial and Quantitative Analysis* 11 (1976), 577–590.

——————. "Temporary Trading Suspensions in Individual NYSE Securities." *Journal of Finance* 33 (1978), 1355–1373.

Kampuis, R., Jr., Kormendi, R. and Watson, J., eds. *Black Monday and the Future of Financial Markets,* the Mid-America Institute for Public Policy Research. Homewood, IL: Irwin, 1989.

Katzenbach, N. "An Overview of Program Trading and its impact on Current Market Practices." A study commissioned by the New York Stock Exchange, December 1987.

Khoury, S. and Jones, G. "Daily Price Limits on Futures Contracts: Nature, Impact, and Justification." *Review of Research in Futures Markets* (1983).

Kryzanowski, L. "The Efficiency of Trading Suspensions: A Regulatory Action Designed to Prevent the Exploitation of Monopoly Information." *Journal of Finance* 34 (1979), 1187–1200.

Ma, K., Rao, R. and Sears, S. "Limit Moves and Price Resolution: The Case of the Treasury Bond Futures." *Journal of Futures Markets* (forthcoming, 1989).

Maberly, E. "The Delivery Period and Daily Price Limits: A Comment." *Journal of Futures Markets* 2 (1982), 105.

Meltzner, A. "Overview." In: R. Kampuis, Jr., Kormendi, R., and Watson, J., eds., *Black Monday and the Future of Financial Markets.* Homewood, IL: Irwin, 1989.

Miller, M., Scholes, M., Malkiel, B. and Hawke, J. "Final Report of the Committee of Inquiry Appointed by the Chicago Mercantile Exchange to Examine the Events Surrounding October 1987." December 1987.

Neiderhoffer, V. "A New Look at Clustering of Stock Prices." *Journal of Business* 39 (1966), 390–413.

Osborne, M.F.M. "Periodic Structure in the Brownian Motion of Stock Prices." *Operations Research* 10 (1960), 345–379.

Parkinson, M. "The Extreme Value Method for Estimating the Variance of the Rate of Return." *Journal of Business* 53 (1980), 61–65.

President's Working Group on Financial Markets. "Interim Report of the Working Group on Financial Markets," May 1988.

Roll, R. "The International Crash of October 1987." In: R. Kampuis, Jr., R. Kormendi, and J. Watson, eds., *Black Monday and the Future of Financial Markets.* Homewood, IL: Irwin, 1989.

Samuelson, P. "Proof that Properly Anticipated Prices Fluctuate Randomly." *Industrial Management Review* 6 (1965), 41–50.

Shiller, R.J. "Do Stock Prices Move Too Much to be Justified by Subsequent Changes in Dividends?" *American Economic Review* 71 (1981), 421–436.

Silber, W. "Innovation, Competition and New Contract Design in Futures Markets." *Journal of Futures Markets*1 (1981), 123–155.

Stoll, H. and Whaley, R. "Stock Market Structure and Volatility." Conference on Stock Market Volatility and the Crash, March 17, 1989.

Telser, L.G. "Margins and Futures Contracts." *Journal of Futures Markets* 1 (1981), 255–255.

——————. "October 1987 and the Structure of Financial Markets: An Exorcism of Demons." In: R. Kampuis, R. Kormendi, and J. Watson, eds., *Black Monday and the Future of Financial Markets.* Homewood, IL: Irwin, 1989.

U.S. General Accounting Office. "Financial Markets: Preliminary Observations on the October 1987 Crash." Report to the Congressional Requesters, January 1988.

U.S. Securities and Exchange Commission. "The October 1987 Market Break." A Report by the Division of Market Regulation, February 1988.

Winkler, R. and Hays, W. *Statistics.* Chicago: Holt, Rinehart and Winston, 1975.

Journal of Financial Services Research, 3: 201–203 (1989)
© 1989 Kluwer Academic Publishers

Commentary: *Volatility, Price Resolution, and the Effectiveness of Price Limits*

MERTON H. MILLER
Robert R. McCormick Distinguished Service Professor
Graduate School of Business
University of Chicago, 60637

I must admit to having somewhat mixed feelings about the Ma-Rao-Sears article. As one of the very few academics to believe that coordinated circuit breakers might even be worth *discussing,* let alone enacting, I was pleased to note the message the three authors drew from their study of what happens in commodity futures markets before and after daily price limits are hit. They conclude that following such limit moves, prices tend to stabilize or reverse; and that volatility also tends to drop off substantially when trading resumes. They thus appear to find, as some of the more enthusiastic supporters of circuit breakers, like the Brady Commission, have argued, that commodity price limits act like the beryllium rods in nuclear reactors. They cool off an overheating market but without permanently damaging market liquidity, since the three authors find also that volume does not drop off substantially once trading resumes.

Provocative as these new empirical findings may seem at first glance, their real probative value in the debates over circuit breakers is far from clear. For one thing, commodity price limits, though they do bring trading to a halt, differ in other important respects from the coordinated circuit breakers proposed after the crash and subsequently installed by the New York Stock Exchange and the Chicago Mercantile Exchange. Furthermore, even if price limits really were the appropriate analog, the attempt to draw valid inferences from the post-resumption activity faces difficult and possibly insuperable obstacles because of selection bias.

Price limit moves, after all, can occur for several days in a row, leaving an investigator of post-limit behavior with several unsatisfactory choices. The most deceptively simple option, of course, is just to throw the multiple-move cases out of the sample. One-day limit moves are already rare events; multiple-day moves are even rarer. Can there be much harm in removing so few points from the sample? The answer, alas, is yes. Trimming out the multiple-move days leaves a sample not just of one-day limit moves, but of limit moves where, by selection, the next day's move could not have been an equally large or larger move in the same direction! Not surprisingly, prices, returns, volatility, and volume would all seem to be going back to normal levels on the days following these selected one-day-only events.

Nor does it help much to put the multiple-move days back in, treating the second move as both the follow-on of a one-day move and the start of a new sequence. When the second limit move in the sequence is considered a post-limit day relative to the first move, the

103

absence of trading on that second day makes volatility and volume necessarily zero, thus biasing downward the post-limit performance of those variables. When the second move is considered the start of a new sequence, the selection bias noted earlier arises again, this time for all sequences involving precisely two limit moves in succession. And so on for three and four or more move cases. There appears to be no solution to these difficulties; they are inherent in the selection process.

I suspect that about the best that can be done to calibrate the after-effects of limit moves is to construct the unconditional distribution of prices, volume, and volatility over intervals longer than one trading day—say, a week or a month. Those distributions might then be contrasted either with the corresponding distributions for the close-out month contract, which is typically not subject to price limits, or perhaps with the relevant spot market in cases of homogeneous commodities like silver or gold. Such intermarket comparisons will require careful interpretation, however, since close-out months and the spot-markets have pecularities of their own. But the contrasting of the constrained and unconstrained markets might throw some light at least on the "spill-over" effects on the substitute markets when one market unexpectedly closed.

The fear that a huge spill-over surge might destory the solvency of its already beleaguered market makers led the CME to halt trading for about 30 minutes in its S&P 500 contract during the morning on October 20, 1987, when the NYSE was rumored about to close. As it turned out, the rumor was false, and the NYSE was able to maintain its proud boast that, like the fabled Windmill Theater during the London Blitz, it never closed (at least not since the prlonged five-month shut-down after the outbreak of World War I in August 1914). But the boast is somewhat hollow in that while the Exchange remains open, trading in particular stocks on the NYSE is halted quite frequently either when major news is to be announced or, more to the present point, when an unusually heavy order imbalance suddenly arises. The accumulation of heavy overnight order imbalances can also lead to delayed openings of anywhere from a few minutes to an hour or more. De facto circuit breakers of these kinds were plentifully in evidence during the fateful days of October 19 and 20, as were many instances, not technically of halts perhaps, but of unusually long delays in effecting (and reporting) transactions.

Although delayed openings and intraday trading halts contributed greatly to the confusion about the true state of the market during the crash, deploring them is pointless. They are an inevitable consequence of the structure of the NYSE and especially of its reliance on regulated, franchised market makers to minimize the frequency of large price jumps between transactions. When large jumps are threatened, the system switches from continuous-market mode, as it were, to discrete-auction mode. Standing alone, this NYSE system of sporadic halts would be of little concern. But, under stress, the system doesn't mesh well with unconstrained continuous market systems like those of the CME's S&P 500 futures contract. Not only do the partial halts on the NYSE threaten spill-over surges to the CME but the pricing (and hedging) of the index futures contract becomes problematic when current prices are not available for major components of the index. Hence the formal circuit breakers negotiated by the two exchanges about a year ago under which sudden and unusually heavy order imbalances will lead to simultaneous, temporary trading halts (and subsequent resumptions) on both exchanges.

Note that while the specific condition triggering the simultaneous shut-down is a price move, the negotiated circuit breakers differ in important respects from the kind of commodity market price-limit moves studied by Ma-Rao-Sears. For one thing, the coordinated circuit breakers are only temporary pauses in trading. Market makers don't just walk off the floor and go home; the point is not to keep them from trading, but to bring them reinforcements, as it were. Nor does the formal information flow from the impacted market grind to a halt, as it does with limit moves. Market participants will still be getting word about the state of the imbalances and about the likely price range at the resumption of trading exactly as they do before the day's open. In fact, the whole procedure is patterned after the regular opening routines in the two markets (as was their earlier joint resolution of the "triple-witching" day problem). The CME has added some additional new wrinkles that allow for "recontracting" after its regular initial open if the opening price move exceeds 5 S&P points. That limit was reached for the first—and so far only—time on March 17 of this year. After a two-minute pause, the day's second opening took place with, from all accounts, no untoward consequences.

All this suggests that if Ma, Rao, and Sears had sought to study what happens when a market resumes trading after an enforced halt, they might better have focused on the daily close rather than on limit moves. They would thus have had a more direct analog to actual current circuit breakers, and since a close occurs every day, an analog that was free of selection bias.

With respect to volatility, at least, we can be pretty sure of what such a study of daily closings and reopenings would show. The day's open typically would have high volatility, and so, presumably, and by extension, would any trading period immediately after an interruption in trading. The more so the longer the delay. But is post-resumption volatility really the key concern about circuit breakers? It might be, perhaps, if the issue were whether to install circuit breakers in an isolated and otherwise unconstrained market. As emphasized earlier, however, circuit breakers, though called by other names, have long been a standard and accepted feature of NYSE procedures. The more operative question about circuit breakers is what kind of rules might be invoked to reduce uncertainties about the initiation and duration of trading halts, particularly when they seriously impact the index futures and options markets. Should the market-wide and intermarket halts be conditioned, for example, on absolute price changes (as under the current agreement) or on the number of stocks not trading (as was the rule on exchanges trading index options even before the crash)? If a price-change standard is to be used, should it be based on the S&P 500 index or the Dow-Jones index or a combination of both as in the current agreement? The two indices are highly but far from perfectly correlated. What if on some given day they should happen to give different signals? Rather than make the switch to auction mode conditional on price changes or other market events, might it make more sense to schedule one or two mid-session call markets every trading day? These and related issues of market interaction have received little or no attention so far, thanks to the widely held view within the economics profession that circuit breakers are either misguided social work or cosmetic devices designed by the exchanges to appease their customers and their congressional critics. That may well be part of the story, but certainly not all of it. Is it too much to hope that someday the serious issues may actually be *discussed?*

Journal of Financial Services Research, 3: 205–209 (1989)
© 1989 Kluwer Academic Publishers

Commentary: *Volatility, Price Resolution, and the Effectiveness of Price Limits*

BRUCE N. LEHMANN
Department of Economics
Graduate School of Business
Columbia University
and National Bureau of Economic Research

Since the market crash on October 19, 1987, it has been commonplace in policy circles to speak of the virtues of circuit breakers—devices for halting or limiting trading when prices have moved "too much." Some see it as self-evident that devices such as price limits curb "excess volatility," while others suggest that circuit breakers interfere with the price discovery process and the impounding of information in market prices. Surprisingly, few empirical researchers have attempted to measure the impact of circuit breakers on price volatility or to examine whether volatility fluctuations arise from "speculative overreaction" or "information arrival."

This article studies price fluctuations in commodities futures markets subject to price limits. As such, the analysis cannot hope to answer questions regarding what impact, if any, circuit breakers would have had on the October crash, since similar crashes did not occur in commodity futures during their sample. However, this research can, in principle, provide useful information about the marginal impact of price limits on volatility.

The purpose of my comments is to question whether the authors provide such information. The next section asks what information can be extracted, in principle, from observed prices in markets subject to price limits. The subsequent section discusses three measurement issues—the occurrence of price limits, and average returns and volatility around them. The final section suggests what conclusions can reasonably be drawn from the evidence in this article.

1. Volatility, liquidity, and price limits

At first blush, the impact of price limits on subsequent price, volume, and volatility is obvious, as suggested by the authors in section 3. Suppose that price limits are set narrow enough to cause appreciable spillover of information or enthusiasm from day to day, an assumption discussed in section 2 below. Informed trading should continue in the day after a price limit is hit, yielding similar pre-limit and post-limit price behavior, since price limits curb "rational" and "informed" trading. Subsequent prices will typically continue past the limit price, subsequent volatility will usually change little, and subsequent volume should remain high. By contrast, if price limits curb "overreaction" or "speculative enthusiasm," subsequent prices will typically stabilize at or "bounce off" the limit price, subsequent volatility will usually fall, and subsequent volume should stabilize or decline because trading halts give giddy traders the time to reflect on their excesses. The authors' hypotheses follow by imagining that one category of trader dominates the order flow.

Unfortunately, this is a deceptively simple view of the effect of price limits on price fluctuations because the authors do not ask one simple question—how will "overly" enthusiastic or "rational" traders behave as prices approach their limits? The authors implicitly assume that market participants do not alter their trading practices in the neighborhood of limit price moves. Yet simple reflections on the market for liquidity in futures markets suggest that observed market prices do not contain the information sought by the authors.

Any model of the market for liquidity must incorporate the factors affecting the supply of and demand for *immediacy* and, hence, answer why the parties to a transaction are trading at that moment. A particularly useful model distinguishes between two kinds of traders (see Treynor, 1981; and Kyle, 1988): long-term, value-based, patient traders, and impatient, short-term, information-based or noise traders. Impatient traders demand the immediate execution of transactions, perhaps impelled by trading strategies, liquidity needs, or real or imagined information. Their demand for immediacy means that they typically confront (and trade in spite of) high transactions costs in the short-run. Patient traders help stabilize markets by buying (selling) when net selling (buying) by impatient traders substantially moves prices. They wait to trade on favorable terms, which they can do because they are providing liquidity to impatient traders.

The spread or liquidity premium between the prices at which one can buy and sell quickly is determined by the balance between patient and impatient traders in the marketplace. Hence, impatient traders need not be a net destabilizing influence on prices—their trading activities generate volume and attract patient traders. Even large and unpredictable fluctuations in their demands need not add to volatility if this generates substantial return to the provision of liquidity.

Price limits have an ambiguous conceptual impact on liquidity around limit price moves. Trading halts let patient traders acquire capital to satisfy unforeseen demand for liquidity by impatient traders. However, the rewards to patient traders are limited in the neighborhood of price limits, which limit the liquidity premium that can be earned. This tends to drive patient traders out of the market in the neighborhood of price limits. The resulting order imbalance between impatient and patient traders may increase both the likelihood of hitting price limits and prior volatility. This occurs irrespective of whether the increased demand for liquidity came primarily from "rational informed" or "overly enthusiastic noise" traders. Put differently, volatility can also rise because of reductions in the supply of liquidity by patient traders around price limits.

Price limits also have no clear implications for the behavior of prices on the day after a limit price move. If the subsequent opening price was not a near-limit move, patient traders will have an incentive to reenter the market, causing prices to stabilize and volatility to fall on average unless another price limit is approached. Once again, it is simply not possible to tell whether any tendency for prices to stabilize following a limit move reflects reductions in the demand for liquidity by reflective impatient traders or increases in the supply of liquidity by patient traders.

In short, price behavior in the neighborhood of limit price moves provides little information about whether price limits are a stabilizing force in futures markets. To be sure, price limits affect the average liquidity premium and the average order balance between patient and impatient traders. Unfortunately, they create a systematic order imbalance between patient and impatient traders in the neighborhood of limit price moves. Studying price behavior around limit moves remains interesting but difficult to interpret without a model of the supply of and demand for liquidity.

2. The measurement of limit price moves and concurrent price behavior

The authors collect price, volume, and open interest data from the *Wall Street Journal.* They use the nearby futures contract, although it is not clear when they switch to the next contract (which should be done before expiration). They obtain intraday tick price data from the Chicago Board of Trade's *Time and Sales File.* For daily data, limit moves occur by definition when measured prices hit their limits. For intraday data, a limit price day occurs when a limit is hit any time within the day.

As noted earlier, the authors' hypotheses hinge on the assumption that price limits are set narrow enough to cause appreciable spillover of the demand for liqudity from day to day. Unfortunately, the data in tables 2 and 3 suggest that price limits are set so high that they are rarely hit. Ignoring the Hunt brothers episode in silver futures, limit moves occur on roughly 3 to 4 percent of the trading days in the sample. Similarly, approximately 0.01 percent of the price ticks in the intraday sample are limit moves. Hitting a price limit is a rare event, suggesting that price behavior will typically be more stable after a limit price move.

The authors treat limit price moves as independent when it is common for limit price moves to be serially correlated, as can be seen in the appropriate panels of tables 2 and 3. A limit price move is followed by at least one other limit price day in approximately 5 percent of the days for corn, 18 percent of the days for soybeans, 32 percent of the days for Treasury bonds, and 46 percent of the days for silver. This alone can cause measured volatility to be relatively low on the day following the first limit price move! Moreover, patient and impatient traders would probably take account of the probability of successive limit price moves, once again affecting the demand of and supply for immediacy with ambiguous implications for price behavior in the neighborhood of limit price moves. The authors suggest that cures for this clustering are worse than the disease. In any event, this evidence indicates that first-time limit days are even more rare.

The authors measure price volatility around limit price days. They use the Parkinson (1980) and Garman and Klass (1980) high/low estimator in their daily data. Like all variance estimators based on the sample range, this estimator is extremely sensitive to measurement errors in the daily high and low prices. Measurement errors are more probable on high volume days like limit price days. There is also an upward bias in these variance estimates on high volatility days to the extent that the bid/ask spread widens in these circumstances.

The authors could estimate the impact of this potential source of measurement error by examining variance estimators based on other order statistics (such as the semi-interquartile range) in their tick data for each day.

The authors also study average price changes following limit price moves. This involves the straightforward examination of log price relatives in their daily data. However, they adopt a very peculiar strategy for examining price changes in their tick data base. Their notion of a limit price day in the tick data is actually two days long in calendar time because a limit price move can occur anytime between the open and the close. If a limit move occurs at the open (close), zeros are recorded for the observations before (after) time zero (the time of the first limit move), and the entire sample path of prices over the remainder of the day constitutes the observations after (before) time zero. If a limit move occurs after k percent of the trading day has elapsed, zeros are generated for the first k percent of the observations before time zero and for the last one minus k percent of the observations after time zero, and the sample path of prices constitutes the observations between these two points.

In constructing figures 1 through 4, the authors average over the observations constructed in this fashion, dividing by the number of nonzero observations at each point in the "day." This practice eliminates virtually all of the information about price behavior around limit moves. For example, the prices sometimes move below the price limit after the time zero for down-limit moves, and above the price limit after time zero for up-limit moves. This happens because there are fewer nonzero observations implicit in the figures as one moves away from time zero on this hypothetical two-day-long limit price day. In fact, the only sample data included in the figures at the beginning (end) of their limit price day are observations for which limit moves occurred at the close (open). Hence, the figures which show large jumps from the close on day zero to the open on day one display the average price difference between the small subsample of observations that closed on a limit move and the average subsequent opening price for all of the sample.

There is a simple way to avoid this problem. Report the difference between the closing (opening) price on the limit price day and the tick prices on the subsequent (previous) day to examine subsequent (previous) price behavior. Similarly, study the joint behavior of intraday prices and the time at which the first limit is hit on the limit price day. This practice would provide meaningful information about price behavior around limit price moves in the tick data.

3. Empirical results

My reading of the evidence in the article is somewhat different from that of the authors. The authors note that measured volatility is higher on the day following a limit price move. However, measured volatility on the day before a limit price movement is typically lower than on the following two days, perhaps representing either lower information arrival or "enthusiasm" before a limit price move. Note also that average volatility over the week before a limit move is higher than that over the subsequent week roughly half of the time—half the time it is less.

The authors find the evidence on reversals most interesting. They observe the following typical intraday pattern—prices usually rise (fall) prior to a limit up (down) day. After hitting the limit, prices appear to stabilize—sometimes tending to reverse somewhat and sometimes tending to continue. They emphasize the former outcomes, concluding that "the triggering of limits appears to give the market *breathing room* . . . ."

As note earlier, the figures are virtually impossible to interpret because of the peculiar strategy the authors employed to average over limit price moves. Moreover, the propensity for limit moves to be followed by limit moves in the same direction suggests a selection bias toward finding stabilization on average. In fact, the daily data suggest their intraday conclusions are erroneous—these data yield more post-limit continuations than reversals. Hence, I see no substantive evidence for price reversals following limit moves in the article.

In summary, three basic interpretations are possible. Maybe price limits stabilize futures markets. Maybe patient traders exit the market near limit moves, making limits a "magnet," diminishing liquidity, increasing volatility slightly, and making it hard to tell whether price limits stabilize futures markets. Maybe price limits occur so rarely that one cannot tell with these data, especially given the potential measurement errors. This article asks good questions but does not provide definitive answers.

References

Garman, Mark and Klass, M. "On the Estimation of Security Price Volatilities from Historical Data." *Journal of Business* 53 (1980), 67–78.

Kyle, Albert S. "Improving the Performance of the Stock Market." *California Management Review* 30/4 (1988), 90–114.

Parkinson, M. "The Extreme Value Method for Estimating the Variance of the Rate of Return." *Journal of Business* 53 (1980), 61–65.

Treynor, Jack L. "What Does It Take to Win the Trading Game?" *Financial Analysts Journal* 37 (1981), 55–60.

Journal of Financial Services Research, 3: 211–246 (1989)
© 1989 Kluwer Academic Publishers

Price Volatility, International Market Links, and Their Implications for Regulatory Policies

RICHARD ROLL
Allstate Professor of Finance and Insurance
University of California
Los Angeles, CA 90024-1481

Disastrous events sometimes engender redeeming social benefits. The international crash of equity markets in mid-October 1987 is a case in point, for it has provoked many scientific papers, both theoretical and empirical, on market volatility, international market links, and market structure, papers that may have never been written without the crash as a catalyst. The purpose of the present article is to provide an assessment of some of the most significant empirical studies and to summarize their implications about possible regulatory reform of the equity and futures markets. In addition, I will present some new evidence about volatility and its relation to existing market regulations across countries.

Specifically excluded from my survey of empirical papers will be reports provided by various "commissions." Some of these reports contain fine empirical work, but they are not really scientific studies in the sense of having been subjected to a thorough review by peers before publication. Kamphuis, Kormendi, and Watson (1989) provide excerpts that include the most important empirical results from six different commission reports.[1]

But even without such commission reports, there are plenty of good papers to examine, some of which have surprising new conclusions. Their technical sophistication is often quite advanced for the general reader, so one of my goals is to summarize their contributions in nontechnical language.

The October 1987 Crash posed three important scientific questions:

1. What were its causes?
2. Why and how did it propagate internationally?
3. Was it related to particular institutional practices, market arrangements, or regulatory policies?

The subsequent three sections of the article are devoted respectively to evidence about these three questions.

The author is grateful for helpful discussions with Franklin Edwards, David Hirshleifer, Merton Miller, and Stephen Ross, and for comments from Dan Nelson, Sushil Wadhwani, and the other participants at the Conference on Regulatory Reform of Stock and Futures Markets, Futures Center, Columbia University, New York, May 12, 1989. None of these individuals would agree to share the responsibility for the contents of the article. Research support has been provided by the Columbia Futures Center.

113

1. Empirical papers on the causes of the crash

1.1. Suggested causes and "triggers"

The first question has been the most difficult to answer. Just after the crash, journalists and politicians (those experts) ascribed it to a variety of sources ranging from portfolio insurance to inadequate computer systems. However, empiricists have since found it difficult to confirm any of these contentions. For instance, though portfolio insurance is a popular culprit in some circles, I was unable to find any evidence that markets where portfolio insurance was widely used declined to a greater extent than markets where portfolio insurance was virtually absent. In fact, countries with portfolio insurance crashed *less* than countries without it, (Roll, 1989, table 4).[2] Bertero and Mayer (1989) confirm this finding.

Another allegation points to *all* uses of stock index futures or other related futures contracts, not just portfolio insurance. The argument seems to be that irrational speculators cause destabilization. However, I could find no evidence that stock markets with related futures markets crashed any more than stock markets in countries without futures exchanges. In a longer term study, Edward (1988a) concludes that the introduction of futures trading on a particular index, the S&P 500, coincided with a period of lower, not higher, volatility. However, a recent paper by Harris (1989) finds evidence that individual stocks that are included in the S&P 500 index have higher volatilities than a control group of similar stocks. The effect is not very large, but it appears to be statistically significant and conceivably could be related to institutional practice such as index arbitrage or widespread S&P 500 index fund investing.

There is better supporting evidence that a particular event in the United States triggered the worldwide crash. According to Mitchell and Netter (1989), the triggering event was the introduction in the U.S. Congress of a tax bill that would have severely penalized corporate takeovers, leveraged buyouts, and other similar activities. These authors provide empirical support in several forms. First, takeover candidates were more severely negatively affected in the week preceeding October 19. Second, takeover candidates subsequently displayed price increases when congressional support for the tax bill waned. Third, in the week before the crash, the U.S. equity market declined more than a value-weighted average of other would markets.[3]

The Mitchell/Netter explanation of the crash, though indeed intriguing, depends on a chain of difficult-to-prove propositions. If the U.S. tax bill caused the worldwide crash (which was much worse in some countries than in the United States), we must accept (1) that heavier taxation of takeovers would cause *all* stocks to be affected; (2) that the U.S. decline on October 14–16 induced an even larger crash on October 19, although tax bill news had already been fully disseminated earlier; and (3) that a stock price decline in the United States *resulting from a proposed U.S. tax bill* caused at least as large a decline on average in other countries.

All of these propositions are possible, but are they really plausible? A persuasive argument can be advanced against each one. Regarding the first proposition, why would even the complete elimination of takeovers, not just a marginally higher tax, cause a 20 percent decline in the aggregate market value of *all* stocks? Takeovers have not often created such a dramatic increase in the combined value of two merging firms.[4] The second proposition is inconsistent with market efficiency; there was no news about the tax bill on October 19. The third proposition seems likely since past increases in U.S. taxes have had no memorable influence on stock markets in *other* countries.

A unique explanation of the crash is suggested by Amihud, Mendelson, and Wood (1989), who argue that investors became persuaded that the stock market was less "liquid" than they had believed previously. Somewhat ingenuously, these authors state that " . . . the main news which led to the prolonged decline in stock prices was the crash itself" (p. 1). In other words, the crash proved that the market was illiquid, and this caused a permanent downward revision in stock values.

This "explanation" is patently circular. The crash can't be explained by the crash! However, Amihud, Mendelson, and Wood might have an explanation for why stock prices failed to completely *recover* after the crash. Given a crash induced by some other influence, it seems quite possible that investors might revise their estimates of market liquidity and therefore permanently write down values, even if the original cause of the crash were reversed.

The absence of an obvious or fully persuasive triggering event has led some to suspect the existence of a speculative "bubble" prior to the crash. Miller (1989) surveys many of the arguments advanced in favor of a bubble but concludes that a fundamentals-based explanation is just as plausible; possible fundamental causes include a revision in risk attitudes or a minor trigger that induced a major shift in expected growth rates. Also, there is suggestive international evidence against a bubble. As Goodhart (1988) notes,

> . . . valiant—but not entirely convincing—efforts have been made to identify Stock Exchange bubbles developing and breaking, simultaneously, in New York, London and Tokyo . . . I would challenge anyone to find a bubble also in Frankfurt, and yet the Stock Market there fell in line with the rest in October (p. 5).

However, the anti-bubble evidence is not entirely convincing either, at least to many authors. Fama (1989) says that the most questionable aspect of 1987 was not the crash itself but the incredible market advance during the previous five years. Telser (1989, p. 102) states, "The most plausible [theory] is that a speculative bubble burst in October 1987." Siegal (1988) presents empirical evidence that fundamental factors from January through September of 1987 would not have been plausible support for such large price increases as were observed in the United States. I found a negative relation between the market increase before the crash in different countries and the size of the crash decline (Roll, 1988, figure 9).[5]

Suspicion about a bubble has been abetted by some theoretical developments, particularly the relatively new literature on "rational" bubbles.[6] Prior to recent papers, many financial economists dismissed bubbles because they seemed inconsistent with rational investor behavior in a realistic setting[7] (Tirole, 1982, 1985), and they were thought to be observationally equivalent to price episodes driven by fundamentals (Hamilton, and Whiteman, 1985). An outstanding survey of this literature is provided by Camerer (1989).

Some bubbles are rational from investors' points of view, although there is usually some other market inefficiency. For example, a rational finite bubble for finite-lived assets in a market with a finite number of traders is demonstrated by Allen and Gorton (1988). In the Allen/Gorton model, all funds are managed by two different types of professionals, and only one type has investment skill. A labor market inefficiency exists in the sense that investors can never tell the difference between worthless and able managers.

An interesting empirical paper in this tradition is by Hardouvelis (1989).[8] He looks for rational bubbles in the United States, Japan, and the United Kingdom, and he finds them, at least to his satisfaction. His argument is that a rational bubble requires an increasing risk premium as the bubble becomes more advanced,[9] and he obtains seemingly impressive empirical evidence that this actually happened in the (approximately) two years ending in September 1987.

How does Hardouvelils obtain ex ante risk premia in this period and then measure their increase? He first builds a model to predict ex post risk premia[10] as functions of various predictor variables such as the price/earnings ratio, the price-to-book-value ratio, lagged values of the observed risk premium, and various interest rate variables. Using a test period ending in March 1985, he finds that the price/earnings ratio and price-to-book-value ratio explain a surprisingly large fraction of the actual stock return in excess of the short-term interest rate over the *subsequent* 12 months. In the United States, the adjusted R^2 is 36 percent, in the United Kingdom it is 32 percent, and in Japan it is an unbelievable 66 percent! The explanatory power is only slightly higher with the other variables included as regressors.

The word *unbelievable* is appropriate. If one could predict 66 percent of *next year's* actual return with the current price/earnings ratio and price-to-book-value ratio, the accumulation of wealth would be immodest. Of course, next year's return would be easier to predict with hindsight, with earnings and book values that are not actually announced to the public until long after the end of the previous year (to which they refer). I suspect that some of Hardouvelis's seeming predictive power may be attributable to using accounting numbers that were not actually available to the market on the forecast date.

Hardouvelis finds that the slope coefficients in his predictive models of ex post risk premia increase during approximately two years before the October 1987 crash. This is consistent with a simple explanation; viz., stock prices increased more than usual over those two years. The conclusion that risk premia actually increased before the crash might be regarded as a munificent interpretation of the results.

Although theorists have concocted models that could conceivably explain bubbles, no one has yet provided completely persuasive evidence that such models have applicability to the crash event. Nonetheless, a bubble is at least as good an explanation of the crash as any other explanation that has thus far been advanced. Further empirical testing for a possible bubble definitely seems worthwhile.

A potentially measurable characteristic of a bubble is positive serial dependence among successive price changes during the bubble's expansionary period. Santoni (1987) used this feature to develop a test for bubbles in 1924–1929 and in 1982–1987. He was unable to find enough evidence of postive serial dependence to conclude that bubbles actually existed during those episodes.

However, as Hardouvelis (1988a, 1989) argues in commenting on Santoni's results, there is so much noise in stock returns that serial dependence is often difficult to uncover. Thus, it might be worthwhile to examine more extensive data, stock returns from the major free market countries, for evidence of positive serial dependence before and after the 1987 crash, in the hope that more observations will overcome the noise problem. The data and some new tests are described in the next section.

1.2. Empirical tests for speculative bubbles in 23 countries before and after the October 1987 stock market crash

In a previous paper Roll (1988), I described and utilized a data set consisting of broad stock market indexes from 23 countries. Except for the absence of Korea and Taiwan, they are *the* major stock markets of the world.[11] Daily price indexes are now available from January 1987 through March 1989 inclusive. Table 1 presents mean daily returns[12] and standard deviations of daily returns for each of the 23 countries and for three periods around the October 1987 crash.[13] In the approximately nine months before the crash, most of the countries exhibited a substantial price increase. The simple average of mean returns in all countries, .1606 percent per day in local currency, can be translated into about 40 percent per annum (even without the outlier of Mexico, the average is about 31 percent per annum). Subsequent to the crash, average returns have been considerably smaller, only .0659 percent per day or about 16.6 percent per annum. Of course, the crash period displays extremely negative returns and extremely large volatilities relative to both the pre- and post-crash periods.

During a speculative bubble, the degree of serial dependence could be highly nonstationary, swinging up and down and yet still being positive during most of the bubble's expansion. Thus, a method robust to departures from a stationary dependence structure would be particularly desirable. Traditional methods for measuring serial dependence, such as autocorrelation methods, usually assume stationarity and, consequently, *may* have weak detecting power.

A volatility comparison test, or variance ratio test, will detect nonstationary serial dependence. A variance ratio test relies on the proposition that a sum of T *independent* identically distributed random variables has a variance T times the variance of a single random variable. *Any* dependence among the variables will make the variance of the sum either larger or smaller depending on whether the dependence is mostly positive or negative. Thus, if we look at multiple day returns (which are sums of daily returns), their volatilities should reveal the presence of any day-to-day dependence and thereby reveal the traces of a bubble.

Volatilities for 23 different countries over several different holding intervals and for pre- and post-crash calendar periods constitute a massive set of numbers. In order to present the essential results in a compact form, I used the following procedure:

First, for each of the 23 countries, volatilities (variances) were calculated for daily returns and for returns over *nonoverlapping* 2, 3, 5, 10, 15, and 20 trading day holding intervals, for calendar periods before and after the crash.

Table 1. Daily returns during the pre-crash period, the crash period, and the post-crash period by country (percent/day)

Calendar Period	Trading Days	Mean	Std. Dev.	Mean	Std. Dev.
		---Local Currency---		-------Dollars------	
		Australia			
1/ 2/87–10/ 9/87	199	0.2239	0.8496	0.2661	1.0887
10/12/87–10/30/87	15	−3.5160	8.3145	−3.9796	8.9462
11/ 2/87– 3/31/89	364	0.0475	1.2160	0.1008	1.4902
		Austria			
1/ 2/87–10/ 9/87	198	−0.0202	0.7363	0.0093	0.9360
10/12/87–10/30/87	15	−0.8255	1.6634	−0.5071	1.7087
11/ 2/87– 3/31/89	361	0.0699	0.5571	0.0453	0.8144
		Belgium			
1/ 2/87–10/ 9/87	198	0.0808	0.8135	0.1156	1.0316
10/12/87–10/30/87	15	−1.6531	4.3161	−1.3836	3.9137
11/ 2/87– 3/31/89	363	0.0906	0.9649	0.0652	1.0516
		Canada			
1/ 2/87–10/ 9/87	200	0.1143	0.6890	0.1421	0.7793
10/12/87–10/30/87	15	−1.5150	5.4126	−1.5613	5.6947
11/ 2/87– 3/31/87	365	0.0405	0.7721	0.0672	0.8576
		Denmark			
1/ 2/87–10/ 9/87	199	0.0710	0.9198	0.0978	1.1514
10/12/87–10/30/87	15	−1.1254	2.6782	−0.8392	3.0185
11/ 2/87– 3/31/89	366	0.1518	0.7152	0.1250	0.8940
		France			
1/ 2/87–10/ 9/87	199	0.0114	0.9177	0.0383	1.0491
10/12/87–10/30/87	15	−1.6526	4.5678	−1.4625	4.3250
11/ 2/87– 3/31/89	365	0.1018	1.2542	0.0784	1.2242
		Germany			
1/ 2/87–10/ 9/87	199	−0.0296	1.2508	0.0000	1.2469
10/12/87–10/30/87	15	−1.5913	4.1776	−1.2696	4.0512
11/ 2/87– 3/31/89	366	0.0254	1.2924	0.004	1.2859
		Hong Kong			
1/ 2/87–10/ 9/87	199	0.2218	1.1213	0.2206	1.1209
10/12/87–10/30/87	11	−5.4174	12.0719	−5.4121	12.1229
11/ 2/87– 3/31/89	362	0.1083	1.3530	0.1089	1.3536
		Ireland			
1/ 2/87–10/ 9/87	199	0.2121	1.1746	0.2364	1.2815
10/12/87–10/30/87	15	−2.6303	5.2557	−2.3895	5.5859
11/ 2/87– 3/31/89	367	0.0852	1.3906	0.0617	1.3317
		Italy			
1/ 2/87–10/ 9/87	200	−0.0338	1.0171	−0.0230	1.1966
10/12/87–10/30/87	15	−1.3943	3.1849	−1.2208	2.9911
11/ 2/87– 3/31/89	367	0.0293	1.1486	0.0064	1.2087
		Japan			
1/ 2/87–10/ 9/87	200	0.1543	1.2743	0.2020	1.4567
10/12/87–10/30/87	15	−0.9777	5.5671	−0.7203	5.8080
11/ 2/87– 3/31/89	366	0.0810	0.9460	0.0929	1.0775
		Malaysia			
1/ 2/87–10/ 9/87	201	0.2821	1.1707	0.2937	1.1869
10/12/87–10/31/87	15	−3.6080	6.0258	−3.5503	6.0397
11/ 2/87– 3/31/89	363	0.1426	1.1363	0.1178	1.1216
		Mexico			
1/ 2/87–10/ 9/87	197	0.9831	2.5085	0.7018	2.6053

10/12/87–10/31/87	15	−3.4050	6.8924	−3.6194	6.9043
11/ 2/87– 3/31/89	360	0.0128	2.7538	−0.0924	2.8612
Netherlands					
1/ 2/87–10/ 9/87	199	0.0672	0.9928	0.1028	0.9258
10/12/87–10/30/87	15	−1.5985	5.6771	−1.2690	5.6945
11/ 2/87– 3/31/89	366	0.0633	1.3012	0.0374	1.1533
New Zealand					
1/ 2/87–10/ 9/87	199	0.0291	1.0908	0.1400	1.2773
10/12/87–10/30/87	15	−2.0473	5.2956	−2.8215	5.9162
11/ 2/87– 3/31/89	363	−0.0755	1.3659	−0.0640	1.5104
Norway					
1/ 2/87–10/ 9/87	199	0.2473	1.2061	0.2997	1.2476
10/12/87–10/30/87	15	−2.5942	7.4383	−2.5134	7.6799
11/ 2/87– 3/31/89	366	0.1063	1.7726	0.0933	1.6964
Singapore					
1/ 2/87–10/ 9/87	201	0.2508	1.0754	0.2685	1.1171
10/12/87–10/30/87	15	−3.9675	10.1823	−3.8900	10.2357
11/ 2/87– 3/31/89	364	0.1004	1.3265	0.1152	1.3033
South Africa					
1/ 2/87–10/ 9/87	197	0.1636	1.0775	0.3243	2.5348
10/12/87–10/30/87	15	−2.0414	3.6262	−2.5031	5.1156
11/ 2/87– 3/31/89	362	0.0610	1.3823	0.0185	2.0956
Spain					
1/ 2/87–10/ 9/87	199	0.2143	1.2761	0.2599	1.4270
10/12/87–10/30/87	15	−2.4154	3.2863	−2.1014	3.7311
11/ 2/87– 3/31/89	367	0.055	0.9266	0.0482	1.0377
Sweden					
1/ 2/87–10/ 9/87	199	0.1272	1.0092	0.1561	1.0296
10/12/87–10/30/87	15	−1.8998	4.5347	−1.7039	4.5496
11/ 2/87– 3/31/89	366	0.1202	1.2421	0.1098	1.2393
Switzerland					
1/ 2/87–10/ 9/87	199	0.0156	0.9166	0.0494	1.0046
10/12/87–10/30/87	15	−2.0706	5.4091	−1.7146	5.2403
11/ 2/87– 3/31/89	364	0.0025	1.3053	−0.0388	1.2560
United Kingdom					
1/ 2/87–10/ 9/87	199	0.1852	0.8654	0.2393	1.1134
10/12/87–10/30/87	15	−2.0759	4.9469	−1.7951	5.0693
11/ 2/87– 3/31/89	367	0.0524	0.9621	0.0470	1.0120
United States					
1/ 2/87–10/ 9/87	199	0.1213	0.9645	0.1213	0.9645
10/12/87–10/30/87	15	−1.4128	7.2527	−1.4128	7.2527
11/ 2/87– 3/31/89	358	0.0428	1.0937	0.0428	1.0937
Mean Returns Over All Countries					
(Simple Cross-Country Average and Standard Deviation)					
1/ 2/87–10/ 9/87	201*	0.1606	0.2041	0.1853	0.1528
10/12/87–10/30/87	15*	−2.2363	1.1032	−2.1583	1.2292
11/ 2/87– 3/31/89	367*	0.0659	0.0500	0.0516	0.0588
Standard Deviations Over All Countries					
(Simple Cross-Country Average and Standard Deviation)					
1/ 2/87–10/ 9/87	201*	1.0834	0.3523	1.2510	0.4453
10/12/87–10/30/87	15*	5.5555	2.3729	5.7215	2.3811
11/ 2/87– 3/31/89	367*	1.2251	0.4264	1.3031	0.4414

*The maximum number of trading days available for any country.

For each country and calendar period, a T-day holding interval sample variance s_T^2 can be written approximately as:

$$s_T^2 = Ts_1^2 + T(T - 1)Rs_1^2,$$ (1)

or,

$$(s_T^{\,2}/T)s_1^2 = 1 + R(T-1),$$ (2)

where s_1^2 is the computed one-day holding interval sample variance and R is a particular *average* of sample autocorrelation coefficients of daily returns (averaged over lags running from 1 to $T-1$).[14] Note that R need not be stationary; it is merely an average autocorrelation during the sample calendar period.

Second, for each country and calendar period, regressions were fit in the following form:

$$(s_T^2/T)s_1^2 = b_0 + b_1(T - 1), \ \{T=2,3,5,10,15,20\}.$$ (3)

The coefficient b_0 should be unity, and the slope coefficient b_1 should be the average sample serial correlation R.[15]

Table 2 gives the cross-country means and standard deviations of the coefficients b_0 and b_1 and t-statistics (from testing b_0 against 1.0 and b_1 against 0). Also shown are the simple averages across countries for mean returns and standard deviations of returns, by holding interval.[16]

Although the mean pre-crash value of b_1 is small (only .0251), the average t-statistic for testing its deviation from zero is substantial. Of the 23 countries, 18 displayed t-statistics for b_1 greater than zero (11 were greater than 2.776)[17] using local currency returns, and 15 were greater than zero using dollar-denominated returns. This seems to imply the existence of small, positive, statistically significant serial dependence in the returns of many countries during the first nine months of 1987. Note that the intercept b_0 is not significantly different from unity, its theoretical value.

The presence of positive serial dependence is revealed also in the pattern of return standard deviations across holding intervals. Note in table 2, pre-crash period, that the average standard deviation is 1.0834 for one-day holding intervals and that it increases to 1.3439 (per day) for 20-day holding intervals. The same pattern was observed in 19 of the 23 individual countries (results not shown).

The contrast is rather striking with the post-crash period. After the crash and up through March of 1989, the average value of b_1 is very close to zero (average t-statistic = .0797). In the post-crash period, the cross-sectional standard deviation of the t-statistic for b_1 is 1.87 (for local currencies), slightly higher than the null value of 1.414.[18] Out of 23 countries, only three (five) of the individual country local currency (dollar-denominated) t-statistics exceeded in absolute value the .05 critical value 2.776, and one of these was negative.[19]

One difficulty with a serial dependence test of a speculative bubble has been recently discovered by Ross (1987). Suppose that prices actually fluctuate randomly. There are no

Table 2. Multiple-day returns and volatilities over 23 countries.

	Mean	Std. Dev.	Mean	Std. Dev.
	---Local Currency---		-------Dollars-------	
Pre-crash period, 1/2/87–10/9/87				
Regression of Variance Ratio on (Holding Period-1)				
[Equation (3) of Text]				
Slope:	0.0251	0.0328	0.0160	0.0349
t-statistic (from zero):	2.6410	3.8122	3.0393	7.1361
Intercept:	1.1478	0.2474	1.0982	0.2094
t-statistic (from 1.0):	0.7762	1.6858	0.5582	2.2861
Cross-Country Simple Averages				
(percent per day)				

Calendar Period	Holding Interval (days)				
1/ 2/87–10/ 9/87	1				
	Mean Returns:	0.1606	0.2041	0.1853	0.1528
	Standard Deviations:	1.0834	0.3523	1.2510	0.4453
1/ 2/87–10/ 8/87	2				
	Mean Returns:	0.1616	0.2019	0.1850	0.1513
	Standard Deviations:	1.1454	0.4060	1.2927	0.4729
1/ 2/87–10/ 9/87	3				
	Mean Returns:	0.1587	0.2004	0.1833	0.1503
	Standard Deviations:	1.2019	0.4095	1.3461	0.4870
1/ 2/87–10/ 8/87	5				
	Mean Returns:	0.1616	0.2019	0.1850	0.1513
	Standard Deviations:	1.2015	0.4594	1.3338	0.5044
1/ 2/87–10/ 8/87	10				
	Mean Returns:	0.1616	0.2019	0.1850	0.1513
	Standard Deviations:	1.2543	0.5770	1.3795	0.6452
1/ 2/87–10/ 1/87	15				
	Mean Returns:	0.1604	0.2001	0.1791	0.1512
	Standard Deviations:	1.2817	0.5598	1.4072	0.6052
1/ 2/87–10/ 8/87	20				
	Mean Returns:	0.1616	0.2019	0.1850	0.1513
	Standard Deviations:	1.3439	0.4796	1.4266	0.6065

Post-crash period 11/2/87–3/31/89				
Regression of Variance Ratio on (Holding Period-1)				
[Equation (3) of Text]				
Slope:	0.0024	0.0160	0.0022	0.0180
t-statistic (from zero):	0.0797	1.8719	−0.0650	2.2838
Intercept:	1.1058	0.1590	1.0424	0.1554
t-statistic (from 1.0):	0.9334	1.7863	0.0223	2.2396
Cross-Country Simple Averages				
(percent per day)				

Calendar Period	Holding Interval (days)				
11/ 2/87– 3/31/89	1				
	Mean Returns:	0.0659	0.0500	0.0516	0.0588

(Continued)

121

Table 2. (Continued)

	Mean	Std. Dev.	Mean	Std. Dev.
	---Local Currency---		-------Dollars-------	
Standard Deviations:	1.2252	0.4264	1.3030	0.4414
11/ 2/87– 3/31/89 2				
Mean Returns:	0.0650	0.0493	0.0510	0.0578
Standard Deviations:	1.3230	0.4946	1.3475	0.4934
11/ 2/87– 3/30/89 3				
Mean Returns:	0.0641	0.0488	0.0503	0.0574
Standard Deviations:	1.2624	0.4414	1.3227	0.4907
11/ 2/87– 3/31/89 5				
Mean Returns:	0.0649	0.0493	0.0509	0.0578
Standard Deviations:	1.2495	0.4399	1.3247	0.5277
11/ 2/87– 3/31/89 10				
Mean Returns:	0.0649	0.0493	0.0509	0.0578
Standard Deviations:	1.2704	0.4646	1.3137	0.5721
11/ 2/87– 3/17/89 15				
Mean Returns:	0.0652	0.0497	0.0531	0.0590
Standard Deviations:	1.3087	0.5204	1.3734	0.6896
11/ 2/87– 3/17/89 20				
Mean Returns:	0.0652	0.0497	0.0531	0.0590
Standard Deviations:	1.2763	0.4974	1.3389	0.6767

true bubbles. Every so often in such a random series, a local peak will occur by chance; interocular examiners have a tendency to focus on the peak as an indication of something unusual in the time series. Conditional on selecting the (random) peak as a sample separation point, Ross shows that the segregated data leading up to the peak will exhibit positive *sample* serial dependence. There is actually no dependence in the true process, and there was actually no bubble prior to the peak, yet choosing such a point ex post has the effect of creating seemingly significant serial dependence in the data preceding the peak.

Given Ross's result, how is one to distinguish a true bubble from a random series that just happened to be selected for study because it was followed by a crash? We are in this very predicament, trying to determine whether a bubble expanded before October 1987. Clearly, attention has been directed to this period because of the crash.

A key to determining the difference between a spurious relation and a true bubble can be developed from Ross's formulae. He shows that the spurious local serial dependence arises from three factors: (1) the height of the peak relative to the starting point in the sample, (2) the volatility of the underlying [random] series, and (3) the time difference between the current data point and the peak. Thus, we can examine the cross-country differences in calculated serial dependence to ascertain whether they are related to these factors. Since all countries crashed at the same time, the third factor can be ignored in a cross-country comparison. As for the first two factors, we can measure the height of the peak by the country's total return from the beginning of 1987 through the week before October 19 and the volatility can be measured by the sample daily standard deviation of returns. Thus, Ross's theory would imply the cross-country model,

$$b_{1j} = a_0 + a_1 r_j + a_2 s_j, \quad \{j=1, \ldots ,23\}, \tag{4}$$

Table 3. Slope from variance ratio regression (3) regressed on mean daily return and volatility during the calendar period [equation (4) of text]

	Mean Return	Standard Deviation	Intercept	Mean Return	Standard Deviation	Intercept
	--------------Local Currency---------------			-------------------Dollars--------------------		
	Pre-Crash Period 1/2/87 through 10/9/87					
Coefficients:	−0.0384	0.0043	0.0266	−0.0203	0.0015	0.0179
t-statistics:	−0.5662	0.1098	0.7712	−0.2774	0.0598	0.7188
	Post-Crash Period 11/2/87 through 3/31/89					
Coefficients:	−0.0073	−0.0070	0.0114	−0.0724	0.0081	−0.0046
t-statistics:	−0.1002	−0.8241	0.8828	−0.9774	0.8255	−0.2977

where b_{1j} is the coefficient estimate of serial dependence from regression (3) for country j, r_j is the mean daily return from January 2, 1987, through October 12, 1987, for country j, and s_j is the standard deviation of daily returns for country j during the same time period. Coefficient a_1 (a_2) should be positive (negative) and statistically significant.

Table 3 presents the results of fitting (4). Somewhat surprisingly, there is no evidence that the serial dependence detected before the crash was related across countries to the size of the price runup or to volatility during the pre-crash period. Both coefficients have the wrong sign, although neither is significant. There are (at least) three possible explanations consistent with this result: (1) there was not enough of a difference among countries in the extent of the bull market before the Crash;[20] (2) the coincidental timing across countries of both the crash and the pre-crash price increase may render a cross-country test problematic;[21] (3) there really was a specculative bubble that burst in October 1987. Further empirical work is required to sort out the appropriate conclusion.

2. International linkages

Given the improvement in electronic coordination across world markets, most casual observers presume that markets are becoming more related. The free flow of capital to locales with the most favorable risk/return tradeoff is certainly a strong force for the alignment of price innovations. Prior to the crash, however, direct empirical estimates have found cross-country correlations to be statistically significant but surprisingly weak even during periods that were clearly affected by international shocks.[22] Indeed, one of the most unusual aspects of the crash was its simultaneous occurrence in every major market. As I pointed out previously,[23] October 1987 was the only month during the decade of the 1980s when every market moved in the same direction.

A recent empirical paper by Dwyer and Hafer (1988) examined the short-term relations among four big markets (Germany, Japan, the United States, and the United Kingdom). The authors find no evidence that correlation has increased *except* for the period immediately around the crash. Over a longer term, they find only a slight increase in correlation from the fixed exchange rate period (January 1957 through April 1973) to the flexible rate period (after April 1973). Bennett and Kelleher (1988) document an increase in international comovements in the 1980s compared to the 1970s, but it was of only a small magnitude.

Parhizgari, Dandapani, and Bhattacharya (1988) provide some interesting evidence about possible lead/lag relations among four markets (London, New York, Singapore, and Tokyo). They find evidence of "bi-directional feedback" between New York and Tokyo and New York and London. However, the temporal "causation" between New York and Singapore goes in only one direction, with New York being the causative force. The strength of the relation is also found to be stronger from New York to both London and Tokyo than the reverse feedback *to* New York.[24]

Three of these markets (London, New York, and Tokyo), were also studied by Hamao, Masulis, and Ng (1989), who had data on opening and closing prices for each exchange. This enables them to measure more accurately the "volatility spillover" from one market to another by examining only those cases where the opening occurs in a market *after* the close in another market. Quoting the authors,

> If the impact of a foreign market is completely absorbed in the subsequent foreign market to open trading, then there should be no significant effect from adding the spillover ... from the foreign market which trades earlier. [Nonetheless] ... for the full sample period [which includes the crash], all three markets are affected by the volatility surprises of the two previously open foreign markets, with the exception that Tokyo has no significant influence on New York. ... The spillover ... from New York is larger than the effect from the other ... markets. [Excluding the crash] there is no significant spillover onto the London and New York markets, but there is an equally significant spillover effect from London and New York onto the Tokyo stock market. The Japanese market is most influenced by spillovers from foreign markets, but the other two major stock markets are only moderately affected, it at all, by volatility spillovers from foreign stock markets (p. 17).

This evidence is consistent with investors evaluating international news events and taking some time to rebalance their portfolios in response. Note that the item being predicted from one market to another is the *volatility* of returns, not the direction of returns. Indeed, for the direction of returns, Hamao et al. find

> ... that there is strong evidence that the most recent open-to-close return in one market has a very large positive influence on the opening price in the next market. ... even the Japanese market return influences the London opening price, which is consistent with informational efficiency across stock markets (p. 20).

Aside from the transmission of international price changes during normal times, several papers have studied the transmission specifically around the October 1987 crash. Bennett and Kelleher, for example, first estimated the usual relations among volatilities across countries[25] and the relation between volatility in one country and approximately contemporaneous correlation of returns between that country and a second country. In the pre-crash period, they found that daily return volatility within a given month *did* tend to be significantly positively related across countries. Also, higher volatility was associated with a larger degree of intercountry correlation.

Then, using the cross-country relations estimated from pre-crash data, Bennett and Kelleher predicted the October 1987 volatility and correlation and compared them with the actual level. For instance, given the observed level of daily volatility during October 1987 in the United States, they predicted the correlation between the United States and Japan, Germany, and the United Kingdom. The predicted value of the correlation was higher than the historical value by a considerable margin; e.g., for Japan, the historical value was .26 while the *predicted* October 1987 value was .97! The actual observed correlation during October was generally lower than predicted (it was actually only .77 with Japan). Nonetheless, the actual correlation was indeed higher for most countries than the historical level.

In contrast, the actual level of volatility during October 1987 was *much* higher than that predicted based on historical estimates of the usual relation between one country's volatility and another's. Although the predicted volatility was roughly twice as high as the historical norm, the actual level was about five times as large. Bennett and Kelleher interpret this evidence as follows:

> These results are consistent with the common view that a wave of panicky selling circled the globe, with traders paying an unusually large amount of attention to price developments in foreign markets in the absence of fundamental news sufficient to account for the disruption [p. 26].

This is a rather bold statement, given the fact that the fitted predictive models were subject to certain econometric problems. To understand these problems let's consider the model used to predict the volatility in one country by the volatility in another country; it was,

$$\ln(s_k) = A + B \ln(s_j) + e \tag{5}$$

where s_j is the observed standard deviation of daily returns in country j, and s_k is the standard deviation in country k, j preceeding k by the partial day by which country j trades before country k.[26] The fitted value of B was uniformly less than unity, no matter which way the regression was run; for instance, when j = U.S. and k = Japan, the fitted value of B was .33 (for data in the 1980s). Conversely, when j = Japan and k = U.S., the fitted value was .13.

There appears to be a classic errors-in-variables problem; indeed, the explanatory variable $\ln(s_j)$ is only a *sample estimate* of the population log standard deviation in returns. In a two-variable model, errors-in-the-variable causes attenuation bias. The coefficient B is biased toward zero. Thus, the model *should be expected* to grossly underpredict, particularly when the explanatory variable is several standard errors outside its historical range, as it was in October 1987.

Based on other tests relating the direction of movement to that predicted by other countries' movements, Bennett and Kelleher conclude that " . . . the basic degree of linkage among monthly average prices in different stock markets during the crash was neither clearly stronger nor weaker than it had been prior to October" (p. 26), a finding curiously at odds with the interpretation of "panicky selling" with traders paying "an unusually large amount of attention . . . to foreign markets."

In the same issue of *The Federal Reserve Bank of New York Quarterly Review,* Aderhold, Cumming, and Harwood (1988) examine the role of cross-border equity investing and stock trading in "centers outside the home market." They conclude that such "direct international linkages cannot explain the worldwide decline in mid-October" (p. 34). According to their data, cross-border selling during the crash was immaterial except in Tokyo (and Tokyo was one of the least affected markets in the world).

Neumark, Tinsley, and Tosini (1988) examine U.S. stocks that are also listed in Tokyo and London. The previous price change in either Tokyo or London is used to predict the New York change. If markets are informationally efficient, the slope coefficient should be unity in the prediction equation; i.e., the price change in Tokyo should be an unbiased predictor of the price change in New York since the previous close, the prediction error reflecting any news between Tokyo's close and the next New York close. Although Neumark et al. find that the estimated coefficients are close to unity (indicating market efficiency), during the crash period, they are significantly less than unity later.

This is consistent with trading costs preventing completely effective arbitrage across countries *except* when volatility is quite large, which it certainly was during the crash period. Their findings for directly arbitragible stocks imply that one might very well observe increased international correlation during every volatile period, without such an increase indicating an augmentation of international linkages. In other words, when markets are highly volatile, transaction costs are less of an impediment to simultaneous price co-movements in response to fundamental factors.

Bertero and Mayer document that return correlations across geographical regions increased dramatically during the period around the crash, and they also interpret the empirical evidence to indicate that the correlations " . . . remained higher *after* the crash" [p. 12, emphasis in original]. Their table 8 shows that three of six geographical region index pairs displayed *lower* correlation, not higher, in the latest reported period (April–May 1988), relative to the crash period, although the correlations do appear somewhat higher on average than in the pre-crash period. However, as was shown in table 1, volatility also has been somewhat higher since the crash.

Bertero and Mayer also find that the degree of intercorrelation between two markets is related to the trading of overseas securities on the domestic market. They reach this finding by regressing a given country's return on (1) a world market index, and (2) indices from other individual countries that have some stocks traded on the local exchange. An F test of significance indicates, for 13 countries out of 22,[27] that foreign individual markets with cross-listed shares explain a significant portion of the local return *beyond* that explained by a world index (using monthly data over the period January 1981 through May 1988).

Using daily data, Bertero and Mayer purport to document a significant increase in the influence of cross-listed share markets during and after the crash. Before the crash, indices from countries with cross-listed shares are statistically significant regressors for 11 countries out of 22.[28] From October 13, 1987, through December 31, 1987, the number of significant countries rises to 19, where it remains from January 1 through May 31, 1988.

Although there seems to be little doubt that empirical connections across markets have increased since the crash, one would be justified in a bit of skepticism about Bertero and Mayer's proposition that cross-listing is an indicator of connectivity. They showed that *individual* foreign country indices improved on the power of a world index in explaining contemporaneous local returns, where the particular indices chosen were from foreign countries with cross-listed shares. One has to wonder whether *any* collection of randomly chosen foreign regressors might not have done just as well. There might simply be more precise information in individual country indices than in a single world index.[29] A better way to test that cross-listing indicates a strong intercountry link would be to regress each country on *all* the other foreign countries and check whether the coefficients are larger and more significant for countries with cross-listed shares.

One of the most innovative and interesting new papers about international linkages is by King and Wadhwani (1989). They develop a "contagion" model of international volatility transmission. The underlying idea is that rational traders in one country *should* use price movements in another country to deduce changes in underlying economic fundamentals, even in the absence of any public news. This implies that a price "mistake" in one country will be transmitted to others almost as if it were an infectious disease. King and Wadhwani point out that weak evidence for contagion in normal times does not preclude contagion being rampant in more volatile times.

King and Wadhwani are motivated by the puzzling uniformity of the crash across countries. As they rightly state,

> ... It is difficult to come up with a credible story that links "fundamentals" to the crash; ... moreover, it is extremely hard to imagine that any [fundamentals based] explanation would be consistent with the uniform decline in equity prices in different countries. ... In a non fully revealing equilibrium, price changes in one market will ... in a real sense depend on price changes in other countries through structural contagion coefficients. Mistakes or idiosyncratic changes in one market may be transmitted to other markets, thus increasing volatility. It is this feature that appeals to us as an alternative to "news" as an explanation of the contemporaneous fall in all major stock markets in October, 1987 (pp. 1–2).

An important part of their theory is that contagion increases with volatility. If this be true, a contagion-based model is consistent with the generally low cross-country dependencies exhibited in "normal" times and with a much greater degree of dependence in periods of major disruption. As mentioned earlier, increased correlation around the crash period has been observed, but King and Wadhwani present a more refined empirical analysis of the phenomenon.

They first develop an explicit bi-country contagion model whose coefficients can be estimated using noncontemporaneous data; an example of noncontemporaneous data point would be the close-to-open London price change and the price change on the previous day in New York *after* the London market closed. Using hourly data from New York, London, and Tokyo from September through November 1987, they fitted the contagion model with cash prices in London and Tokyo and futures prices for the S&P index from the United States.[30] The evidence is quite striking that increased volatility around the crash coincided with increased contagion coefficients. King and Wadhwani conclude, "The pattern of correlations between markets that is revealed by the data seems easier to reconcile with the contagion model than with a fully revealing or purely 'fundamental' model" (p. 24).

Perhaps so, but regardless of the fine quality of their empirical work and the ingenuity of their contagion model, there remain some unanswered questions about the King/Wadhwani interpretation of the crash episode; viz., if the crash was caused by a mistake or perturbation in a given market that went on to infect other markets, where did it originate? If the United States was the original infectee, its price decline on October 14–16 was transmitted to other countries in sequence. Yet this seems inconsistent with the very large declines in October 19 in the Far East (excluding Japan), in continental Europe, and in the United Kingdom, declines that were far larger than the U.S. decline during the previous week and that preceded in time the big U.S. decline on its October 19. Indeed, in deciphering the global sequencing of declines in the context of the contagion model, one would be obliged to conclude that the crash was caused by investor "mistakes" in Hong Kong, Malaysia, and Singapore! This seems a bit far-fetched.

A second question involves whether contagion as measured by King and Wadhwani is really inconsistent with fundamental news. Imagine, for instance, that many different and important news items happened to arrive at random intervals during the crash period, some arriving when London was open and New York and Tokyo were closed, and vice versa in all combinations. Then, to the extent that these news items had importance for all markets, a price change in, say, New York would indeed be highly related to the next opening price change from the previous close in Tokyo, and so on. And, to the extent that there were more important news events around the crash than in a quieter period, the King/Wadhwani contagion coefficients would be larger. The coefficients are clearly a positive function of the number of news items arriving per unit of calendar time and of the international significance of the news relative to the background news idiosyncratically concentrated in each local country.

Unfortunately, such a conjecture may not help very much, for, as King and Wadhwani argue, if such news items really had been forthcoming during the crash period, one might have thought they would stand out[31] as possible candidates for causing the crash.

Searching for possible triggering mistakes, King and Wadhwani examine a practice that is often indicted by the popular press, computer-driven portfolio insurance in the United States. During periods of high volatility, they argue that portfolio insurance might induce negative serial dependence in very short-term price movements; thus, during the crash period, there should have been more detectable negative dependence in the United States, with its widespread use of portfolio insurance, than in the United Kingdom where formal portfolio insurance schemes were not common. Both U.S. and U.K. cash prices and U.K. futures prices showed more negative dependence during the crash, but U.S. futures prices did not (see their table 6). Their conclusion: " . . . time-honoured practices such as stop-loss orders had as significant an effect on share prices as formal dynamic hedging strategies" (p. 25); i.e., whatever the source of the "mistake," if any, it wasn't U.S. portfolio insurance.

This conclusion is buttressed with results by Goodhart (1988), who constructs a number of different tests exploiting both foreign exchange and stock returns. His overall conclusion: " . . . once the Crash week itself is past, . . . the main increase in the strength of linkage [among international markets] appear to have been from the rest of the world to asset price changes in New York" (p. 22).

3. Market regulations and volatility

The third important question arising around the crash episode concerns the influence, if any, of various regulations and institutional rules on price volatility. Three that are prominently mentioned are: (1) some form of circuit breaker, (2) margin requirements, and (3) transaction taxes.[32] To be sure, other possible regulations are sometimes mentioned, such as short-sale rules, restrictions on the DOT system, enhanced capital requirements for market makers, and so on,[33] but margin requirements, circuit breakers, and trading taxes are discussed most often, they are actually in place in many markets and countries, and they undoubtedly are the most likely to be implemented.

3.1. Empirical literature on margin requirements

Margin requirements are one of the most intensely studied market regulations. In the United States, initial margin requirements for equity purchases are set under law by the Federal Reserve using regulations G, T, U, and X. The regulations differ depending on whether the lender is a broker/dealer, a bank, or another type of lender. They apply only to the *initial* margin, (at the time of original purchase), and do not apply to all stocks. Maintenance margins on stocks (after original purchase) are set by the exchanges and the National Association of Securities Dealers with the approval of the Securities Exchange Commission (SEC). Stock index futures, stock options, stock index options, and stock index futures options are set by various authorities, mostly the exchanges and clearing houses (with the approval of regulatory agencies). A good description of the various margins is provided by Sofianos (1988).

Many of the earlier studies of margin requirements failed to find a significant impact on anything. A classic paper of this genre is by Largay and West (1973). Using data from January 1933 through January 1969 on the S&P 500 index, Largay and West fail to uncover an impact of changes in margin requirements on stock price levels. They do, however, uncover striking evidence of what induces the Fed to change margins; decreases in margin tend to occur after price declines and increases in margins follow price rises, a tendency confirmed and discussed by Garbade (1982). Note that this typical Federal Reserve behavior before 1970 seems to conform to what many persons thought (with hindsight) might have been a good policy in the pre-crash period of 1987.

Officer (1973) also found evidence that the Fed responded to changes in the market, concluding that margins were increased *after* stock volatility had fallen. In connection with a comprehensive study of stock return volatility over more than a century, Schwert (1988)

129

put together the Largay and West and Officer conclusions into a coherent explanatory package. Noting that there is a general tendency for increases in stock price levels to be associated with decreases in volatility, and vice versa, Schwert pointed out that a tendency for the Fed to increase (decrease) margin requirements after a price increase (decrease) would induce an inverse correlation but *not a causation* between return volatility and margin requirements.

Schwert also conducted empirical tests that confirmed that margin requirements were increased "*after* prices have risen and volatility is relatively low . . . [but that] There is no evidence that stock return behavior is different from normal in the 12 months following a change in margin requirements" (p. 28, emphasis in original).

Grube, Joy, and Panton (1979) examine almost the same set of data as Largay and West (there are four additional changes in margin requirements), and they also investigate abnormal volume around margin changes. The pattern of prices during days before and after margin changes is very similar to that found by Largay and West. However, Grube, Joy, and Panton place more emphasis on the price increase observed in just the few days around a margin decrease. The average pattern prior to a margin decrease is generally downward, but there is a sharp reversal just prior to the margin decrease announcement, which Grube, Joy, and Panton interpret to imply that margin decreases are good news (and that there is either anticipation or leakage about the decrease a few days in advance). After the margin decrease announcement date, there is no perceptible change in either prices or volume. No abnormal price movements were found around margin increases. However, there is evidence of abnormal volume both before and after an increase.

The exchanges are free to impose margin requirements in excess of those required by the Federal Reserve and on some occasions in the past, the exchanges *have* chosen higher margins for given individual stocks. The impact of exchange-imposed 100 percent margin requirements was studied by Largay (1973), who found a significant price impact:

> . . . the restricted stocks all rose in price prior to 100% margins being imposed. On the imposition date, the restricted stocks declined in price and over 70% of the individual price relatives were less than one . . . [A control sample of] non margin stocks also rose in price but did not decline on what would have been the imposition date if [100%] margins had been imposed (p. 982).

Largay also found an effect on volume. "The imposition of the margins dampens trading volume while their removal is associated with a revival of somewhat higher levels of trading activity" (p. 984). However, the Largay evidence on volume is not all that clear-cut.[34] In his figures 7 and 8 (p. 985), which show plots of average volume around 100 percent margin imposition, it appears that post-imposition volume is roughly on a level with previous volume *except* for a few days just preceding the imposition. But this could imply that the exchange imposes 100 percent margin *in response* to a sudden and inexplicable flurry of trading, not that margin has a causative influence.

Of course, volume is merely a proxy for price volatility and it may not be a very good one. Largay does report that price volatility decreased after the imposition of 100 percent margins, but the empirical results are not given.[35]

The direct effectiveness of the Fed's margin requirements on reducing borrowing (in broker margin accounts) was presented by Luckett (1982). Luckett does find evidence that increased margin requirements reduced borrowing in the 1966–1979 period; his empirical estimates indicate "...that a 10 percent change in the Federal Reserve's margin requirement will change investor equities on stocks held in margin accounts at security dealers by about 1 1/2 to 2 percent" (p. 794). Of course, this does not necessarily imply that it has a significant impact on volatility, but Luckett argues that reducing volatility is not the appropriate goal of margin regulations anyway. In an interesting passage that remains germane for present purposes, Luckett states,

> The Federal Reserve is not (nor should it be) in the business of influencing volume of credit, volume of trading, or stock prices *per se*. ... none of [these] taken by itself, is inherent cause for official concern. Rather, the power over the margin requirement given the Federal Reserve in 1934 was meant to prevent a repetition of the disastrous events that culminated in the Crash of '29—specifically, the pyramiding of margin credit in a rising market and margin calls in a falling market.... [Even] pyramiding *per se* is not troublesome; its significance lies, rather, in the derivative fact that it makes the market *vulnerable* to margin calls" (p. 787, emphasis in original).

Yet the crash of 1987 is unlikely to have been prevented by the Fed's having imposed higher initial margin requirements (than the current 50 percent) during the pre-crash expansion. Most of the selling in the cash market during the crash episode was by institutions, who rarely use margin, and the actual percentage of stock held on margin was very small.

Negative conclusions about the actual or likely efficacity of margin requirements can be found in a number of other papers, including the Federal Reserve's own "Evaluation" (1984). Hartzmark (1986) goes even further, arguing that margin requirements can "backfire," driving sophisticated investors from the market and leaving unsophisticated traders who might cause even more "aberrant price movements" (p. S148).[36] Grossman (1988) makes a similar point in discussing portfolio insurance:

> These [margin] requirements make it more difficult ... to take the opposite side of portfolio insurance trades. These requirements grew out of an effort to curb speculation, but it is exactly speculation by traders that can provide the other side of portfolio insurance trades and serve to lessen volatility (p. 8).

Because of this uniformly negative literature about margin requirements, recent papers by Hardouvelis (1988b, 1988c) came as quite a surprise. Hardouvelis claims to have found a surprisingly large and significant effect,

> ... over the entire sample, [1934–1987], an increase in the margin requirement by 10 percentage points from, say 50 percent to 60 percent decreases the monthly volatility of large stocks by 1.10 percentage points. The effect ... on small stocks is even greater (1.91 percentage points). To put these numbers in perspective, observe that the average monthly

131

volatility of large stocks . . . is 4.8 percentage points and of small stocks, 7.4 percentage points (1988b, p. 85).

According to this, if margin requirements were raised to 100 percent from their current 50 percent level, large stock volatility would decline to zero!

The second paper by Hardouvelis (1988c) is more complete than the one quoted above (1988b) and contains fancier econometrics. The conclusions, too, are somewhat different. For instance, the 10 percentage point increase in margin now only causes a reduction in small stock volatility of .77 percentage points, but the effect is still highly significant. From a rather complex set of tests, Hardouvelis concludes that margin requirements also reduce "excess" volatility (defined as volatility "that cannot be explained by the variation of current and future dividends and discount rates" (p. 11); see also 1988b, p. 88).

Finally, Hardouvelis studies long-term swings in stock prices, presumably occasioned by long-term changes in expected returns. He finds no effect of margin requirements. Everything together, he concludes, " . . . is consistent with the hypothesis that an increase in margin requirements mitigates the presence of fads, while a decrease in margin requirements exacerbates the presence of fads and excessive speculation (p. 19); i.e., long-term trends are not affected very much by higher margin requirements, but speculatively driven short-term swings are reduced.

Hardouvelis's results are mighty suspicious on their face, not only because he finds a large and significant margin effect where no one else ever did but also because his results are difficult to understand owing to their econometric complexity. There have been only 23 changes in margin requirements since the Federal Reserve system received its margin authority in 1934, yet Hardouvelis uses *monthly* data 14 years of which are included since 1974, the last time margin requirements were changed! He also controls for the influence of nuisance variables, whose impact might mask the influence of margin requirements, variables such as lagged changes in industrial production and in stock prices. He measures volatility by a moving standard deviation of returns over the past year, updated monthly. Thus, each successive estimate of volatility shares 11/12ths of the underlying monthly returns data with its neighbors. It would take an econometric wizard to figure out what is really going on.

Fortunately, two wizards have stepped forward. Hsieh and Miller (1989) have replicated Hardouvelis's results and found them spurious. First, Hsieh and Miller conduct a detailed study of their own using the 23 historical margin regulation changes and estimated volatilities before and after each change. They calibrate their test statistic with a "bootstrap," or simulation procedure, so that the measured level of statistical significance is reliable. Their conclusion:

We find only three occasions in which the modified Levene statistic lie in the upper 5% tail of the bootstrap distribution. In one case, the volatility increased when margins declined. In the other two cases, the volatility declined when margins declined. This absence of strong and consistent impact effects of margin changes is particularly relevant for policy discussions. Margin requirements are not [at] all like the beryllium rods used to control nuclear reactors (p. 7).

Hsieh and Miller also present a "long-term" investigation that comes to the same conclusion.

Give these result, Hsieh and Miller then set out to solve a detective problem: viz., how did Hardouvelis get such different results with the same data? After an extensive examination of Hardouvelis's methods, Hsieh and Miller conclude that the basic problem is autocorrelation in the moving standard deviation that is not adequately expunged by the anti-autocorrelation method employed by Hardouvelis. Using a simulation, they show that the coefficient in a simplified version of Hardouvelis' model " . . . converges to a non-degenerate distribution, so that *any test of the hypothesis of no correlation between* [volatility and margin] *will be rejected with probability 1* (as the sample size goes to infinity)" (p. 15, emphasis in original), even if there is no true relation between the two variables.

Hardouvelis recognizes that his overlapping observations are subject to autocorrelation problems, and he employs the well-accepted Newey/West method of correction. However, again using simulation, Hsieh and Miller show that Hardouvelis's implementation of Newey/West employs an insufficient number of lags to remove the danger of spuriously finding "significance." As a final tribute to Occam, they run the Hardouvelis model in first difference form and find " . . . that margins and volatility are positively rather than negatively correlated, although the coefficients are not reliably different from zero" (p. 16)!

Hardouvelis's results were found wanting also by Schwert (1988) (cited already above) and by Salinger (1989).[37] Salinger presents new evidence that there is a connection between volatility and the level of margin *debt*, but that margin requirements appear to have no direct effect on volatility. Both debt and requirements meet head-to-head in Salinger's regressions, and debt is the winner during most periods. Of course, a proponent of margin requirements would probably assert that increased margin requirements reduce margin debt so that such requirements actually are effective in reducing volatility. Furthermore, Salinger finds that inclusion of the pre-1934 period (before the Fed had margin authority), reverses the relative strength of margin debt and margin requirements; if the regressions include data from January 1927 through December 1987, margin requirements have a significant negative impact on volatility above and beyond the influence of margin debt.[38]

It seems to me, however, that Salinger's results are subject to some of the same criticisms that Hsieh and Miller and Schwert aimed at Hardouvelis. There is a danger of spurious regression. Also, there seems every reason to think a priori that Salinger's measure of margin debt, dollar amount of debt *divided by NYSE market value,* would decrease (increase) *after* a rise (fall) in stock prices. Since a rise (fall) in stock prices is related to a (fall) rise in volatility. Schwert's argument about Hardouvelis's results applies with equal force to Salinger's results. Both margin requirements *and* margin debt display a lagging and spurious relation to volatility changes. They are not causes.

3.2. Empirical evidence on price limits and volatility

In futures markets, price limits are often employed, but they do not appear to be directed toward dampening volatility; instead, limits seem to be useful for ensuring contract compliance. A theory of price limits developed by Brennan (1986) focuses on their effectiveness in preventing futures traders from reneging on contracts. Brennan's theory predicts that limits will disappear in futures markets that have closely correlated cash markets, a prediction more or less satisfied by the existing markets in the United States. This is suggestive evidence against the proposition that limits are used to reduce volatility.

There is a relative paucity of empirical literature on circuit breakers. Price limits in commodity markets have sometimes been studied in connection with other phenomena, and they have displayed perceptible influences on short-term price behavior.[39] If a market has limits on price movements that are occasionally encountered, *measured* volatility over a short enough interval is bound to be affected. During the October 1987 crash, daily volatility in Japan could have been reduced to the extent that some stocks hit their daily limit. Certainly in Hong Kong, which closed during the day of the crash, measured daily volatility was lower than it would have been without the closure.

Of course, most investors would see little difference between a market that went down 20 percent in one day and a market that hit a 5 percent down limit four days in a row. Indeed, the former might very well be preferable. The measurement problem with price limits and circuit breakers is to detect their *long*-run impact on volatility, if any. A reduction in short-term volatility could be spurious and immaterial.

An illustration of this pitfall is given by Bertero and Mayer (1988), who find a mitigating influence of "circuit breakers" on the cross-country extent of the crash. They say,

> The results reported here are similar to those in Roll (1988) in finding no relation [between the size of the Crash and futures trading or portfolio insurance] but it [sic] differs in finding some influence from circuit breakers and capital controls on domestic residents. This may be because Roll's results relate to the *month* of October, not the days immediately surrounding the crash. Repeating our regression for the month of October, we too find that most variables become significant . . . (p. 11).

In their introduction, however, they state that their study differs from mine partly because they used daily data. "This allows the period of the crash to be identified more precisely and ... suggests a different interpretation of the role of some of the structural characteristics of markets."

Actually, I used and reported daily data too, but in evaluating the impact of various market arrangements, returns were calculated over a longer period around the crash *explicitly to assure the inclusion of all crash-related returns.* It seems sensible that any investigation of factors relating to the crash should include *all* related price movements. Again using the example of Hong Kong, its observed price decline October 19 grossly understates the true impact of the crash.

Several past studies, though not directly about price limits, may bear on their potential effectiveness. Hopewell and Schwartz (1978) examined trading suspensions on individual New York listed stocks and concluded that post-suspension price movements offered no profit opportunities and that the behavior of prices around the suspension was consistent with significant news. They could not ascertain whether the suspension per se had any influence on volatility.

Kryzanowski (1979) examined trading halts effected by Canadian exchange officials who were suspicious that corporate information had been withheld from the market. On average over all such halts, stock prices declined more than 26 percent from the last transaction price prior to the suspension. Some of this drop occurred between the last transaction and the first trade after resumption, but the greatest part of the drop, more than 24 percent, occurred even later. Although we cannot know whether prices might have declined even more had there *not* been a cooling-off period, such a period evidently does not preclude an impressive price change.

A recent study by Ma, Rao, and Sears (1989) of price limits in futures markets contains some striking and surprising results. Using minute-by-minute data, they seem to find that limit moves are *not* followed by an increased probability of price moves in the same direction during subsequent periods,[40] this result is hard to believe since any limit move induced by significant news (and there surely must be some occasional important news) almost certainly alters the subsequent conditional expected return in the same direction as the limit move.

Ma et al. also produce evidence that limit moves are followed by reduced volatility and by normal levels of volume but the results may have been affected by novel methods. Even if their results were impeccable, however, they would not constitute unambiguous evidence that price limits reduce volatility. Reduced volatility after a limit move is equally consistent with a reduction in the amount of news received relative to the pre-limit move period and the limit move period. We really need information about whether the imposition of a limit move *system* reduces *overall* volatility in (all periods.)

3.3. Transaction taxes

Transaction taxes are the least studied of the three most serious proposals for dampening volatility. In fact, two recent papers by academics urging such a tax, Stiglitz (1989) and Summers and Summers (undated) cite *no* empirical studies bearing directly on this question. However, both Stiglitz and the Summers cite empirical work which allegedly finds that stock prices are excessively volatile, too volatile to be explained by "fundamental" determinants of value.

Accepting this alleged excess volatility as fact, Stiglitz develops a theory based on "noise" traders who believe (irrationally) that trading systems, horoscopes, etc., are beneficial in forecasting prices. (Arbitrageurs are unable to completely remove the noise induced by such traders.) In a taxonomy of traders, Stiglitz portrays the noise-causing group as " . . . dentists and doctors in the midwest and the retired individuals in the sunbelt . . . " (p. 7) who are essentially using the stock market to amuse themselves, as they would in a casino. Why do such traders not eventually lose all their money and disappear? Because, says Stiglitz, quoting P.T. Barnum, " . . . a fool is born every moment. For every fool that is weeded out, a new one enters the market" (p. 9).[41]

Other traders such as those who possess no information and even those who do possess valuable information trade less frequently than noise traders and would therefore be less affected by a transaction tax. Indeed, such a tax would be a smaller fraction of total return the longer the holding period, and this would supposedly induce investors to take a more long-term view. Finally, according to Stiglitz, a transaction tax might actually increase liquidity since it would reduce the influence of noise traders and lower volatility. Not only can the government raise revenue but it can promote the efficacity of capital markets in the process! (This conclusion is based entirely on theory.)

Summers and Summers argue that there is too much trading, too much volatility to be explained by fundamentals, and too many "resources devoted to financial engineering." Furthermore, many other countries have transaction taxes in place, so why should the United States be different? The authors complain that "talented human capital is devoted to trading paper assets rather than actually creating wealth. . . . one fourth of the Yale senior class [applied] for a job at First Boston" (p. 13).

Summers and Summers seem to regard securities transactions and the entire securities industry as a pernicious activity that should be taxed heavily along with other vices such as gambling, alcohol, tobacco, and the teaching of economics. No evidence is offered that a tax would actually be beneficial to investment and saving, but that seems secondary to raising revenue anyway.

3.4. Conclusions about the existing empirical literature on market regulations and volatility

My overall interpretation is that the empirical literature has failed to uncover any solid evidence that margin requirements are effective in reducing price volatility, at least for U.S. data, nor has it found uncontrovertible evidence that price limits are effective in reducing true (as opposed to measured) volatility. There have been demonstrable effects of margin requirements on the equity levels in margin accounts (Luckett and Hsieh and Miller), and possibly on trading volume (Largay), but volatility itself has thus far escaped un-scathed.[42] Perhaps this is not too surprising given how easily an investor can evade the initial Federal Reserve margin requirements (by borrowing from someone other than a broker/dealer or allegedly for some purpose other than equity investing).[43]

However, I retain some sympathy for the view that any effect might be awfully difficult to detect, given the enormous background noise in equity markets. A cross-country comparison could possibly help overcome a locally weak signal-to-noise ratio, and we now turn to the international data to find out if it will. In the process of examining the international data, some new evidence will be presented concerning the influence on volatility of price limits and transaction taxes.

3.5. The cross-country influence of margin requirements, price limits, and transaction taxes on market volatility

Official margin requirements for cash equity positions and official price limits on cash equity transactions[44] are given by country in table 4 for the pre-crash and post-crash periods. (They are mostly unchanged in the two periods.) Taxes on round-trip transactions are also shown.

Table 4. Official price limits, margin requirements, and transaction taxes

	Price Limits	Margin Requirements	Price Limits	Margin Requirements	Roundtrip Transaction Tax
	---------Before Crash--------------		---------After Crash---------------		
			Percent		
Australia	none	0.	none	0.	.6
Austria	5.	100.	5.	100.	.3
Belgium	10.	100.	10.	100.	.375
Canada	none	50.	none	50.	0
Denmark	none	0.	none	0.	1.0
France	7.	20.	7.	20.	.3
Germany	none	0.	none	0.	.5
Hong Kong	none	0.	none	0.	.6
Ireland	none	100.	none	100.	1.0
Italy	15.	100.	15.	100.	.3
Japan	10.	70.	10.	50.	.55
Malaysia	none	0.	none	0.	.03
Mexico	35.	0.	35.	0.	0
Netherlands	24.	0.	24.	0.	1.2*
New Zealand	none	0.	none	0.	0
Norway	none	100.	none	100.	1.0
Singapore	none	71.	none	71.	.5
South Africa	none	100.	none	100.	1.5
Spain	10.	40.	20.	50.	.11
Sweden	none	40.	none	40.	2.0*
Switzerland	5.	0.	12.5	0.	.9
United Kingdom	none	0.	none	0.	.5
United States	none	50.	none	50.	0

Notes about Transaction Taxes:
  Belgium: tax on forward contracts is .195 percent.
   France: .15 percent above FF 1 million.
    Japan: .18 percent on dealers.
Netherlands: tax on nondealers only.
   Sweden: additional .5 percent if transaction is through a market maker.
Switzerland: different tax rate applies to foreigners.
*Does not agree with tax rate in Summers and Summers, 1989.

In many countries, there is a different margin requirement for futures as opposed to cash transactions. Given the variety of margin rules, a single number may be an inadequate portrayal of reality, yet it *would* be a policy variable that could conceivably be altered. As mentioned in the table's notes, a similar situation exists in some countries with respect to transaction taxes, different rates being applied to different instruments and/or traders. Thus, if we find an influence of margin requirements, price limits, or taxes in the tests below, we could legitimately interpret this as indicating the potential impact of a particular policy change, *but only while holding constant the plethora of other rules and regulations.*

The first results are shown in table 5, which contains a series of cross-country OLS regressions of the following form:

Table 5. Standard deviation of returns regressed on price limits, margin requirements, and trading taxes

Holding Period (Days)		Local Currency			Dollar		
		Pr Limits	Margin	Taxes	Pr Limits	Margin	Taxes
	Estimated values of price limits, margin, and taxes used as regressor [equation (6) of text]
	Pre-Crash Period
	1/2/87 through 10/9/87
1	Coefficients:	−0.0088	−0.1049	−0.1127	−0.0117	0.1092	0.0264
	t-statistics:	−0.7225	−0.5598	−0.7417	−0.7476	0.4519	0.1347
2	Coefficients:	−0.0041	−0.1114	−0.2154	−0.0092	0.0784	−0.1095
	t-statistics:	−0.2990	−0.5233	−1.2479	−0.5521	0.3035	−0.5230
3	Coefficients:	−0.0066	−0.0840	−0.1949	−0.0134	0.1097	−0.0761
	t-statistics:	−0.4719	−0.3871	−1.1082	−0.7812	0.4145	−0.3547
5	Coefficients:	−0.0098	−0.0915	−0.2598	−0.0143	0.0241	−0.1883
	t-statistics:	−0.6314	−0.3823	−1.3392	−0.8141	0.0890	−0.8585
10	Coefficients:	−0.0085	−0.0508	−0.3165	−0.0131	0.0681	−0.1756
	t-statistics:	−0.4288	−0.1667	−1.2818	−0.5776	0.1937	−0.6164
15	Coefficients:	−0.0009	−0.0011	−0.3538	−0.0045	0.0300	−0.2236
	t-statistics:	−0.0452	−0.0038	−1.4924	−0.2121	0.1003	−0.8387
20	Coefficients:	−0.0074	−0.1089	−0.2126	−0.0210	0.0725	−0.0791
	t-statistics:	−0.4489	−0.4269	−1.0282	−0.9940	0.2215	−0.2981
	Post -Crash Period
	11/2/87 through 3/31/89
1	Coefficients:	−0.0205	−0.0852	−0.0067	−0.0208	0.0125	0.0204
	t-statistics:	−1.1365	−0.3638	−0.0360	−1.1023	0.0511	0.1051
2	Coefficients:	−0.0210	−0.0572	−0.0198	−0.0210	−0.0110	−0.0495
	t-statistics:	−0.9908	−0.2074	−0.0911	−0.9902	−0.0398	−0.2266
3	Coefficients:	−0.0243	−0.0004	−0.0306	−0.0200	−0.0073	−0.1046
	t-statistics:	−1.3020	−0.0017	−0.1597	−0.9440	−0.0264	−0.4819
5	Coefficients:	−0.0222	0.0476	−0.0821	−0.0188	−0.0031	−0.1735
	t-statistics:	−1.1823	0.1950	−0.4255	−0.8277	−0.0106	−0.7437
10	Coefficients:	−0.0200	0.0307	−0.1059	−0.0217	0.0035	−0.2207
	t-statistics:	−1.0024	0.1182	−0.5155	−0.8882	0.0111	−0.8781
15	Coefficients:	−0.0216	0.0952	−0.1393	−0.0115	−0.0107	−0.3247
	t-statistics:	−0.9634	0.3265	−0.6046	−0.3878	−0.0279	−1.0679
20	Coefficients:	−0.0098	−0.0683	−0.0641	−0.0078	−0.1765	−0.2286
	t-statistics:	−0.4475	−0.2409	−0.2864	−0.2665	−0.4655	−0.7626
	Dummy Variables for Price Limits, Margin, and Taxes used as Regressors [Equation (7) of Text]
	Pre-Crash Period
	1/2/87 through 10/9/87
1	Coefficients:	0.1868	−0.1673	−0.2969	0.0963	−0.0437	−0.2014
	t-statistics:	1.2620	−1.1565	−1.5769	0.4697	−0.2178	−0.7719
2	Coefficients:	0.2961	−0.1658	−0.3958	0.1970	−0.0592	−0.3200
	t-statistics:	1.8128	−1.0385	−1.9043	0.9342	−0.2874	−1.1929
3	Coefficients:	0.2410	−0.1317	−0.3778	0.1303	−0.0119	−0.3035
	t-statistics:	1.4042	−0.7853	−1.7300	0.5900	−0.0551	−1.0796
5	Coefficients:	0.2434	−0.1334	−0.4553	0.1752	−0.0676	−0.4218
	t-statistics:	1.2660	−0.7100	−1.8611	0.7896	−0.3117	−1.4945
10	Coefficients:	0.3986	−0.1052	−0.6880	0.3065	0.0017	−0.6099
	t-statistics:	1.7494	−0.4724	−2.3729	1.1083	0.0064	−1.7330
15	Coefficients:	0.4534	−0.0731	−0.6663	0.3687	−0.0218	−0.6261
	t-statistics:	2.1002	−0.3466	−2.4254	1.4687	−0.0889	−1.9600

Table 5. (*Continued*)

Holding Period (Days)		Local Currency			Dollar		
		Pr Limits	Margin	Taxes	Pr Limits	Margin	Taxes
20	Coefficients:	0.3108	−0.1228	−0.6282	0.1098	0.0571	−0.5252
	t-statistics:	1.6855	−0.6811	−2.6770	0.4095	0.2179	−1.5396
		Post-Crash Period 11/2/87 through 3/31/89					
1	Coefficients:	0.0917	−0.2031	−0.3280	0.0522	−0.1537	−0.3329
	t-statistics:	0.4965	−1.1252	−1.3961	0.2679	−0.8074	−1.3439
2	Coefficients:	0.1169	−0.2185	−0.3343	0.0752	−0.1948	−0.3664
	t-statistics:	0.5374	−1.0271	−1.2074	0.3470	−0.9188	−1.3281
3	Coefficients:	0.0710	−0.1729	−0.3121	0.1446	−0.1968	−0.4402
	t-statistics:	0.3644	−0.9075	−1.2584	0.6880	−0.9579	−1.6463
5	Coefficients:	0.1029	−0.1400	−0.3361	0.2010	−0.2063	−0.5067
	t-statistics:	0.5300	−0.7376	−1.3608	0.9018	−0.9469	−1.7868
10	Coefficients:	0.0966	−0.1853	−0.2857	0.1856	−0.2380	−0.4888
	t-statistics:	0.4667	−0.9160	−1.0850	0.7551	−0.9907	−1.5630
15	Coefficients:	0.1444	−0.1640	−0.4046	0.4022	−0.2782	−0.6824
	t-statistics:	0.6305	−0.7330	−1.3889	1.4186	−1.0037	−1.8914
20	Coefficients:	0.2358	−0.2392	−0.3358	0.4078	−0.3508	−0.6043
	t-statistics:	1.0989	−1.1399	−1.2296	1.4682	−1.2921	−1.7099
		Dummy Variables for Price Limits, Margin, and Taxes used as Regressors [Equation (7) of Text] With Mexico Deleted from Sample Pre-Crash Period 1/2/87 through 10/9/87					
1	Coefficients:	0.1010	−0.1806	0.2139	0.2399	−0.0166	0.2606
	t-statistics:	0.6041	−1.1426	0.8987	1.1463	−0.0840	0.8747
2	Coefficients:	0.1681	−0.1737	0.2240	0.2819	−0.0001	0.2253
	t-statistics:	0.8722	−0.9533	0.8165	1.2679	−0.0007	0.7119
3	Coefficients:	0.1386	−0.1559	0.3015	0.2677	0.0174	0.3074
	t-statistics:	0.7183	−0.8542	1.0975	1.1798	0.0810	0.9518
5	Coefficients:	0.1200	−0.1706	0.2916	0.2228	−0.0349	0.3094
	t-statistics:	0.5414	−0.8143	0.9246	0.9250	−0.1535	0.9025
10	Coefficients:	0.2130	−0.1501	0.2488	0.3327	0.0001	0.2357
	t-statistics:	0.7518	−0.5602	0.6167	1.0624	0.0003	0.5288
15	Coefficients:	0.2798	−0.0287	0.2442	0.3558	0.0533	0.2485
	t-statistics:	1.0289	−0.1115	0.6307	1.2329	0.1952	0.6049
20	Coefficients:	0.2983	−0.1871	0.0618	0.4093	0.0211	0.0224
	t-statistics:	1.2945	−0.8589	0.1885	1.3953	0.0760	0.0536

$$s_{jT} = c_0 + c_L L_j + c_M M_j + c_{TX} TX_j \quad \{j=1, \ldots ,23\} \tag{6}$$

where s_{jT} is the computed sample standard deviation of returns for country j using T-day nonoverlapping holding intervals, L_j is an inverse measure of country j's price limits,[45] M_j is the level of margin requirements in country j, TX_j is country j's tax rate on transactions (in %/100), and c_0, c_L, c_M, and c_{TX} are regression coefficients.

All of the tests are repeated using zero/one dummy variables for countries that that do not/do have price limits, official margin requirements (whatever the size), and transaction taxes. These regressions, shown in the second part of each table, have the following form:

$$s_{jT} = h_0 + h_L D_{jL} + h_M D_{jM} + h_{TX} D_{jTX}, \quad \{j=1,\dots,23\} \tag{7}$$

where D_{jK} is one (zero) if country j has (does not have) feature K, $\{K=L, M,$ and TX for price limits, margin requirements, and transaction taxes, respectively.$\}$

For the pre-crash and post-crash periods, table 5 contains absolutely no evidence that margin requirements have an influence on volatility, regardless of whether returns are measured in local currency or in dollars and regardless of the length of the holding interval. In local currency, c_M from regression (6) is negative for all holding intervals during the pre-crash period while it is positive for three of seven of the holding intervals in the post-crash period (the holding periods are obviously not independent). In a common currency (dollars), the margin requirements coefficient is uniformly positive in the pre-crash period and mainly negative in the post-crash period. The dummy variable margin coefficient, h_M, is similarly insignificant, though it is mostly negative.

The results for price limits are also insignificant, though their sign pattern makes at least some sense. Price limits *should* have a larger impact on *measured* volatility, the shorter the holding interval. Using the L_j measure of limits, we do observe slightly smaller (absolute) values of c_L the longer the holding interval, particularly in the post-crash period, although there is undoubtedly no statistical significance in the pattern. The dummy variable coefficient, h_L, is mostly positive.[46]

Transaction taxes display negative coefficients as they should if taxes reduced volatility, and there are even a few significant t-statistics, for the dummy variable regressions using local currency in the pre-crash period. However, these results are somewhat questionable because a possible outlier. Notice in table 4 that only four countries out of 23 have a zero transaction tax and thus a zero valued dummy variable D_{jTX}; these countries are Canada, Mexico, New Zealand, and the United States. The fact that the coefficient is significant only in the pre-crash period, only for local currency, and only for the dummy variable version of the regression makes one suspect that Mexico is the culprit, the reason being that Mexico had an extremely large and volatile *local* currency return in the pre-crash period.

To check for a possible overweaning influence of Mexico, these regressions were repeated with Mexico excluded, and the results are shown in the final panel of table 5. The tax effect is no longer significant, and the coefficient has changed signs. This seems to be evidence against taxes really having any material impact on volatility during relatively normal periods.

There remains a possibility that margin requirements, price limits, or taxes might have an influence on volatility during particularly disruptive periods. To check this out, regressions (6) and (7) were repeated for all possible nonoverlapping holding intervals during the 1987 crash period, the 15 trading days between October 12 and October 30 inclusive.[47] Table 6 gives the results.

Margin requirements still display no statistically significant effect, though both c_M and h_M, the fitted coefficients using numerical values and dummy variables, respectively, are

Table 6. Standard deviation of returns regressed on price limits, margin requirements, and trading taxes

Holding Period (Days)		Local Currency			Dollars		
		Pr Limits	Margin	Taxes	Pr Limits	Margin	Taxes
		Estimated values of price limits, margin, and taxes used as regressors [equation (6) of text] Crash Period 10/12/87 through 10/30/87					
1	Coefficients:	−0.1444	−0.8544	−0.5257	−0.1658	−0.7156	−0.3830
	t-statistics:	−1.9117	−0.7321	−0.5558	−2.2382	−0.6253	−0.4129
2	Coefficients:	−0.1302	−0.8080	−1.0769	−0.1544	−0.3827	−0.9718
	t-statistics:	−1.6033	−0.6442	−1.0592	−1.8593	−0.2982	−0.9341
3	Coefficients:	−0.1252	−0.1924	−0.8451	−0.1376	−0.1241	−0.6516
	t-statistics:	−1.8634	−0.1854	−1.0044	−2.0470	−0.1195	−0.7740
5	Coefficients:	−0.1483	−0.6151	−0.4713	−0.1509	−0.6535	−0.3364
	t-statistics:	−2.0726	−0.5565	−0.5261	−2.0757	−0.5817	−0.3695
		Dummy Variables for Price Limits and Margin Used as Regressors [Equation (7) of Text]					
1	Coefficients:	−1.5440	−0.7787	−0.4707	−1.8726	−0.6986	−0.4967
	t-statistics:	−1.5159	−0.7820	−0.3632	−1.8856	−0.7196	−0.3931
2	Coefficients:	−0.8665	−0.8624	−1.8705	−1.2746	−0.5905	−1.8792
	t-statistics:	−0.8059	−0.8205	−1.3671	−1.1682	−0.5536	−1.3535
3	Coefficients:	−1.4077	−0.1722	−1.3586	−1.6943	−0.1535	−1.2931
	t-statistics:	−1.6185	−0.2025	−1.2276	−1.9896	−0.1843	−1.1933
5	Coefficients:	−2.2196	−0.9887	0.7574	−2.2852	−0.9577	0.8086
	t-statistics:	−2.5376	−1.1564	0.6805	−2.5737	−1.1034	0.7157

uniformly negative as they should be if margin requirements reduced volatility. Transaction taxes are similarly negative but insignificant.

Price limits are another matter. Using both the numerical limits and dummy variables, more stringent limits are associated with lower volatility, and the effect is significant for some holding intervals. Remember that very short-term intervals might display a significant impact of price limits for a spurious reason, yet the five-day intervals in table 6 are generally more significant than the shorter intervals.

This unexpected pattern is suspicious and made me wonder whether the results had been unduly influenced by the Hong Kong case. Notice in table 4 that Hong Kong does not have official price limits, yet the closing of the Hong Kong market on October 19 after about an 11 percent decline (cf. footnote 13), had the same effect as a price limit since the registered return on that day was smaller than it otherwise would have been. Hong Kong's estimated crash period volatility is extremely large; see table 1.

This unusual situation suggests that the tests be repeated with Hong Kong counted as if it had had price limits. Thus, Hong Kong was assigned a price limit of 11 percent, the price decline before trading was suspended on October 19. The results are given in table 7 which shows that the significance for price limits has disappeared. This is consistent with Hong Kong's closure (for five days) being entirely responsible for the seemingly significant long-term effect of price limits found in table 6.

Table 7. Standard deviation of returns regressed on price limits and margin requirements with Hong Kong assumed effectively to have had price limits (crash period, 10/12/87 through 10/30/87)

Holding Interval (Days)		Local Currency			Dollars		
		Pr Limits	Margin	Intercept	Pr Limits	Margin	Intercept
	Estimated Values of Price Limits and Margin Used as Regressors						
	[Equation (6) of Text]						
1	Coefficients:	−0.0821	−1.1181	−0.3806	−0.1038	−0.9990	−0.2356
	t-statistics:	−1.0345	−0.9112	−0.3796	−1.3179	−0.8197	−0.2366
2	Coefficients:	−0.0711	−1.0516	−0.9404	−0.0933	−0.6537	−0.8276
	t-statistics:	−0.8477	−0.8098	−0.8863	−1.0767	−0.4875	−0.7554
3	Coefficients:	−0.0751	−0.4130	−0.7272	−0.0870	−0.3578	−0.5308
	t-statistics:	−1.0713	−0.3806	−0.8202	−1.2309	−0.3273	−0.5943
5	Coefficients:	−0.0924	−0.8694	−0.3386	−0.0960	−0.9084	−0.2052
	t-statistics:	−1.2264	−0.7456	−0.3554	−1.2555	−0.7676	−0.2122
	Dummy Variables for Price Limits and Margin Used as Regressors						
	[Equation (7) of Text]						
1	Coefficients:	−0.3721	−0.9977	−0.6343	−0.7027	−0.9513	−0.6399
	t-statistics:	−0.3535	−0.9602	−0.4608	−0.6710	−0.9202	−0.4672
2	Coefficients:	0.2563	−1.0092	−2.0644	−0.1079	−0.7815	−2.0580
	t-statistics:	0.2397	−0.9563	−1.4765	−0.0976	−0.7159	−1.4229
3	Coefficients:	−0.4240	−0.3674	−1.4891	−0.6979	−0.3789	−1.4090
	t-statistics:	−0.4694	−0.4121	−1.2605	−0.7733	−0.4252	−1.1936
5	Coefficients:	−1.2271	−1.2679	0.6742	−1.3039	−1.2431	0.7319
	t-statistics:	−1.2913	−1.3517	0.5425	−1.3520	−1.3058	0.5803

4. Conclusions

The October 1987 stock market crash spawned an abundance of research papers, as scholars attempted to explain what seemed at the time, and to some extent remains, an inexplicable event.

Except for the period immediately around the crash, there is only meager evidence that international linkages across markets have become tighter over time. Yet the crash was worldwide in scope, and its similarity across countries was uncanny. Just on the face, this international similarity puts doubt to such explanations as particular macroeconomic events in one country, failure of a given country's market system, or simultaneous changes in underlying fundamentals (which were quite different across countries).

Assigning the origination of the crash to one country cannot be entirely ruled out, however, because of the possibility of a non-fully revealing equilibrium "contagion" process of the type suggested by King and Wadhwani (1988). Such a process *would* allow a world-wide crash to begin by a particular news event or even by a market "mistake" in one country. Evidence in favor of this process is that international correlations of returns increased dramatically during the crash period. However, this increase is consistent with other explanations, such as transaction costs hindering international arbitrage except during periods of high volatility.

Was the crash the bursting of a bubble? Some evidence seems to support this proposition: for example, in the majority of countries, the pre-crash period displayed significant serial dependence in stock returns, dependence that was definitely *not* present in the post-crash period. However, further work is necessary to ascertain whether this *measured* serial dependence is unusual relative to what one would have expected to find, even in a perfectly random process, by choosing a sample period that happened to culminate in a random peak. Ross (1987) shows that such ex post sample period selection will induce upward bias in estimates of serial dependence. Cross-country tests failed to detect this bias, but there are several ambiguities in the tests that will have to be resolved in future work.

The crash is history. What implications, if any, does it have for regulatory policy? Is there evidence that popular regulations or rules would have mitigated the crash, or that they would decrease price volatility in general? There is very little evidence in favor of the efficacy of margin requirements, price limits, or transactions taxes. Despite a large number of empirical studies, no one has provided evidence that margin requirements have an impact on volatility. There has been at least one recent paper claiming the contrary, but a careful examination of its methods have uncovered enough problems to cast those results into doubt.

As for price limits, there *must* be a very short-term impact on *measured* volatility, for the measured market price at a trading halt is likely to understate the direction of movement. Yet even for daily data, the cross-country evidence is slim that price limits reduce volatility, and there is no evidence at all that they work over periods as long as a week. In other words, trading halts caused by limits seem to have no effect on true volatility.

Transaction taxes are inversely but insignificantly correlated with volatility across countries, and the effect is too questionable for taxes to be used with confidence as an effective policy instrument.

Notes

1. The reports covered by Kamphuis, Kormendi, and Watson include those by the Presidential Task Force on Market Mechanisms, the Chicago Mercantile Exchange, the International Stock Exchange of London, the Commodity Futures Trading Commission, the Securities and Exchange Commission, and the U.S. General Accounting Office.

2. However, no one (including me) argues that the existence of portfolio insurance actually *mitigated* the extent of the crash.

3. The authors show that other potentially damaging news events, such as a worse-than-expected U.S. trade deficit announcement on October 14, were unable to explain the extent of the price decline.

4. However, as my colleague David Hirshleifer has pointed out, even a seemingly small event such as increased tax on takeovers could conceivably trigger a large crash if it were expected to foster more management malfeasance (because of the decreased threat of takeover).

5. However, this cross-country relation is also consistent with some countries simply being more sensitive to fundamental factors than other countries (and with such factors increasing over the first part of 1987 and falling in October).

6. This finance literature had its antecedents in some of the earlier literature on optimal growth along unstable paths. Samuelson (1967) speaks of the "tulip mania" in this context, and Ross (1975) gives an example of a bubble under a dynamic jump process.

7. Bubbles were known to be possible even under rationality with unrealistic assumptions such as an infinite time horizon or an infinity of traders.

8. Some of the results in Hardouvelis (1989) have been published in Hardouvelis (1988a).

9. As the bubble inflates, the probability of a crash increases; this increase in potential volatility (or risk) must be accompanied by an increased reward.

10. That is, the observed difference between actual stock returns and short-term interest rates.

11. The data are from Goldman Sachs & Co. and are widely publicized as the Goldman Sachs/FT-Actuaries World Indices.

12. A daily return is defined as $\log_e(P_t/P_{t-1})$ where P_t is the price index level on trading day t. Dividends are *not* included; dividend yields are available in the data base but their addition to the return makes virtually no difference in volatility. The log first difference was used so that returns over multiple days would be additive.

13. Table 1 brackets the major crash day of October 19 by a week before and two weeks afterward. This window is somewhat arbitrary, of course, but it is justified by allowing the inclusion of substantial and perhaps related price movements in the week prior to October 19, and it allows the capture of crash-related price movements after October 19 in countries with price limits or closures. In Hong Kong, for example, the observed major price decline did not occur until October 26 because the Hong Kong market was closed for the rest of the week after substantial price declines on October 19. The Hong Kong index declined 11.4 percent on October 19 and then the market was closed. On the day the market reopened, October 26, the index fell an *additional* 39.7 percent.

14. R is actually the simple average of the off-diagonal elements of the $(T \times T)$ sample autocorrelation matrix.

15. The regression is not well specified under all possible serial dependence structures. For example, if there were stationary first-order dependence, the coefficient b_1 would be a known function of T. However, the regression is simply meant to be a compact way to present a lot of evidence, and it should not be regarded as anything more meaningful, such as a method of testing for a given dependence structure.

16. For the cross-country simple averages given in table 2, everything is scaled to percent per day. Thus, for multiday returns, every mean return and variance of returns is divided by T, the number of days in the multiday holding period.

17. The regression has 4 degrees of freedom. A two-tailed test for significance at the 5 percent level has a critical value of 2.776 (i.e., the .975 fractile of Student's t distribution with four d.f.).

18. The t distribution with d degrees of freedom has variance $d/(d-2)$; see Johnson and Kotz (1970, p. 96).

19. The negative significant coefficient, indicating negative serial dependence, was for the United States. The two positive significant coefficients were for Austria and Belgium.

20. However, this explanation seems unlikely. As shown in table 1, there were large differences across countries in pre-crash mean returns.

21. Imagine, for instance, that returns in each country were driven by some common world factor, but that the degree of response to that factor differs among countries. Suppose in addition that the pre-crash period was simply a realization of a random process for the factor. Then the degree of measured [spurious] serial dependence would be the same in every country because it would be the same as the serial dependence in the factor itself. The observed serial dependence would not be cross-country related to the magnitude of the price rise in the pre-crash period.

22. See the paper by Hilliard (1979), which examined international stock price comovements during the OPEC crisis, July 1973–April 1974.

23. See Roll (1989, p. 39).

24. The empirical results of Parhizgari et al. are somewhat implausible because they find lead/lag relations from two to eight days. This would seem to imply the possibility of predicting one market's return up to eight days in advance by using the return in another market as a predictor. Their test involves a complicated multivariate statistic and it is not clear (at least to me) how to transform their results into a practical trading rule.

25. Using Germany, Japan, the United States, and the United Kingdom.

26. If, for example, j = U.S. and k = Japan, and the standard deviation is calculated from March 1 through March 31 in the U.S., it would be calculated from March 2 through April 1 in Japan.

27. Bertero and Mayer also use the Goldman Sachs/FT Actuaries data which cover 23 countries, but Mexico is excluded from the tests for the effect of cross-listed countries because no Mexican shares are traded abroad and no foreign shares are traded in Mexico.

28. At the 1 percent level of significance.

29. This is probably true for several reasons. For example, if there is more than one world "factor" in the

Arbitrage Pricing Theory context, just about any set of multiple regressors will beat a single regressor. Also, Bertero and Mayer *are* undoubtedly justified in thinking that some countries are much more closely attuned than others, and, as a consequence, a global index masks individual country relations.

30. King and Wadhwani present evidence that the contemporaneous correlation during hours when both London and New York are open for trading was much higher between U.S. futures prices and London cash prices than between New York and London cash prices. They interpret this to imply that cash prices in New York were out of date part of the time during the crash period, and thus they use the apparently more accurate U.S. futures prices in all subsequent tests.

31. However, Miller (1989) argues that the triggering event might not be all that obvious; an analogy to the crash is " . . . an avalanche . . . an increasingly unstable buildup of snow on a mountainside, triggered finally by some trivial and normally harmless event like the snapping of a twig (p. 3)."

32. A transaction tax should be distinguished from the currently-in-place tax on trading profits. The former is levied on every trade at the time it occurs. Less credible proposals have also been made about the latter; for instance, a 50 percent surtax on short-term trading profits is proposed by Rohatyn (1988) to curb volatility induced by the "proliferation of speculative financial instruments" wielded by institutional investors who " . . . no longer invest . . . they *speculate*" (p. 50, emphasis in original). With a 100 percent surtax, volatility might be *entirely* eliminated, along with trading!

33. See Edwards (1988b). Also, an interesting survey of many suggested reforms is given from a legal viewpoint by Becker and Underhill (1988).

34. There is a very clear-cut impact on price *level:* imposition by the exchange of 100 percent margin causes an immediate price decline. But this could be attributed to the conveyance of information about the company implicit in the imposition of such a severe margin. For instance, investors could interpret the exchange's move to imply that the exchange itself possesses privileged information to the effect that previous price advances have been unwarranted.

35. Largay's price impact and volume results were confirmed with a bigger sample in a replication study by Eckardt and Rogoff (1976).

36. Hartzmark's paper is unique in several respects. He studies the impact of margins on the *type* of trader and he uses data for commodity futures. He finds no systematic influence of margin changes on price volatility (p. S177), but he points out that much larger margins than are currently in effect in the futures market could conceivably have an effect (though perhaps in the "wrong" direction). Merton Miller pointed out to me, however, that empirical studies of margin requirements with futures data might not be entirely applicable to cash markets because, unlike the Federal Reserve, futures exchanges explicitly tie margin levels to volatility. The Fed does the opposite since it decreases (increases) margin requirements when price levels decrease (increase), and there is a well-documented inverse relation between volatility and price level.

37. Salinger argues that Schwert's criticism of Hardouvelis " . . . has several problems . . . it suggests that the Federal Reserve reduces margins in response to volatility increases, which would be odd" (p. 17). Actually, Schwert finds that the Fed responds to price *levels* and that levels happen to be inversely related to volatility (evidently unbeknownst to the Fed). Salinger also says that Schwert's test "arguably has low power" since it is based on first differences. On the other hand, a test based on levels such as Hardouvelis's is subject to gross bias induced by the spurious regression fallacy, as documented by Hsieh and Miller.

38. However, when 12 lags of volatility are included in the model, neither debt nor margin requirements remains significant in the 1928–1987 period.

39. For instance, in studying orange juice futures (Roll, 1984), I found that limits impeded prices from responding to weather.

40. The Ma et al. results using daily *do* show a tendency for continuation of price movements in the same direction.

41. One might ask if Barnum's proposition applies also to economists.

42. This conclusion is supported in the recent detailed examination provided by Salinger (1989).

43. Easy avoidance is related to the problem of harmonization of margin rules across markets, although the latter also a question of inter-market competition. An interesting analysis of avoidance and harmonization is given by Estrella (1988).

44. In the single exception of France, the margin requirements and price limits are given for the short-term futures market. There most stock is traded for delivery within the month (i.e., the purchase contract is technically a future).

145

45. If there are no price limits in country j, $L_j = 0$, while if there are price limits, $L_j = 100/$(Price Limits in %). The rationale for L_j is that the absence of price limits is essentially a wider band than any level of imposed limits; thus, L_j represents an attempt to combine countries without limits into the same data set as countries with limits having numerical values.

46. If price limits reduced volatility, the coefficient would be negative.

47. Holding intervals are limited to five trading days. Intervals of 10 and 20 days used in previous results are not feasible here because there would be only one complete nonoverlapping interval during the 15-day crash period and thus the standard deviation of returns could not be computed.

References

Aderhold, Robert, Cumming, Christine and Harwood, Alison. "International Linkages among Equities Markets and the October 1987 Market Break." *Federal Reserve Bank of New York Quarterly Review* 13 (2, Summer 1988), 34–46.

Allen, Franklin and Gorton, Gary. "Rational Finite Bubbles." The Wharton School, University of Pennsylvania, No. 41–88, November 1988.

Amihud, Yakov, Mendelson, Haim and Wood, Robert A. "Liquidity and the 1987 Stock Market Crash," Graduate School of Business, New York University, April 1989.

Becker, Brandon and Underhill, David L. "Market Reform Proposals and Actions," IIT/Chicago-Kent College of Law, Eleventh Annual Commodities Law Institute, October 1988, pp. 20–21.

Bennett, Paul and Kelleher, Jeanette. "The International Transmission of Stock Price Disruption in October 1987." *Federal Reserve Bank of New York Quarterly Review* 13 (2, Summer 1988), 17–33.

Bertero, Elisabetta and Mayer, Colin. "Structure and Performance: Global Interdependence of Stock Markets around the Crash of October 1987." London: Centre for Economic Policy Research Discussion Paper No. 307, March 1989.

Brennan, Michael J. "A Theory of Price Limits in Futures Markets." *Journal of Financial Economics* 16 (2 June 1986), 213–233.

Camerer, Colin. "Bubbles and Fads in Asset Prices: A Review of Theory and Evidence." *Journal of Economic Surveys* 3 (1, 1989 forthcoming).

Dwyer, Gerald P., Jr. and Hafer, R.W. "Are National Stock Markets Linked?" *Federal Reserve Bank of St. Louis Review* 70 (6, November/December 1988), 3–14.

Eckardt, Walter L., Jr. and Rogoff, Donald L. "100% Margins Revisited." *Journal of Finance* 31 (3, June 1976), 995–1000.

Edwards, Franklin R. "Does Futures Trading Increase Stock Market Volatility?" *Financial Analysts Journal* (January–February 1988a), 63–69.

————. "Policies to Curb Stock Market Volatility." Columbia Business School, Center for the Study of Futures Markets, Working Paper CSFM #176, August 1988b.

Estrella, Arturo. "Consistent Margin Requirements: Are They Feasible?" *Federal Reserve Bank of New York Quarterly Review* 13 (2, Summer 1988), 61–79.

Fama, Eugene F. "Perspectives on October 1987 or What Did We Learn from the Crash." In: R.W. Kamphuis, R.C. Kormendi, and J.W.H. Watson, eds., *Black Monday and the Future of Financial Markets.* Homewood, IL: Irwin, 1989.

Federal Reserve System, Staff of the Board of Governors. "A Review and Evaluation of Federal Margin Regulation." Washington, D.C.: Federal Reserve, December 1984.

Garbade, Kenneth D. "Federal Reserve, Margin Requirements: A Regulatory Initiative to Inhibit Speculative Bubbles." In: P. Wachtel, ed., *Crises in The Economic and Financial Structure.* Lexington, MA: D.C. Health, 1982, ch. 12.

Goodhart, Charles. "The International Transmission of Asset Price Volatility." London School of Economics Financial Markets Group, 1988.

Grossman, Sanford J. "Insurance Seen and Unseen: The Impact on Markets." *Journal of Portfolio Management* 14 (4, Summer 1988), 5–8.

Grube, R. Corwin, Joy, O. Maurice and Panton, Don B. Market Responses to Federal Reserve Changes in the Initial Margin Requirement, *Journal of Finance* 34 (3, June 1979), 659–673.

Hamao, Yasushi, Masulis, Ronald W. and Ng, Victor. "Correlation in Price Changes and Volatility Across International Stock Markets." University of California, San Diego, February 1989.

Hamilton, James D. and Whiteman, Charles H. "The Observable Implications of Self-Fulfilling Expectations." *Journal of Monetary Economics* 16 (3, November 1985), 353–373.

Hardouvelis, Gikas A. "Evidence on Stock Market Speculative Bubbles: Japan, the United States, and Great Britain." *Federal Reserve Bank of New York Quarterly Review* 13 (2, Summer 1988a), 4–16.

—————. "Margin Requirements and Stock Market Volatility." *Federal Reserve Bank of New York Quarterly Review* 13 (2, Summer 1988b), 80–88.

—————. "Margin Requirements, Volatility, and the Transitory Component of Stock Prices." First Boston Working Paper Series FB-88-38, Columbia University, Barnard Collage, November, 1988c.

—————. "Stock Market Bubbles Before the Crash of 1987." First Boston Working Paper Series #FB 89-07, Columbia University Graduate School of Business, 1989.

Harris, Lawrence. "S&P Cash Stock Price Volatilities." School of Business Administration, University of Southern California, February, 1989.

Hartzmark, Michael L. "The Effects of Changing Margin Levels on Futures Market Activity, the Composition of Traders in the Market, and Price Performance." *Journal of Business* 59 (2, part 2, April 1986), S147–S180.

Hilliard, Jimmy E. "The Relationship Between Equity Indices on World Exchanges." *Journal of Finance* 34 (1, March 1979), 103–114.

Hopewell, Michael H. and Schwartz, Arthur L. Jr. "Temporary Trading Suspensions in Individual NYSE Securities." *Journal of Finance* 33 (5, December 1978), 1355–1373.

Hsieh, David A. and Miller, Merton H. "Margin Regulations and Stock Market Volatility." Graduate School of Business, University of Chicago, April, 1989.

Johnson, Norman L. and Kotz, Samuel. *Continuous Univariate Distributions-2.* New York: Wiley, 1970.

Kamphuis, Robert W., Jr., Kormendi, Roger C. and Watson, J.W. Henry, eds., *Black Monday and the Future of Financial Markets.* Homewood, IL: Irwin, 1989.

King, Mervyn and Wadhwani, Sushil. "Transmission of Volatility Between Stock Markets." London School of Economics Financial Markets Group, November 1988.

Kryzanowski, Lawrence. "The Efficacy of Trading Suspensions: A Regulatory Action Designed to Prevent the Exploitation of Monopoly Information." *Journal of Finance* 34 (5, December 1979), 1187–1200.

Largay, James A. III. "100% Margins: Combatting Speculation in Individual Security Issues." *Journal of Finance* 28 (4, September 1973), 973–986.

Largay, James A. III and West, Richard R. "Margin Changes and Stock Price Behavior." *Journal of Political Economy* 81 (2, part 1, March/April 1973), 328–339.

Luckett, Dudley G. "On the Effectiveness of the Federal Reserve's Margin Requirement." *Journal of Finance* 37 (3, June 1982), 783–795.

Ma, Christopher K., Rao, Ramesh P. and Sears, R. Stephen. "Volatility, Price Resolution and the Effectiveness of Price Limits." Columbia Futures Center, Conference on Regulatory and Structural Reform of Stock and Futures Markets, May 1989.

Miller, Merton H. "The Crash of 1987: Bubble or Fundamental?" Keynote Address, First Annual Pacific-Basin Finance Conference, Taipei, March 1989.

Mitchell, Mark L. and Netter, Jeffrey M. "Triggering the 1987 Stock Market Crash: Antitakeover Provisions in the Proposed House Ways and Means Tax Bill?" Washington, D.C.: U.S. Securities and Exchange Commission, January 1989.

Neumark, David, Tinsley, P.A. and Tosini, Susan. "After-Hours Stock Prices and Post-Crash Hangovers." Washington, D.C.: Federal Reserve Board, Division of Research and Statistics, Finance and Economics Discussion Series 50, November 1988.

Officer, Robert R. "The Variability of the Market Factor of the New York Stock Exchange." *Journal of Business* 46 (3, July 1973), 434–453.

Parhizgari, A. M., Dandapani, K. and Bhattacharya, A. K. "Global Market Place and Causality." Finance Department, Florida International University, 1988.

Rohatyn, Felix. "A Financial House of Cards." *Time,* (October 17, 1988), 48–50.

Roll, Richard. "Orange Juice and Weather." *American Economic Review* 74 (5, December 1984), 861–880.

——————. "The International Crash of October, 1987." In: K.W. Kamphuis, R.C. Kormendi, and J.W.H. Watson, eds., *Black Monday and the Future of Financial Markets.* Homewood, IL: Irwin, 1989, also printed in *The Financial Analysts Journal,* (September/October, 1988).

Ross, Stephen A. "Uncertainty and the Heterogeneous Capital Good Model." *Review of Economic Studies* 42 (1, January 1975), 133–146.

Ross, Stephen A. "Regression to the Max." Yale School of Organization and Management, December 1987).

Salinger, Michael A. "Stock Market Margin Requirements and Volatility: Implications for Regulation of Stock Index Futures." Graduate School of Business, Columbia University, April 1989.

Samuelson, Paul A. "Indeterminancy of Development in a Heterogenous-Capital Model with Constant Saving Propensity." In: Karl Shell, ed., *Essays on the Theory of Optimal Economic Growth.* Cambridge, MA: MIT Press, 1967.

Santoni, G. J. "The Great Bull Markets 1924–29 and 1982–87: Speculative Bubbles or Economic Fundamentals?" *Federal Reserve Bank of St. Louis Review* 69 (9, November 1987), 16–29.

Schwert, G. William. "Business Cycles, Financial Crises and Stock Volatility." Working Paper BC 88-06, Bradley Policy Research Center, University of Rochester, October 1988.

Siegal, Jeremy J. "The Stock Market Crash of 1987: A Macro-Finance Perspective." The Wharton School, University of Pennsylvania, July 1988.

Sofianios, George. "Margin Requirements on Equity Instruments." *Federal Reserve Bank of New York Quarterly Review* 13 (2, Summer 1988), 47–60.

Stiglitz, J.E. "Using Tax Policy to Curb Speculative Short-Term Trading." Conference on Regulatory Reform of Stock and Futures Markets, Columbia University Futures Center, May 1989.

Summers, Lawrence H. and Summers, Victoria P. "When Financial Markets Work Too Well: A Cautious Case for a Securities Transactions Tax." Mimeo, undated.

Telser, Lester G. "October 1987 and the Structure of Financial Markets: An Exorcism of Demons." In: R.W. Kamphuis, R.C. Kormendi, and J.W.H. Watson, eds., *Black Monday and the Future of Financial Markets.* Homewood, IL: Irwin, 1989.

Tirole, Jean. "On the Possibility of Speculation Under Rational Expectations." *Econometrica* 50 (5, September 1982), 1163–1181.

——————. "Asset Bubbles and Overlapping Generations." *Econometrica* 53 (5, September 1985), 1071–1100.

Wachtel, Paul. *Crises in the Economic and Financial Structure.* Lexington, MA: D.C. Health, 1982.

Journal of Financial Services Research, 3: 247–254 (1989)
© 1989 Kluwer Academic Publishers

Commentary: *Price Volatility, International Market Links, and Their Implications for Regulatory Policies*

DANIEL B. NELSON
University of Chicago
Graduate School of Business
1101 East 58th St.
Chicago, IL 60637

The crash of October 1987 has produced a flood of interesting econometric studies of its origins, of stock market volatility, and of its international transmission. I am pleased to have been asked to comment on Richard Roll's clear and insightful review of this literature. Indeed, there is much of the literature that I never would have learned about without Roll's review.

I have two main comments to make with regard to Roll's article and to the literature he reviews: First, I think that one of Roll's points deserved re-emphasis. We have now more than 100 years of daily returns data on Market indices (Schwert, 1989). Of all the market moves made in the approximately 28,000 trading days during this period, the crash of 1987 was by far the largest. Many of the papers that Roll reviews examine a fairly narrow period surrounding the crash. This introduces a potentially serious sample selection bias problem, since the sample period was selected precisely to bracket the largest outlier in the data. To take a trivial example, suppose we generate 28,000 i.i.d. $N(0,1)$ draws and then pick out the largest draw. Say that this occurs in element 21,804. Then we regress our randomly generated variables on a constant and on a dummy variable that equals zero except at element 21,804. Such a dummy variable will certainly have a huge t-statistic associated with it, a t-statistic that is meaningless and that is an artifact of our sample selection procedure. Of course, none of the authors cited makes such an elementary error. I can't help but wonder, however, what the effect is on our estimates of regression coefficients when we carefully choose our sample period to coincide with the crash.

Of all the papers that I was introduced to in Roll's review, the most useful one was Ross (1987) precisely because Ross looks carefully at the effects of sample selection bias on tests for serial correlation and speculative bubbles in returns. I think more work along these lines would be very useful.

My second comment is more of a question: we know that volatility on the market changes dramatically over time. To what extent can the high volatility of October 1987 be explained by the same factors that govern less dramatic volatility shifts? If a single model can forecast different episodes of high volatility over a long historical period, then we might conclude that the crash of 1987 was governed by the same market forces that caused previous periods of high volatility, rather than by forces unique to the 1980s.

149

In the finance literature, three main factors have been isolated in explaining shifts over time in market volatility:

1. Volatility is positively serially correlated (e.g., see Mandelbroit, 1963; Fama, 1965; French, Schwert, and Stambaugh, 1987; and Officer, 1973). As Mandelbroit (1963) put it, " ... large changes tend to be followed by large changes—of either sign—and small changes tend to be followed by small changes ...." Sharper-than-expected market movements are, therefore, a signal of higher future volatility.

2. As first noted by Fischer Black (1976), the direction of recent market movements strongly influence volatility. When the market goes up (down), volatility tends to go down (up), at least temporarily. To a certain extent, this can be explained by leverage effects. For example, if a firm has both debt and equity outstanding, or if the firm has other fixed costs besides debt, a change in the value of the firm will affect the degree of leverage in the firm's equity. So, for example, when the value of the firm rises (falls) the firm's equity becomes less (more) highly levered, and the volatility of equity returns falls (rises). Black argued, however, that the effect of returns on volatility is too powerful to be explained by leverage changes.

3. As noted by French and Roll (1986), nontrading days also contribute to volatility. For example, the typical Monday is more volatile than the typical Wednesday, since returns on a typical Monday reflect information arriving between the Friday close and the Monday close, a period of 72 hours, while returns on a typical Wednesday reflect information arriving from the Tuesday close to the Wednesday close, a period of only 24 hours.

A number of econometric models have been proposed that use one or more of these three factors to forecast volatility. For example, the family of ARCH models introduced by Engle (1982), and developed by many authors since, uses factor (1) to forecast volatility, and can easily be modified to use factor (3) as well. Recently, Nelson (1989) has proposed a variant of ARCH (Exponential ARCH) which also uses factor (2). Can these models succeed in forecasting periods of extremely high volatility? To check this, I fit an Exponential ARCH model to daily capital gains on the S&P 500[1] from January 1928 to April 1989. (I also estimated the model using only the January 1928 through September 1987 period. Perhaps surprisingly, it made little difference in the coefficients.) I chose a specification in which the log of the conditional variance of daily market returns follows an ARMA (2,1) process, since this specification had been found to work reasonably well with other daily returns data sets. The model is exactly the same as the models estimated in Nelson (1989).

The estimated coefficients are reported in table 1. I would like to call your attention, however, to figures 1–6. Here we pick out several episodes of very high volatility in 60 years of stock returns and see how well our simple model was able to forecast them. In each figure, the solid lines represent the ex-ante, one-day-ahead, 99 percent confidence intervals for returns. The black squares represent the realized returns. When the lines are close together, the model is forecasting low volatility, and when the lines are far apart, it is forecasting high volatility. Notice that many more than 1 percent of the realized returns lie outside these lines. This is not surprising because of our sample selection: we've deliberately picked out the outliers.

Figures 1 and 2 plot the crashes of 1929 and 1987, respectively. It is in these two crashes

Table 1.

Formally, the model is

(T.1) $\xi_t = \sigma_t z_t$,

(T.2) $z_t \sim$ i.i.d. with

     $E(z_t) = 0$, $\mathrm{Var}(z_t) = 1$, and GED density

(T.3) $f(z) = \dfrac{v \exp[-0.5 \times |z/\lambda|^v]}{\lambda \, 2^{(1 + 1/v)}\Gamma(1/v)}$, where

(T.4) $\lambda = [2^{(-2/v)}\Gamma(1/v)/\Gamma(3/v)]^{1/2}$.

(T.5) $\ln(\sigma_t^2) = \alpha_t + \Delta_1 \ln(\sigma_{t-1}^2) + \Delta_2 \ln(\sigma_{t-2}^2) + g(z_{t-1}) + \psi g(z_{t-2})$,

(T.6) $\alpha_t = \alpha + \ln(1 + N_t\delta)$,

where N_t is the number of nontrading days between the trading days $t-1$ and t,

(T.7) $R_t = a + bR_{t-1} + c\sigma_t^2 + \xi_t$, and

(T.8) $g(z_t) = \theta z_t - \gamma[\,|z_t| - E\,|z_t|\,]$.

The model makes $\ln(\sigma_t)$ follow an ARMA (2,1) process. See Nelson (1989) for details.

PARAMETER	ESTIMATE	STANDARD ERROR
α	−9.919302	0.2476
δ	0.228157	0.0200
γ	0.190060	0.0098
Δ_1	1.905719	0.0110
Δ_2	−0.905824	0.0038
ψ	−0.975941	0.0038
θ	−0.109967	0.0066
a	0.000448	$6.1817 \cdot 10^{-5}$
b	0.116587	0.0075
c	−1.459826	0.7759
v	1.373277	0.0155

that the performance of the model is poorest, since both "Black Mondays" are associated with very large outliers. Even in this failure, however, the partial success of the model is striking; on October 28, 1929, the market dropped about 13 percent,[2] whereas the ex-ante 99 percent confidence intervals were [−7.5 percent, 7.3 percent], up from about [−2 percent, 2 percent] a few weeks before. On October 19, 1987, the index dropped about 23 percent, whereas the 99 percent confidence intervals were [−9 percent, 7.6 percent]—clearly not wide enough, but very wide compared to the ±2 percent of a few weeks before. What was it that signaled high volatility on the two Black Mondays? In each crash, there had been a series of unexpectedly large, downward moves in the market, an indication that factors (1) and (2) were working together. According to the simple model just estimated, large, downward moves are warning signals of very high volatility ahead. Factor (3) also played a very minor role in the two crashes (i.e., both crashes were on Mondays).

In the very large market moves of 1932, 1933,[3] and 1974, the model does extremely well—i.e., there are relatively few outliers. In the downturn of 1962, there is one fairly substantial outlier, May 28, when the market dropped 6.9 percent. On this day, the ex-ante 99 percent confidence interval generated by the model was [−4.86 percent, 4.42 percent], up from around ±1.1 percent a few weeks before. Again, the model succeeded in predicting high volatility on this day.

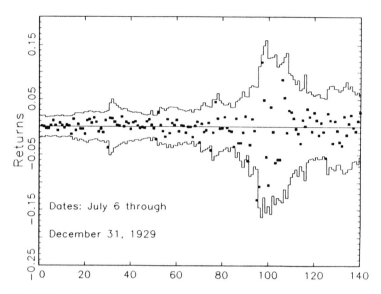

Fig. 1. The crash of 1929

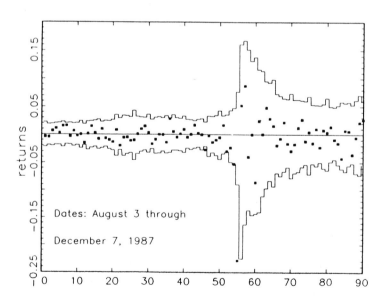

Fig. 2. The crash of 1987

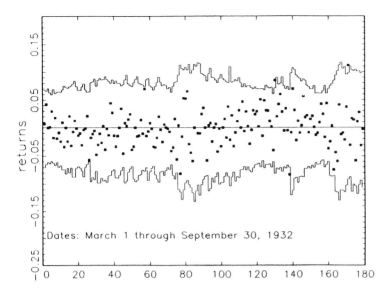

Fig. 3. The crash and rise of 1932

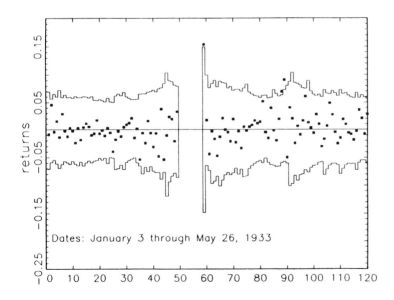

Fig. 4. Bank panic, market recovery

153

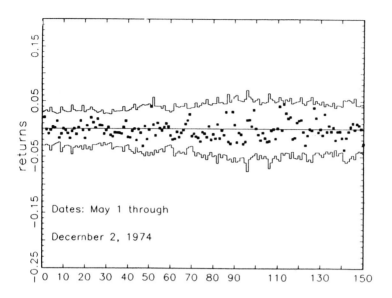

Fig. 5. The downturn of 1974

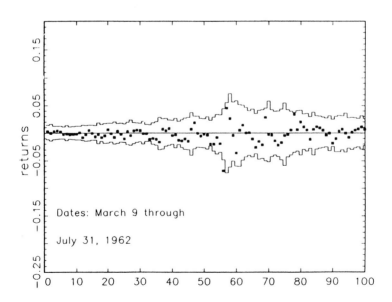

Fig. 6. The downturn of 1962

154

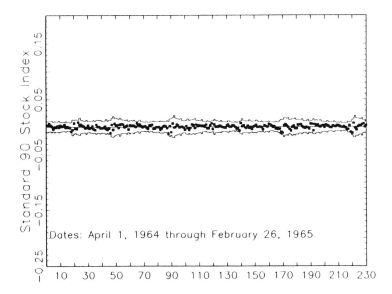

Fig. 7. The doldrums, 4/64–2/65

By way of contrast, figure 7 portrays a period of very low volatility (though by no means a period barren of important news),[4] in which the 99 percent confidence intervals hover at around ±1 percent.

The model examined here was only an initial guess about what an appropriate model would be, and a more refined model might have done much better at forecasting volatility. There does seem to be reason to hope, however, that spectacularly high levels of market volatility may be explainable by the same forces that explain lower levels of volatility. These forces themselves are not well understood, and much work remains to be done in this context. I think that Roll's article, and many of the works he cites, help us to understand these factors and how they operate, not merely during huge market moves, but day to day.

Notes

1. The S&P 500 index was introduced in 1956, replacing the Standard 90 stock index, which we use in the period 1928–1956.

2. All return figures are given in Log form—i.e., $r_t = \ln(SP_t/SP_{t-1})$, where SP_t is the closing level for the S&P index for day t.

3. The points of zero returns and zero volatility in figure 4 are for March 4 through March 14, when the stock markets were closed in conjunction with the national banking holiday that was occurring at the same time. Because this was an unusual market closure (i.e., not like the usual weekend closing), it is included in the figure.

4. For example, the Gulf of Tonkin incident and the passage of the Gulf of Tonkin Resolution occurred during this period, but seemed to have little or no impact on the market.

References

Black, F. "Studies of Stock Market Volatility Changes." *Proceedings of the American Statistical Association, Business and Economic Statistics Section,* 1976, 177–181.

Engle, R.F. "Autoregressive Conditional Heteroskedasticity With Estimates of the Variance of United Kingdom Inflation." *Econometrica,* 50 (4, 1982), 987–1008.

Fama, E.F. "The Behavior of Stock Market Prices." *Journal of Business* 38 (1965), 34–105.

French, K.R. and Roll, R. "Stock Return Variances: The Arrival of Information and the Reaction of Traders." *Journal of Financial Economics* 17 (1986), 5–26.

French K.R., Schwert, G.W. and Stambaugh, R.F. "Expected Stock Returns and Volatility." *Journal of Financial Economics* 19 (1, 1987), 3–30.

Mandelbroit, B. "The Variation of Certain Speculative Prices." *Journal of Business* 36 (1963), 394–419.

Nelson, D.B. "Conditional Heteroskedasticity in Asset Returns: A New Approach." University of Chicago Graduate School of Business, Working Paper Series in Economics of Chicago Graduate School of Business, Working Paper Series in Economics and Econometrics #89–73, 1989.

Officer, R.R. "The Variability of the Market Factor of the New York Stock Exchange." *Journal of Business* 46 (1973), 434–453.

Roll, R. "Price Volatility, International Market Links, and Their Implications for Regulatory Policies." *Journal of Financial Services Research* (1989, this issue).

Ross, S.A. "Regression to the Max." Mimeo, Yale School of Organization and Management, 1987.

Schwert, G.W. "Indexes of United States Stock Prices from 1802 to 1987." Mimeo, William E. Simon Graduate School of Business, University of Rochester, 1989.

Journal of Financial Services Research, 3: 255–259 (1989)
© 1989 Kluwer Academic Publishers

Commentary: *Price Volatility, International Market Links, and Their Implications For Regulatory Policies*

SUSHIL WADHWANI
London School of Economics
Department of Political Science
London WC2A 2AE

Roll's article is interesting and contains an impressively comprehensive discussion of the issues at hand. I agree with much of what is said, although there are some issues on which, inevitably, our judgment differs.

In discussing the hypothesis that there was a speculative bubble before the crash, the author argues that " . . . the verdict . . . has to be: *neither confirmed not denied.*" The evidence for the existence of a bubble is based, in the main, on the existence of positive serial correlation in price changes before the crash. However, evidence for positive serial correlation is not robust across studies. Mullins (1988), using a similar sample, did not find any evidence for positive serial correlation when using a runs test instead of the author's preferred formulation of a variance-ratio test. Further, positive serial correlation in returns may arise for a myriad of reasons unrelated to the existence of a speculative bubble.

On the other hand, there are several reasons for believing that the existence of a speculative bubble is implausible. There is the difficulty of explaining why Frankfurt fell, even though it hardly rose through 1987, as the author notes. In the same vein, if there were a market with a bubble before the crash, then Tokyo, with its sky-high price-earnings ratios, would surely be it. Yet Japan declined less than other major markets, and also recovered more quickly. While it is possible to "explain" this by superimposing the existence of a "new" bubble on the pricking of the "old" bubble, we are in danger of making a bubbles-based explanation tautological.

As a bubble inflates, there is an increase in potential volatility. Therefore, in the period before the crash, we should have seen an increase in the volatility perceived by market participants. An indicator for changes in the market's perceived volatility is provided by movements in the measure of "implied volatility" inferred from options on a stock index. We present such a measure, for the FTSE 100 index, in figure 1 (the original series was constructed by Franks and Schwartz, 1988). Notice that in the days before the crash, volatility was lower than it had been at several points earlier that year. Further, there was no perceptible trend increase in volatility during the sample period. Hence, the prediction of bubbles-models, that we should see increased perceived volatility, does not appear to hold.

Many of the popular "explanations" of the crash, including that of a speculative bubble, fail to account for the relative uniformity of price declines in all markets. However, the man in the street is probably content to believe that some initial factor helped precipitate a fall in U.S. stock prices, which then *caused* a fall in prices elsewhere. This is certainly consistent

Fig. 1. Volatility implied by index options

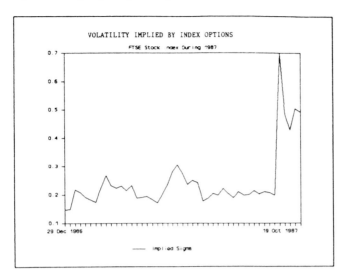

Source: Franks and Schwartz, 1988.

with survey evidence: Shiller, Konya, and Tsutsui (1988) found that the vast majority of Japanese investors felt that the most important reason for the decline in share prices on October 20 (the day when the Japanese market declined most) was the crash of the London and New York markets on October 19.

Mervyn King and I have recently formalized the above notion in a "contagion" model. Because of the existence of asymmetric information, traders in one market rationally react to price changes in other markets because the latter are correlated with the "news" only observed in other markets. In practice, examples of such private information include superior insight into how a particular piece of economic news will be interpreted and a better feel as to how "market sentiment" is changing. For this reason we expect the existence of some "contagion" to be the normal state of affairs. Moreover, the degree of contagion may vary over time. Thus, in periods like the crash, when there is no obvious news event to explain price declines, and what matters more for share price determination is the perceptions of other investors (as in the Keynesian beauty contest parable), price changes in other markets provide a good indicator of changes in such perceptions. Consequently, they rationally receive a higher weight in share price formation.

The existence of the possibility of contagion is also important for policy purposes. For example, one can no longer logically argue that the existence of portfolio insurance played no role in the crash, because markets without formalized portfolio insurance fell as much as the U.S. (which is one of the arguments in Roll, 1988). Instead, it is at least theoretically possible that a U.S. price decline which was exacerbated by portfolio insurance could have been spread to markets without formal portfolio insurance. Of course, in order to make that case, one would still have to find direct evidence that portfolio insurance did contribute to the U.S. price decline.

What of the argument that there is no true contagion, but that the observed links between markets arise from the fact that there are common, observable, fundamental news events that are relevant to all markets? It is not easy to discriminate between these hypotheses, as the author notes. The fundamentals explanation, however, could not plausibly account for the worldwide decline in prices during the crash.

One possible test is to examine the behavior of U.K. share prices around the time that the U.S. stock market opens. If markets are moved by commonly observed fundamentals, then there is no reason to expect anything unusual in London share prices when New York opens. In contrast, the contagion model predicts higher volatility in share prices in London at the New York open because the opening value of the Dow Jones contains information that is not easily observable to market participants in London.

Figure 2 presents some evidence on this issue, using 15-minute data on the FTSE 100 price index. Notice that volatility is high around the open, and again around 11.30 a.m.—the time at which all official U.K. economic statistics are released. Further, it is also high during the period 2.15 p.m.—3.15 p.m. There is, therefore, some support for the contagion model, in spite of the fact that there are reasons to believe that much information regarding the opening value of U.S. stock prices is available to market-makers in London: an S&P 500 futures contract that is traded (albeit in a thin market) in Amsterdam prior to the opening of Wall Street, and there is information about the state of the order books of specialists on the New York Stock Exchange.

An alternative test relies on the fact that the U.S. stock markets were closed on Wednesdays in the second half of 1968 in order to help clear a settlement backlog. These exchange holidays have already been used in some ingenious work on the determinants of

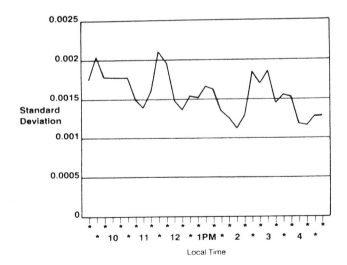

Fig. 2. Intraday volatility in London (FTSE 100 price index) (1 July to 13 October 1987)
Source: King and Wadhwani, 1988.

stock market volatility (see French and Roll, 1986). For our purposes, the contagion model would predict that share prices in London would be less volatile on these U.S. exchange holidays. This would not be an implication of a fundamentals model, in that these exchange holidays did not stop the release of normal economic news—e.g., official economic statistics. The relevant statistics are presented in table 1. They are fairly striking. While there is no difference in daily return volatility on Wednesdays versus other days through 1969–1971 (124.5 against 123.9), volatility in London on Wednesdays in the second half of 1968 was only about two-thirds of its average daily level on other days of the week. We view this as providing fairly strong support for the contagion model.

Returning to the crash, we concede the author's point that the United States may not have been the original infectee because several markets fell on the 19th before the U.S. opened. However, one needs to be careful here. Imagine that one is in a valley, and that echoing has begun. It is, then, extremely difficult to tell where the original noise originated. In the same way, once markets begin to feed off each other, one may lose sight of where the initial shock occurred. Turning to the markets that fell before the United States opened on the 19th (in the main, the United Kingdom, Hong Kong, and Singapore), we know that they fell very little in the preceding week (see table 2). However, once the United States fell by as much as 5 percent on Friday, the 16th, the contagion model predicts that the other markets would now sit up and take notice. The first opportunity that these markets had of reacting to the U.S. fall of the 16th was Monday the 19th. (The U.K. market was closed on the 16th because of a hurricane, while Hong Kong and Singapore were already closed on the 16th before the United States opened.) It is true that Singapore and Hong Kong fell more on the 19th than the U.S. price decline of the 16th. However, this just suggests that there were influences other than contagion that may have played a role—in Hong Kong, the fall in prices might

Table 1. Daily returns variances in the United Kingdom (FTSE 100 price index)

	Wednesdays	Other Days
1968	57.2	83.2
1969–1971	124.5	123.9

Table 2. Stock price changes in selected countries

Date	Hong Kong	Singapore	United States
14th Oct	−0.3%	−0.04%	−2.8%
15th Oct	−0.3%	−0.4%	−2.3%
16th Oct	−1.9%	−2.7%	−4.9%
19th Oct	−10.8%	−13.8%	−20.0%
20th Oct	CLOSED	−25.3%	+3.8%

have triggered a fear of insolvency and, more generally, stop-loss selling can exacerbate an initial price fall. Further support for the notion that Singapore was following the United States (not leading it) is provided by the fact that it continued on falling on the 20th (in response to the United States price fall of the 19th), while the United States recovered somewhat on the 20th. For all these reasons, I do not believe that the notion that the United States was the original infectee, and that the crash was then transmitted to other markets through contagion effects, can be ruled out.

Finally, I would like to congratulate Richard Roll for writing a stimulating and thoroughly sensible article.

References

Mullins, Mark. "Bursting Bubbles and Bleeding Bulls: Does the Evidence Support the Rhetoric?" LSE, Financial Markets Group. Mimeo, 1988.

Franks, J.R. and Schwartz, E.S. "The Stochastic Behaviour of Market Variance Implied in the Prices of Index Options: Leverage, Volume, and Other Effects." London Business School. Mimeo, 1988.

Shiller, R.J., Konya, F. and Tsutsui, Y. "Investor Behaviour in the October 1987 Stock Market Crash: The Case of Japan." NBER Working Paper No. 2684, 1988.

King, M.A., and Wadhwani, S.B. "Transmission of Volatility Between Stock Markets." LSE, Financial Markets Group Discussion Paper No. 48, 1988.

Roll, R. "The International Crash of October 1987." *The Financial Analysts Journal* (September/October 1988).

French, K.R. and Roll, R. "Stock Return Variances: The Arrival of Information and the Reaction of Traders." *Journal of Financial Economics* 17 (1, 1986), 5–26.

Journal of Financial Services Research, 3: 261–286 (1989)
© 1989 Kluwer Academic Publishers

When Financial Markets Work Too Well: A Cautious Case For a Securities Transactions Tax

LAWRENCE H. SUMMERS
Professor of Economics
Littauer 229
Harvard University
Cambridge, MA 02138

VICTORIA P. SUMMERS
Deputy Director, International Tax Program
Harvard University, Cambridge, MA 02138

Abstract

Unlike most major industrialized nations, the United States does not impose an excise tax on securities transactions. This article examines the desirability and feasibility of implementating a U.S. Securities Transfer Excise Tax (STET) directed at curbing excesses associated with short-term speculation and at raising revenue. We conclude that strong economic efficiency arguments can be made in support of a STET that throws "sand into the gears," in James Tobin's (1982) phrase, of our excessively well-functioning financial markets. Such a tax would have the beneficial effects of curbing instability introduced by speculation, reducing the diversion of resources into the financial sector of the economy, and lengthening the horizons of corporate managers. The efficiency benefits derived from curbing speculation are likely to exceed any costs of reduced liquidity or increased costs of capital that come from taxing financial transactions more heavily. The examples of Japan and the United Kingdom suggest that a STET is administratively feasible and can be implemented without crippling the competitiveness of U.S. financial markets. A STET at a .5% rate could raise revenues of at least $10 billion annually.

Technological and institutional innovations have radically transformed financial markets in the United States and around the world. These changes have permitted and encouraged spectacular increases in the volume of trade in securities of all kinds. In 1960, 766 million shares were traded on the New York Stock Exchange; by 1987, more than 900 million shares changed hands in the average week. More shares were traded on the lowest-volume day in 1987 than in any month in 1960. And more shares changed hands in the first 15 minutes of trading on October 19 and 20, 1987, than in any week in 1960.

Increases in trading have been even more spectacular in other markets. In 1960 or 1970 there were no organized markets in derivative securities. Today, the dollar value of contracts traded on the stock market futures market alone significantly exceeds the volume of trade

We wish to thank David Cutler, Thomas Kalil, James Poterba, Jonathan Evans, and Charles Perry for useful discussions, and Jeffrey Mantz for dedicated research assistance.

163

on the stock market itself, and the volume of trade in stock market futures is nearly equalled by trade in index options. Explosive increases in trading volumes have not been confined to corporate equities. While the value of shares traded on the New York Stock Exchange averages less than $10 billion a day, the daily value of trade in government bonds averages more than $25 billion and the daily value of trade in foreign exchange approaches $300 billion. There is every reason to expect trading volumes to continue to increase. Already, the New York Stock Exchange is planning for a billion share day. And with increasing international linkages between markets, an increasing variety of securities will soon be tradable 24 hours a day.

In the narrow sense of permitting trade to take place between consenting adults, it is obvious that our financial markets have become much more efficient over time. Unloading a million dollar portfolio of stock might easily have cost $10,000 or more in 1960; today a functionally equivalent transaction can be carried out in the futures market for a couple of hundred dollars or less. There are, however, increasing concerns that financial markets may have deteriorated over time in performing their social functions of spreading risk and efficiently guiding the allocation of capital, despite their increased transactions efficiency.

On the question of risk taking, First Boston's Albert Wojnilower (1980) expressed the fears of many in financial markets when he wrote that: "The freeing of financial markets to pursue their casino instincts heightens the odds of crises . . . . Because unlike a casino, the financial markets are inextricably linked with the world outside, the real economy pays the price." Treasury Secretary Brady (1988) has expressed concerns about the costs of our financial system: "We are headed in the wrong direction, when so much of our young talent and so much of this nation's resources are aimed at financial engineering when the rest of the world is laying the foundation for future growth." And the proposition is widely endorsed that American business needs to be freed from market pressures that prevent it from taking the long view.

Concern about the consequences of rapid turnover in financial markets is hardly new. In one of the most famous chapters of *The General Theory,* Keynes questioned the benefits of more liquid and smoothly functioning financial markets:

As the organization of investment markets improves, the risk of the predominance of speculation does increase. In one of the greatest investment markets in the world, namely New York, the influence of speculation is enormous. Speculators may do no harm as bubbles on a steady stream of enterprise. But the position is serious when enterprise becomes the bubble on a whirlpool of speculation. When the capital development of a country becomes the by-product of the activities of a casino, the job is likely to be ill-done. The measure of success attained by Wall Street, regarded as an institution of which the proper social purpose is to direct new investment into the most profitable channels in terms of future yield cannot be claimed as one of the outstanding triumphs of laissez-faire capitalism—which is not surprising if I am right in thinking that the best brains of Wall Street have been in fact directed towards a different object.

He continues the same passage by suggesting a possible remedy for the problems caused by excessive speculation:

These tendencies are a scarcely avoidable outcome of our having successfully organized "liquid" investment markets. It is usually agreed that casinos should in the public interest be inaccessible and expensive. And perhaps the same is true of stock exchanges . . . . The introduction of a substantial government transfer tax on all transactions might prove the most serviceable reform available, with a view to mitigating the predominance of speculation over enterprises in the United States.

Today, 50 years after Keynes wrote these words, the United States is one of the only major industrialized countries that does not levy a significant excise tax on the transfer of financial securities. Such taxes raised more than $12 billion in Japan in 1987, and raised significant amounts of revenue in most European countries despite the fact that their stock markets are much smaller than that of the United States. In light of concerns about both the large federal deficit and the pace and volatility of the markets, it is hardly surprising that the idea of imposing some form of Securities Transaction Excise Tax (STET) in the United States has received serious attention in recent years. James Tobin (1982) has urged adoption of such a tax to curb excessive volatility in international financial markets. Former House Speaker Jim Wright proposed a .5 percent tax on all securities transactions. An alternative approach to curbing speculation through the use of the tax system has been advocated by Felix Rohatyn, Warren Buffett, and Henry Kauffman, among many others. They have called for raising the tax rate on short-term capital gains and reducing the tax rate on long-term gains.

This article analyzes some of the economic and administrative issues raised by proposals to use a transactions tax to curb speculation. We conclude that there are strong economic efficiency arguments to be made in support of some kind of STET that throws "sand into the gears," to use James Tobin's (1982) phrase, of our excessively well-functioning financial markets. The efficiency benefits from curbing speculation are likely to exceed any costs of reduced liquidity or increased costs of capital that come from taxing transactions more heavily. The examples of Japan and Britain suggest that transactions taxes are administratively feasible and would not unduly interfere with our international competitiveness in the provision of financial services. International cooperation and coordination in setting STET rates could increase the ability of all countries to tax financial transactions fairly, in a manner designed to achieve the goals of curbing speculation and raising revenue.

Our article is organized as follows. Section 1 contrasts the Panglossian, theoretical, efficient markets view of the operation of financial markets with the way they work in practice. This section focuses on three concerns—excessive volatility caused by destabilizing speculation; the diversion of human and capital resources away from more socially profitable pursuits into the financial sphere; and the impact of rapid financial turnover on the way in which corporate investment decisions are made. It also examines the extent to which these problems can be addressed by taxes that curb speculation. Possible adverse economic effects of transactions taxes are considered. Section 2 describes international experiences with transactions taxes and considers the historical United States' experience. It considers a number of aspects of the operation of a U.S. STET, and concludes that such a tax would be workable and could yield significant new government revenues. Section 3 offers some concluding policy observations.

1. How well do our financial markets function?

American financial markets are extremely successful, as measured by the narrow test of facilitating free trade in a huge array of securities. Capital market participants today enjoy a degree of flexibility that would have been inconceivable even a decade ago. Large institutions are able to reallocate their portfolios between stocks and bonds in a matter of hours. Well-developed futures and options markets enable investors to hedge all kinds of risks. Starting with relatively little capital, it is now possible to take over all but the largest companies within a matter of weeks.

The difficult question about our financial markets, however, concerns how well they perform their ultimate social functions of spreading risks, guiding the investment of scarce capital, and processing and disseminating the information possessed by diverse traders. Financial innovators and their academic champions argue that the facilitation of trading necessarily contributes to economic efficiency. They therefore see innovations that reduce trading costs as clearly beneficial and regard as badly misguided proposals, such as those of Keynes and Tobin, to throw "sand into the gears" of financial markets.

The belief that facilitating trading improves the social functioning of financial markets is premised on the acceptance of the efficient markets hypothesis. If prices in unfettered financial markets closely track fundamental values, then they will provide proper economic signals, guide investment appropriately, and facilitate the spreading of risks. If, on the other hand, easy trading encourages speculation that drives prices away from fundamental values, there is cause for concern about the social functioning of financial markets. Excessive speculation that increases volatility would create rather than reduce risk, distort the allocation of investment, and limit the information content of asset prices. In this case, benefits would be derived from tax measures that would help to curb speculation.

This section begins by summarizing the available evidence on the market efficiency hypothesis. It then considers three possible adverse consequences of excessive short-term trading: increases in volatility; the excessive diversion of resources into rent-seeking activities; and the shortening of the investment horizons of corporate managers.

1.1. Do prices track fundamental values?

Although it has never been completely accepted among practitioners, the efficient markets view that stock prices will always reflect fundamental values has, until recently, commanded widespread allegiance from academic students of financial markets. The logic of efficient markets is compelling. If a stock's price diverges from the fundamental value of the company at any point, there would be a profit opportunity for anyone who recognized this fact. If a stock were underpriced relative to the underlying value of the assets it represents, for example, then efforts to profit by purchasing it would continue until its price was pushed up to the point where it equalled that underlying value. If one assumes that stock prices move quickly to eliminate easy profit opportunities, then it must be the case that prices closely mirror fundamental values. Changes in stock prices should, then, reflect changes in the fundamental value of the underlying assets, or at least in the market's estimate of those underlying values based upon changing information regarding the assets.

166

Furthermore, in the efficient markets model, investors who drive prices toward the fundamental value of a company that is undervalued by the market, by buying low and selling high, will prosper over time. Those who destabilize prices by buying high and selling low will lose money. Accordingly, "good money" will drive out "bad money" and markets will come to function better over time.

This logic has historically been supported by a vast amount of empirical literature demonstrating the difficulty of making predictable excess profits in the stock market. In 1978, Michael Jensen was able to label the efficient markets hypothesis "the best established empirical fact in economics." More recently, however, the efficient markets hypothesis, and its implication that the tremendous volatility of stock prices reflects corresponding movements in the fundamental value of assets, has been subjected to unfavorable scrutiny. As a matter of theory, critics have noted that even speculators who recognize a deviation of prices from fundamental values will be reluctant to trade on the basis of their observation as long as there is the possibility that the deviation will get larger before it gets smaller. For example, many people thought the market was undervalued at 1700 on the afternoon of October 19, 1987, but were reluctant to buy stock for fear that the market would fall further before stabilizing. More important, several types of empirical studies have questioned the presumption that movements in stock prices reflect movements in fundamental values.

First, the difficulty of isolating the news that drives stock prices even with the benefit of hindsight is well documented. Table 1, reproduced from Cutler, Poterba, and Summers (1988), describes the news events on the 50 days since World War II on which the largest market moves were observed. On many of the days, it is difficult to point to any event at all that should have had a major impact on fundamental values. The example of the 1987 crash is particularly striking. It is difficult to imagine what news that occurred on that day was sufficient to cause a 22 percent decline in the value of the American corporate sector.

This method of examining the ability of "news" to account for stock market volatility is inherently subjective, since there are always many possible factors that could have affected fundamental values. A sharper test is possible using simpler markets. Roll (1985) examined the futures market in frozen orange juice, in which prices are substantially determined by predictions about the weather in Florida. Even in this simple market, it is not possible to account for a large fraction of the observed volatility based upon any changes in external information. Roll (1988) later reached a similar conclusion with respect to the stock market, by examining the relative movements of individual corporate stocks.

Perhaps the clearest evidence that something other than fundamental values drives stock prices comes from French and Roll's (1987) ingenious study of volatility over periods when the market is open and when it is closed. It has long been observed that the market's variability between Friday's close and Monday's close is much less than three times as great as its variability between Monday's close and Tuesday's close. In the efficient market theory, this fact is attributed to the observation that less relevant news is revealed on weekend days than on weekdays. However, French and Roll examined volatility during a period in 1968 when the market was closed on Wednesdays because of the pressures caused by heavy volume. Remarkably, they found that the market volatility between Tuesday and Thursday was approximately halved when the market was closed on Wednesday! If Thursday's prices always reflected "fundamental" news generated since the last market

167

Table 1. Fifty largest postwar movements in S&P index and their "causes"

	Date	Percent Change	New York Times Explanation
1	Oct. 19, 1987	−20.47%	Worry over dollar decline and trade deficit; Fear of U.S. not supporting dollar.
2	Oct. 21, 1987	9.10%	Interest rates continue to fall; deficit talks in Washington; bargain hunting.
3	Oct. 26, 1987	−8.28%	Fear of budget deficits; margin calls; reaction to falling foreign stocks.
4	Sep. 3, 1946	−6.73%	" . . . no basic reason for the assault on prices."
5	May 28, 1962	−6.68%	Kennedy forces rollback of steel price hike.
6	Sep. 26, 1955	−6.62%	Eisenhower suffers heart attack.
7	Jun. 26, 1950	−5.38%	Outbreak of Korean War.
8	Oct. 20, 1987	5.33%	Investors looking for "quality stocks."
9	Sep. 9, 1946	−5.24%	Labor unrest in maritime and trucking industries.
10	Oct. 16, 1987	−5.16%	Fear of trade deficit; fear of higher interest rates; tension with Iran.
11	May 27, 1970	5.02%	Rumors of change in economic policy: " . . . the stock surge happened for no fundamental reason."
12	Sep. 11, 1986	−4.81%	Foreign governments refuse to lower interest rates; crackdown on triple witching announced.
13	Aug. 17, 1982	4.76%	Interest rates decline.
14	May 29, 1962	4.65%	Optimistic brokerage letters; institutional and corporate buying; suggestions of tax cut.
15	Nov. 3, 1948	−4.61%	Truman defeats Dewey.
16	Oct. 9, 1974	4.60%	Ford to reduce inflation and interest rates.
17	Feb. 25, 1946	−4.57%	Weakness in economic indicators over past week.
18	Oct. 23, 1957	4.49%	Eisenhower urges confidence in economy.
19	Oct. 29, 1987	4.46%	Deficit reduction talks begin; durable goods orders increase; rallies overseas.
20	Nov. 5, 1948	−4.40%	Further reaction to Truman victory over Dewey.
21	Nov. 6, 1946	−4.31%	Profit taking; Republican victories in elections presage deflation.
22	Oct. 7, 1974	4.19%	Hopes that President Ford would announce strong anti-inflationary measures.
23	Nov. 30, 1987	−4.18%	Fear of dollar fall.
24	Jul. 12, 1974	4.08%	Reduction in new loan demands; lower inflation previous month.
25	Oct. 15, 1946	4.01%	Meat prices decontrolled; prospects of other decontrols.
26	Oct. 25, 1982	−4.00%	Disappointment over Federal Reserve's failure to cut discount rates.
27	Nov. 26, 1963	3.98%	Confidence in President Johnson after Kennedy assassination.
28	Nov. 1, 1978	3.97%	Steps by Carter to strengthen dollar.
29	Oct. 22, 1987	−3.92%	Iranian attack on Kuwaiti oil terminal; fall in markets overseas; analysts predict lower prices.
30	Oct. 29, 1974	3.91%	Decline in short-term interest rates; ease in future monetary policy; lower oil prices.
31	Nov. 3, 1982	3.91%	Relief over small Democratic victories in House.
32	Feb. 19, 1946	−3.70%	Fear of wage-price controls lowering corporate profits; labor unrest.
33	Jun. 19, 1950	−3.70%	Korean War continues; fear of long war.
34	Nov. 18, 1974	−3.67%	Increase in unemployment rate; delay in coal contract approval; fear of new mid-East war.
35	Apr. 22, 1980	3.64%	Fall in short-term interest rates; analysts express optimism.

36	Oct. 31, 1946	3.63%	Increase in commodity prices; prospects for price decontrol.
37	Jul. 6, 1955	3.57%	Market optimism triggered by GM stock split.
38	Jun. 4, 1962	−3.55%	Profit taking; continuation of previous week's decline.
39	Aug. 20, 1982	3.54%	Congress passes Reagan tax bill; prime rate falls.
40	Dec. 3, 1987	−3.53%	Computerized selling; November retail sales low.
41	Sep. 19, 1974	3.50%	Treasury Secretary Simon predicts decline in short-term interest rates.
42	Dec. 9, 1946	3.44%	Coal strike ends; railroad freight rate increase.
43	Jun. 29, 1962	3.44%	"...stock prices advanced strongly chiefly because they had gone down so long and so far that a rally was due."
44	Sep. 5, 1946	3.43%	"Replacement buying" after earlier fall.
45	Oct. 30, 1987	3.33%	Dollar stabilizes; increase in prices abroad.
46	Jan. 27, 1975	3.27%	IBM wins appeal of antitrust case; short-term interest rates decline.
47	Oct. 6, 1982	3.27%	Interest rates fall; several large companies announce increase in profits.
48	Jul. 19, 1948	−3.26%	Worry over Russian blockade of Berlin; possibility of more price controls.
49	Nov. 30, 1982	3.23%	"...analysts were at a loss to explain why the Dow jumped so dramatically in the last two hours...."
50	Oct. 24, 1962	3.22%	Khrushchev promises no rash decisions on Cuban Missile Crisis; calls for U.S.-Soviet summit.

Note: The last column is per the *New York Times* financial section or front page.

close and nothing else, one would not expect the opening or closing of the market on Wednesday to have any effect at all on the total price movements between Tuesday and Thursday. The implication of French and Roll's findings is that Wednesday's trading is itself a source of market volatility with lasting effects.

A second type of evidence has been derived from studies that seek to compare stock price movements with movements in fundamental values. Shiller (1981) developed a statistical method of comparing the volatility of stock prices with the volatility of fundamental values, as estimated from a study of the movement of dividend levels. He concluded that the stock market was far more variable than could be reasonably attributed to the observed behavior of dividends. Shiller's work is controversial because of its assumption that valid inferences about the variance of the fundamental value of a company's equity can be drawn from its dividend behavior. Other evidence on this point is, however, more clear-cut.

Consider the example of closed end mutual funds. Since the only asset of a closed end mutual fund is its stock portfolio, which is easily valued, the fundamental value of the fund shares is easily evaluated. Interestingly, closed end funds typically sell for less than the aggregate market value of their underlying assets. Further, these discounts vary widely and inexplicably from fund to fund, in a manner that is extremely hard to square with the theory that stock market prices always reflect fundamental values. Similarly, it is very difficult to see how the extremely rapid fluctuations in the price of shares of companies that are active takeover targets could reflect actual changes in the fundamental value of the company over

169

the course of a few days or weeks, or even the availability of new information that allowed the market to make better estimates of such value.

Practical evidence that stock prices fluctuate more than fundamental values comes from the success of investment strategies that seek to exploit the long-term tendency of the price of individual securities and the market as a whole to return toward fundamental values. The success of noted investor Warren Buffett and of the Value Line trading system is based on the pursuit of an approach of this type. Statistical studies reveal that stocks whose prices are low relative to dividends, earnings, capital assets, or even past prices consistently outperform other securities.

None of the foregoing is intended to suggest that stock prices are entirely unrelated to fundamental values or that they are driven only by speculation. Indeed the evidence suggests that the stock market probably is efficient according to the rather weak definition offered by noted financial economist Fischer Black:

> We might define an efficient market as one in which price is within a factor of two of value, i.e., the price is more than half the value and less than twice the value. By this definition, I think almost all markets are efficient almost all the time. "Almost all" means at least ninety percent.

Variable divergences of price from value obviously suggest the presence of substantial excess volatility in the stock market. We turn next to the question of whether excessively liquid financial markets are responsible.

1.2. Does speculation contribute to excess volatility?

Even if one accepts that stock prices are excessively volatile, it does not necessarily follow that this is due to excessive short-term speculation. Indeed, excessive volatility is often ascribed to *insufficient* short-term speculation. In markets that are demonstrably extremely illiquid, such as those for certain types of art or real estate, prices are observed to be extremely volatile. Volatility arises because sellers cannot find buyers or buyers cannot find sellers except after large price changes. However, it does not follow that once an adequate level of liquidity has been attained, as must have been the case with the stock market many years ago, further increases in liquidity are stabilizing. Indeed, Keynes was at pains to argue that excessive liquidity actually encourages destabilizing speculation.

The evidence reviewed above suggests that a significant part of market volatility reflects "noise trading"—trading on the basis of something other than information about fundamental values. Those who seek to gauge "market psychology" or to guess how the guesses of others will evolve might be labelled as noise traders. Measures discouraging such noise trading should contribute to reductions in volatility and improve the functioning of speculative markets, as Delong, Shleifer, Summers, and Waldmann (1988) have demonstrated. Reductions in noise trading will cause prices to fluctuate less violently about fundamental values, both because there will be less speculative pressure on prices and because speculative pressures will be more easily resisted because risk inherent in irrational noise trader demands will be reduced.

170

In considering the relationship between speculation and volatility, it is helpful to distinguish between two types of speculative strategies. The first type, which might be called "value investing," involves negative feedback. Traders who purchase stocks on the basis of comparisons of stock prices with some relatively stable estimate of fundamental values will normally find themselves selling when prices rise and buying when they fall. This strategy, when pursued by any substantial number of players, will tend to reduce volatility by returning stock prices to the (perceived, stable) fundamental value of the underlying company. Stabilizing negative feedback will also arise when traders rebalance their portfolios, following a risk-reducing strategy of buying and selling equity in order to maintain specified fractions of their assets in the form of equity versus debt, and when they trade against the market on the theory that the market typically initially overreacts to news in either direction.

The second type of trading strategy involves positive feedback. Traders following such a strategy buy when markets rise and sell when they fall. Such positive feedback traders tend to increase volatility. Strategies based upon the slogan "the trend is your friend," the placement of stop-loss orders, and the use of certain complex dynamic hedging strategies to provide "portfolio insurance" all contribute to the destabilization of market prices.

Those following negative feedback trading strategies have no need to trade frequently—portfolio assets are expected to earn abnormally high returns in a manner of months or more likely years, not in days or weeks. On the other hand, frequent trading is the essence of positive feedback trading strategies. Any sort of curbs on short-term speculative trading through reductions in liquidity are, therefore, more likely to discourage positive feedback investing to a greater extent than negative feedback investing and may reduce price volatility.

The theoretical effects of reductions in transactions costs on asset price volatility are ambiguous. However, as an empirical matter the evidence cited earlier regarding the extent of price movements over periods of comparable length when the market is open and when it is closed does suggest the possibility that trading itself may be a source of volatility. This possibility is also highlighted by the events of 1929 and 1987. In both cases, stock prices increased dramatically on very high volume, as investors reinvested their market gains while assuming they could quickly extricate themselves from the market in the event of a decline. In fact, the presumption of universal liquidity proved to be an illusion. In both cases, prices collapsed as traders sought to liquidate their positions quickly. The association between high turnover and volatility is not confined to periods of market breaks. Statistical studies such as Schwert (1988) inevitably find a positive relationship between turnover and volatility, although the direction of causation is far from clear. It is striking that on the American stock market, turnover has increased very substantially because of declining transactions costs over the last several decades, with no concomitant decrease and perhaps a trend increase in volatility.

On balance, this evidence suggests that there is little basis for concern that volatility would increase if short-term trading in financial markets were discouraged, and some basis for concluding that taxes that discouraged turnover might reduce volatility in general and the risk of fluctuations like those in 1987 in particular.

1.3. Are too many resources devoted to financial engineering?

Perhaps the most frequent complaint about current trends in financial markets is that so much talented human capital is devoted to trading paper assets rather than to actually creating wealth. The spectacle of one-fourth of the Yale senior class applying for a job at First Boston generated more than a little comment to this effect. Even after the 1987 crash, financial jobs remain extraordinarily popular among top business school students. This situation is very different from that in Japan, where top graduates vie for positions in large manufacturing companies such as Toyota, and less successful students typically enter the financial services industry.

In many sectors where productivity increases have been far greater than those in the overall economy, for example, in agriculture and manufacturing, the share of employment has declined over time. However, the demand for financial services seems to be so elastic that, as figure 1 demonstrates, the share of American employment in the securities industry has increased sharply over time. Increases in trading volumes have been so dramatic that they have more than offset sharp declines in commission rates and other trading costs, causing the total real transaction costs associated with securities trading to have risen significantly in recent years, as figure 2 indicates. Perhaps James Tobin (1984) is correct in his assessment that "the immense power of the computer is being harnessed to the paper economy not to do the same transactions more efficiently but to balloon the quantity and variety of financial exchanges."

It is striking to contemplate the costs of operating our financial system. Its primary social function is the allocation of capital among corporations. These corporations had a combined income of about $310.4 billion in 1987. The combined receipts of member firms on the New

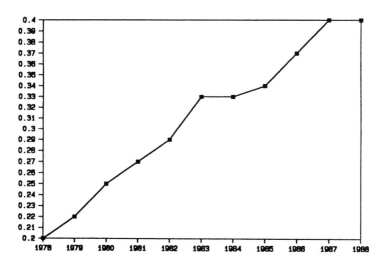

Fig. 1. Securities industry personnel as a percentage of the civilian U.S. labor force, 1978–1987
Source: New York Stock Exchange *Fact Book* (1988).

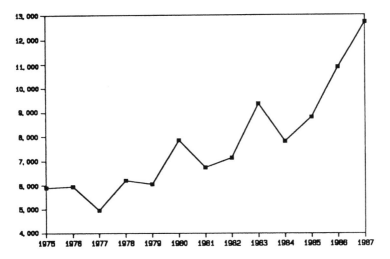

Fig. 2. Income from securities commissions of NYSE member firms (in millions of dollars)
Note: Adjusted to fourth quarter 1987 dollars; commissions for 1987 do not include fourth quarter earnings and are adjusted.
Source: New York Stock Exchange *Fact Book* (1988).

York Stock Exchange in that year was $53 billion. This figure takes no account of the costs borne by individuals and institutions in monitoring their portfolios, acquiring information about securities, or actually making investment decisions. Nor does it take any account of the costs corporations incur in seeking to attract investors in their securities. It is not uncommon for the chief executive officers of major U.S. corporations to spend a week or more each quarter telling their corporate story to security analysts. If we assume that these latter costs are even half as great as direct payments to securities firms, it follows that the cost of operating our securities market was over $75 billion in 1987. This represented one-fourth of total corporate profits, and close to half of corporate net investment.

Is this too much? It is hard not to agree with James Tobin's (1984) judgment that "[w]hat is clear is that very little of the work of the securities industry, as gauged by the volume of market activity, has to do with the financing of real investment in any very direct way." This provides a strong case for reducing the volume of resources flowing into trading activities. Tobin, speaking of the recent proliferation of new financial markets, raises the consideration that "[e]very financial market absorbs private resources to operate and government resources to police. The country cannot afford all the markets that enthusiasts may dream up." It is true that many attempts to start financial markets fail, just as many new casino games fail to catch on. But the fact that the private market test eliminates some markets itself hardly establishes that those that succeed should be able to inflict the costs of regulation on the government.

There is, however, a more fundamental reason for concern about the diversion of human and capital resources into the trading of securities than the costs of additional government regulation or the absolute size of the financial sector. While well-functioning securities

173

markets produce the socially desirable byproducts of sharing risks and allocating capital to high value uses, it is nonetheless true that speculative trading is a zero-sum game in terms of its direct effects. When A buys stock from B, because he has a good tip, or good information, or even a particularly trenchant analysis of the current situation, and the stock subsequently rises sharply he wins a zero-sum game. His gain from trading is exactly matched by B's loss. Individuals each gain from acquiring information and trading on it, but much of the gains come at the expense of others. Therefore, the social gains are much less than the private ones. As Hirschleifer pointed out years ago, in such situations there is likely to be excessive investment in gathering information. Consider the question of how the social return to research directed at gauging track conditions at Churchill Downs compares with the social return to research directed at developing a better mousetrap. What about personally profitable research directed at predicting Carl Icahn's next move, or anticipating GM's earnings announcement hours early, or finding patterns in past stock prices that help to predict future stock prices?

When I stand up at a football game, I see better. When everyone stands up, tall people see better and short people see less well than they did before. Overall, however, the game cannot be viewed any more clearly. The same is largely true when everyone seeks to gather information to guide their trading on the stock market. There is, of course, a potentially important difference between the stock market and the race track. There is no social utility to knowing about track conditions. On the other hand, if individuals gather information and trade on it, stock prices will reflect this information and perhaps contribute to the efficient allocation of capital by moving toward their fundamental values. This may well be an important beneficial effect of long-term investment strategies. It is hard to believe, however, that investments made with a horizon of hours reveal much socially beneficial information to the market place.

A transactions tax is a natural policy for alleviating this market failure. While it would not have much impact on long-term investors who invest on the basis of judgments about the true value of assets, it would have a significant impact in making it less attractive to invest resources in various short-term prediction activities, since the tax cost would increase with the frequency of trading. By encouraging investment research directed at long-term rather than short-term prediction, such a tax might help to solve the conflict noted by Keynes between the privately and socially most desirable investment strategies.

1.4. Does excessive speculation shorten managerial horizons?

In his discussion of the stock market in *The General Theory,* Keynes was at pains to stress that most investors did not focus on gauging long-term fundamentals, but instead concentrated on assessing market psychology and the likely direction of short-run movements in markets. He attributed this to the temperament of those likely to go into money management and to the way in which money managers are evaluated. Keynes stressed the fact, no less true today, that those who are orthodox and wrong are often more richly rewarded than those who are unorthodox and right. Probably the most common complaint of corporate executives about financial markets is that the stock market forces them to take the short rather than the long view. The usual statement of the argument goes something like this. "Portfolio managers are evaluated and hired or fired on the basis of their quarterly performance. They therefore care only about maximizing the performance of their portfolio over the very near term. This makes them focus only on companies' reported earnings and their near-term prospects. As a consequence, managers who are concerned about maximizing their stock price, either in the interests of current shareholders or because they want to avoid being taken over, are forced to slight long-term investment in favor of managing short-term earnings." Treasury Secretary Brady has adopted this position and has stated that changing this situation is his highest priority.

The image created is one of contagious myopia. Those who hire portfolio managers are myopic; therefore, the managers of the companies in which portfolio managers invest are myopic. The argument linking these different forms of myopia is less than transparent, however. For example, shouldn't portfolio managers who are concerned with long-run performance nonetheless hold the assets today the total return on which they think will be highest over the next week or month? Even if it is granted that portfolio managers care only about returns over a short horizon, they nonetheless necessarily must care about the price at which they can unload their stock. This will depend on tomorrow's demand for that stock, which will in turn depend upon tomorrow's expectations about corporate performance thereafter. It should be clear that a holder of corporate stock today who anticipates quickly selling to a sequence of future short-term holders should nonetheless be concerned about his company's profitability over the long term, at least as long as it will exert some influence on its stock market price.

The connection between the horizons of portfolio managers and of corporate managements is a rich subject for future investigation. Here we indicate possible mechanisms through which tax measures that discourage short-term speculative trading might serve to lengthen managerial horizons.

First, if transactions taxes drove irrational investors who do not look beyond quarterly earnings reports out of the market, companies might be more willing to accept reductions in quarterly earnings that reflected investments with long-term payoffs. Firms might take a longer view when their stock price is less sensitive to their current quarterly performance. Further, lengthening portfolio holding periods by discouraging speculation may well induce investors to focus more on fundamental values—on confronting "the dark forces of ignorance," to use Keynes's phrase—rather than on gauging market psychology. To the extent that this change in investment practices was conveyed to corporate managers through their observation of the market treatment of their stock, they might pursue more long-term strategies. Or, perhaps more plausibly, in the different environment that would result if speculation were reduced, different types of managers would be selected to run major companies.

Second, as Lowenstein (1988) and other have argued, transaction taxes that tie shareholders to firms may induce shareholders to take a more active role in monitoring management and insuring that proper planning and investment activities take place. In Albert Hirschman's famous phrase, transactions taxes tend to substitute shareholder "voice" for shareholder "exit." With significant transactions costs, it is possible that dissatisfied shareholders would seek to influence or displace corporate managements rather than simply to buy other companies. The importance of this effect is open to question. Even for relatively large passive investors, the free rider problem is likely to discourage efforts to control managerial behavior.

There is not much empirical evidence beyond abundant anecdotes on the importance of these mechanisms. And the available anecdotes do not always distinguish sharply between the consequences of rapid turnover in financial markets and the rather different issue of takeover threats. It may be relevant that there is a general sense that managers are more myopic in America than they used to be and that stock market turnover has increased dramatically over time. It may also be suggestive that the American stock market has relatively high turnover by world standards and American managers are thought to be more myopic than most.

1.5. Conclusion

The three economic arguments presented in this section support the presumption that it would be desirable to curb short-term speculation if this could be done without adverse side effects. We conclude this section by considering possible economic arguments against transactions taxes. Two stand out. First, such taxes may reduce market liquidity, which may discourage investment and increase the risks borne by the owners of capital. Second, transactions taxes may reduce the supply of funds available for investment by increasing the costs of investment.

We have argued that, beyond a certain point, increased liquidity may have costs that exceed its benefits. Further, as we note below, transactions taxes are in place with respect to most of the world stock markets, and have apparently not reduced liquidity sufficiently to create severe problems. The introduction of even quite substantial transaction taxes would raise trading costs in the American marketplace back only to their levels in the 1950s, 1960s, and early 1970s. Major liquidity problems were not evident at that time. Finally, to some degree, the perceived liquidity of the U.S. market is an illusion. When all investors tried to move in the same direction in October 1987, the tenuous nature of market liquidity became painfully apparent. At this late date, it is fair to throw the challenge back to the supporters of financial innovation. Trading opportunities have multiplied enormously. Whose risks have been reduced relative to those that existed ten years ago? Whose access to capital has been augmented?

The concern is legitimate that transactions taxes, like any tax that falls upon investment income, would discourage investment. A first reponse is that transactions taxes could be matched by reductions in other taxes on corporate income, so that the total tax burden on investment income was not increased. Even if this were not done, a modest transaction tax would not have a major impact on the return to the long-term investors who are the primary suppliers of capital in the U.S. market. A tax of .5 percent on the purchase or sale of stock is not likely to stop an investor with a horizon of several years from investing in the stock market. Certainly any behavioral effects with respect to those investors could be expected to be dwarfed by those caused by, for example, the 1987 increase in the maximum capital gains tax rate from 20 to 28 percent.

2. How would a STET work?

Most other major industrialized countries presently impose some form of STET. As table 2 indicates, such taxes are in place in West Germany, France, Italy, the Netherlands, Sweden, Switzerland, the United Kingdom, and Japan, among other places. These taxes collect a significant amount of revenue. In 1985, revenue collections ranged from .04 percent of gross national product (GNP) in Germany to .48 percent of GNP in Switzerland. This would correspond to a range from about $2 billion to $25 billion in the United States. Similar figures are suggested by the comparisons of STET revenues with total tax revenues and with the market value of outstanding equity.

A brief comparison of the administrative approaches used in other countries suggests that the problems that arise in structuring a STET may be resolved in a number of different ways. The overall lesson to be drawn from international comparisons is that a STET can be made to work in a modern financial economy without insurmountable distortions, and without crippling the national securities industry.

We note here certain aspects of the Japanese and British systems, as well as the former United States documentary stamp tax, imposed until the end of 1965. We then examine in more detail some of the issues raised in creating an administrable STET and potential resolutions of those issues.

Table 2. Transactions taxes and tax revenue

		Tax Revenue as a Percent of		
Country	*Tax*	*Total Revenue*	*GNP*	*Market Value of Equity*
Canada	None	NA	NA	NA
France	0.3% below FFr 1 mill. 0.15% above FFR 1 mil.	0.26%	0.12%	1.19%
Germany	0.25%	0.14%	0.04%	0.28%
Italy	0.15%	1.10%	0.38%	6.10%
Japan	0.18% on dealers 0.55% on individuals	1.42%	0.17%	0.34%
Netherlands	0.5% below Dfl 1200	0.63%	0.32%	1.17%
Sweden	1.0% on sales	0.87%	0.36%	1.55%
Switzerland	0.15% (Swiss issuer) 0.30% (Foreign issuer)	2.33%	0.48%	0.94%
United Kingdom	0.5%	0.80%	0.30%	0.01%
United States	Document and stock transfer tax (State and Local)	0.17%	0.03%	0.08%

Source: Revenues and market capitalizations are for 1985. Transaction tax rates are from Spicer and Oppenheim, *Securities Markets Around the World* (New York: John Wiley & Sons, 1988). Revenue statistics are from OECD, *Revenue Statistics,* various issues. Market values are from Morgan Stanley, *Capital International Perspectives,* various issues.

2.1. The Japanese tax

The Japanese transactions tax is situs-based, falling upon the transfer within Japan of "securities," including both equity and debt instruments. It is imposed upon a base determined by the sale price of the instrument. The rate applicable to the transfer depends upon the nature of the interest transferred; that applicable to debt interests, .03 percent, is one-tenth that applicable to equity interests, .3 percent (reduced from .55 percent in the recent 1988 tax reform). Derivative instruments that are not deemed to fall within the meaning of a "security"—for example, stock index futures—are not subject to the tax. National bonds, as well as privately issued debt securities, are, however, covered.

The tax is collected from the seller by the securities firm making the transfer. Certain transfers of covered securities, including gifts and some corporate mergers, are exempt from the tax. The Japanese securities transfer tax raised 1.7 trillion yen in fiscal year 1987–1988, translating into more than $12 billion.

2.2. The British tax

The present British system of documentary transfer taxes was instituted in 1891. It was drastically revised in 1986 in order to widen the base of transactions that are subject to transfer tax and to lower the rate of tax applicable to many transactions. The original tax ("Stamp Duty") is a documentary stamp tax. It falls upon the issuance or transfer of stampable instruments. These instruments include corporate securities, although in 1988 Stamp Duty ceased to apply to the initial issuance of corporate stock. The 1986 Budget augmented the Stamp Duty by imposing the new "Stamp Duty Reserve Tax" (SDRT). This tax, despite its name, is not a stamp duty at all, but rather a pure transfer tax, designed to fall upon transfers of beneficial ownership of certain rights and securities which in the modern financial system may not be reflected in any "stampable" instruments.

The current British system has several notable features. Unlike the Japanese tax, the rate applicable to all taxed transfers is now the same, .5 percent of value. However, the British tax exempts pure debt securities. Exemptions are also provided for options and futures traded on the Stock Exchange Traded Options Market and the London International Financial Futures Exchange, as well as for government gilt securities, purchases by charities, and bearer securities (although these are subject to a special higher "bearer instrument duty" upon issuance). Securities subject to SDRT include stocks and shares and rights to stocks and shares in a United Kingdom company or in a foreign company that keeps a register in the United Kingdom. Because SDRT applies to transfers of beneficial ownership of chargeable securities, transfers in street name, or between brokerage accounts without changing the street name, are picked up. The tax is imposed upon nonresidents of the United Kingdom if their acquisition of chargeable securities occurs within the United Kingdom, through a broker or an agent there.

The potential to avoid the tax on transfers of beneficial ownership of U.K. chargeable securities by U.K. residents by making such transfers outside the United Kingdom is addressed under British company law. British corporations are in general required to maintain a corporate register of their stock within Britain. Thus, transfers of actual registered stock ownership must occur within Britain in order to be effective, and may therefore be picked up by the tax.

The development of modern financial instruments permitted the avoidance of this constraint, however, by permitting the transfer of beneficial ownership in an enforceable way without the need to transfer actual stock ownership. U.K. securities are transferred into a "depository" or "clearance system," and rights to the underlying stock then traded (outside Britain) through that system. The SDRT legislation dealt with these systems by creating a toll charge, at the rate of three times the normally applicable transfer tax, upon the transfer of chargeable securities into such a depository or clearance system. The subsequent transfer of the depository receipts or beneficial interests within the clearance system outside Britain is then free from SDRT. A similar charge applies upon the issuance of bearer instruments which are of a type which would have been subject to the tax if issued in registered form. These toll charges are intended to serve as a proxy for imposing tax on the unrecorded subsequent transfers of rights to British equity interests which, it was felt, could not be monitored or enforced in Britain.

2.3. The former United States documentary stamp tax

Until 1965, the United States imposed a federal stamp tax on the transfer of certain securities in the United States. The repeal of this tax occurred as a part of the 1965 legislation repealing almost all of the hodge-podge of federal retail and manufacturers' excise taxes which had accumulated over the course of three decades. At that time, the repeal of the tax on securities transfers was estimated to result in revenue loss of approximately $195 million annually (in 1965 dollars). The dollar volume of transactions on the New York Stock Exchange has increased about 20-fold since that time; thus the imposition of an identical tax, ignoring any effects on behavior, could be estimated to collect about $4 billion annually today.

The tax was imposed upon the transfer and issuance of capital stock, shares in mutual funds, certificates of indebtedness, and rights to acquire these interests. Like the current Japanese tax, the rates of tax applicable to different types of interests differed. Interestingly, however, the differences were reversed; the charge on the issuance or transfer of certificates of indebtedness exceeded that on the issuance or transfer of equity.

The tax contained an exemption for state and federal obligations, similar to that contained in the British tax. Foreign stock exchanged in the United States was also not subject to the stamp duty. Perhaps significantly for the current debate over the feasibility and wisdom of such a tax, transfers of U.S. equities that took place entirely outside the United States were exempt from the tax. Certain exemptions also existed for transfers occurring in corporate mergers and consolidations; however, the issuance of new equity instruments in such transactions was in general subject to the tax. Notably, tax-exempt entities were not exempt from paying the stamp tax on their transfers of covered instruments.

2.4. Designing a STET[2]

A number of fundamental questions must be answered regarding the structure of a STET, including:

1. What assets should be subject to the tax?
2. How should transactions by U.S. persons taking place outside the United States be treated? Does the answer differ depending upon the nature of the asset being traded, i.e., whether the asset represents an interest in a U.S. entity? How should transactions by non-U.S. persons taking place within the United States be treated?
3. What, if any, exemptions based upon the identity of the persons transferring or receiving the assets should be permitted? Should any exemptions based upon the nature of the transfer itself be provided?
4. How and by whom should the tax be collected?

2.5. Assets subject to the STET

Perhaps the most important issue involved in the adoption of a STET is the question of what assets should be subject to the tax. Decisions must be made regarding the treatment of debt (as opposed to equity), of bearer instruments, of tax-exempt obligations, and of obligations of the federal government. The economic arguments discussed above suggest that a STET should cover the transfer of marketable securities or their equivalents. By this we mean debt or equity interests in corporations or business enterprises in other forms, debt of governmental entities, rights to acquire title or beneficial ownership to such assets, and other financial assets. None of the considerations raised above suggests the adoption of a tax applicable to every contract for the transfer of other types of assets, such as documents of conveyance for real or personal tangible property or trust instruments. Further, interests in privately held corporations for which there is no ready market could likewise be exempt from the STET.

We see no argument for a blanket exemption from the tax for all debt instruments, though a lower rate for such instruments, such as is imposed under the Japanese transfer tax, may be appropriate because of the tremendous volume of trading in fixed income markets. A complete exemption for debt would merely exacerbate the existing problems under the income tax in distinguishing debt from equity interests. Further, an exemption for debt, even if it could be easily administered, would create additional distortions of capital structure in favor of debt financing. Although the use of a lower rate of tax with respect to debt instruments might arguably lead to these distortions as well, albeit to a lesser extent, the purpose of such a lower rate is actually to equalize the economic effects of the tax with respect to debt and equity, because of the much greater trading frequency and shorter average maturity of debt. A sliding scale for different forms of debt could theoretically be introduced to take more specific account of these differences, like the scale that was used for this purpose between differing maturities of debt under the former U.S. Interest Equalization Tax.

To some degree the omission of a blanket exemption for debt merely pushes back to another level the decision as to what instruments should be covered by the tax. If debt securities are to be covered in at least some forms, the issue arises as to which loan contracts will fall within the ambit of the tax. For example, should the issuance of a promissory note be taxable? What features of a bank loan for a corporate acquisition would distinguish it from corporate bonds in a way sufficiently significant to draw an administrable line? The issue of what debt should be chargeable is a very real one; this question was addressed repeatedly by the courts, including the Supreme Court, in the administration of the old U.S. documentary stamp tax. Then, the question was answered largely by reference to the degree and ease of marketability of the instrument in question. Such distinctions are neither impossible to make, nor unique to the transfer tax issue; distinctions between "securities" and nonsecurity debt contracts are formally drawn in both the income tax and the securities laws. For the purposes suggested here, a marketability test would be appropriate. However, it should be noted that this approach under the old U.S. documentary stamp tax led to a distortionary pattern of avoidance of the tax by the use of private financings through banks or other lenders in circumstances where debentures would otherwise have been used.

If readily marketable debt is in general to be covered by the STET, the question of whether government debt should be exempt must be addressed. The old U.S. tax exempted federal, state, and municipal obligations. Similarly, the British system exempts transfers of government debt obligations. The Japanese, however, do impose their transfer tax upon national bonds. The distortionary effects of allowing an exemption for government obligations are probably much lower than those involved in the decision whether to exempt all "pure" debt from the reach of the tax. Such an exemption would, however, significantly reduce the revenue raised by the tax and might make the cost of capital to corporations somewhat higher than if the tax were imposed upon government bonds as well as privately issued debt. Further, speculation in government obligations and government-backed obligations is probably at least as serious a problem (on the arguments presented in this article) as that with respect to privately issued instruments.

It is clearly desirable to impose the tax upon rights to acquire or to control, currently or in the future, assets that are themselves subject to the tax. Failure to do so could lead to avoidance of the transfer tax by the use of economically equivalent derivative securities. However, the taxation of the transfers of options, futures, and other derivative financial assets does introduce considerable complexity. In particular, if the STET is to be imposed on an ad valorem basis, the value of the right to acquire the asset must itself be valued. The decision whether, and how, to apply such a value-based tax in the case of various derivative securities is not at all straightforward. As we have seen, traded financial futures and options are exempt from the U.K. transactions tax, and the Japanese exempt derivatives such as stock index futures. In examining the issue, however, it is important to distinguish between arguments that such an application of the tax would be feasible and arguments that domestic financial business in these sectors would be harmed by imposing such a tax. The latter issue is discussed below.

In the case of commodity and currency futures, the question arises whether the transfer of such rights should be subject to the STET when a contract for the transfer of the underlying tangible asset itself would not be subject to the transfer tax contemplated here.

181

Perhaps a rule could be drawn that distinguished rights with respect to which delivery of the commodity itself may be taken or required and those more purely financial assets with respect to which the underlying asset is not deliverable. Further, the fact that such futures are used as hedging devices against changes in values or exchange rates with respect to assets used in or produced by the nonfinancial sector raises the possibility that the imposition of a transactions tax curbing such hedging could create undesirable distortions in sectors other than the capital markets. Finally, enforceability issues, discussed below, arise where there is no intrinsic connection between the market and the United States; such financial futures may be traded as easily worldwide as in the United States.

2.6. Issues raised by international markets

The global marketplace raises several issues that must be addressed in the creation of a workable STET. First is the possibility that such a tax would harm the competitiveness of the U.S. financial industry, both with respect to trades and investments by U.S. persons and by foreigners. Second is the question of whether trades occurring "outside" the United States but involving U.S. persons should be taxed. Finally, the mechanism for and feasibility of enforcing the tax in the context of trades occurring outside the U.S. markets must be resolved.

Perhaps the principal objection raised to a STET by its opponents is that such a tax would cripple the United States securities industry by driving much of the activity of the U.S. financial markets offshore. We tentatively conclude that fears regarding a drastic reduction in the size of the U.S. securities industry are unwarranted. As the significant revenue collections realized from similar taxes in many other countries attest, such a tax can actually be enforced without resulting in the elimination of national stock markets. Trading in derivative securities and commodities may, however, pose a greater problem in this regard. Evidence for this may be found in the exemption from transfer tax of certain of such products in both the United Kingdom and Japan, as well as, for example, the downfall of the small Sweden Options and Futures Exchange, attributed by some to the Swedish government's decision to increase turnover taxes on options transactions. The imposition of a significant STET would clearly exert market pressure to move trading beyond its reach; the question, which has not yet been definitively answered, is whether such a tendency would be sufficiently great to prevent the tax from raising significant revenue or to harm U.S. competitiveness in financial services.

At least two possible approaches to this problem present themselves. First, and perhaps most ambitious, harmonization of the STET structure and enforcement among the financial center countries would minimize the potential gains from shifting trading to those nations. Of course, the possibility would remain for tax-haven countries to provide sanctuary in this case as well as in the case of direct taxes. Second, the STET could be imposed upon transactions occurring outside the United States but involving U.S. persons as principals, on a residency, rather than a situs, basis. This would minimize the advantages of such offshore trading. Conversely, with respect to the competitiveness of the U.S. markets for foreign participants, transactions by foreigners within the United States could be partially or wholly exempted.

As a theoretical matter, we conclude that the STET should be imposed upon any transaction involving a U.S. beneficial owner, regardless of the location of the transaction. Such an approach, if it were administratively feasible, would minimize the attractiveness of offshore trading of U.S. assets by such persons and would increase the revenue raised by the tax. Avoiding a shift to offshore trading of U.S. assets is important for reasons other than protecting the competitiveness of the U.S. securities industry. One of the goals of imposing a STET is to curb speculative trading, through the imposition of an extra marginal cost on each trade. This goal clearly would not be achieved merely by moving the location of such trades. Furthermore, the United States has additional interests in regulating the markets for domestic assets and their derivatives, which would be undermined if those markets moved beyond U.S. jurisdiction to a greater extent than they already have.

Several considerations support the view that trades in non-U.S. assets by U.S. persons should also be taxed, whether here or abroad. First, of course, is the revenue issue. Second, in interlinked markets the United States may be concerned with excess volatility not only of the U.S. stock market but of world markets; excessive speculation by U.S. persons in those markets may contribute significantly to such volatility. The connections between the world's markets were made dramatically apparent during the events of October 19, 1987. Finally, the definition of a "U.S. asset" would add an additional layer of complexity to the STET system. For example, should publicly traded debentures of a wholly owned foreign subsidiary of a U.S. corporation be considered different for this purpose from similar debentures of a domestic subsidiary doing business abroad?

Nonetheless, such taxation of foreign assets would be a departure from past U.S. practice, as well as that of most other established STET systems. Furthermore, inclusion of foreign transfers of assets, especially in the case of non-U.S. assets, is likely in some cases to subject such transfers to a double STET, that of the United States and of the country where the trade takes place. This could be addressed through a treaty or credit system, or, alternatively, that result could be allowed. Double taxation of offshore trading would certainly serve as an additional disincentive to moving parts of the U.S. securities industry out of the United States.

It would be possible to exempt from the tax either or both the transfer of U.S. assets or foreign assets on U.S. markets by foreign persons; this approach would minimize the anti-competitive nature of the STET with respect to the use of the United States as a world financial center. We conclude, however, that the registration of foreign stock or debt on U.S. markets or the use of U.S. markets or brokers by foreign persons should subject trades in such assets or by such persons to the STET. The STET is not an inappropriate price to pay for access to the U.S. markets. Furthermore, the fact that a speculative trader has his tax residency outside the United States will not serve to limit the destabilizing effect of his frequent trades which (as argued above) increase U.S. market volatility. Finally, providing exemptions for foreign assets or trades by non-U.S. persons through U.S. markets or brokers would merely complicate further the already complex administrative issues surrounding the imposition and enforcement of a new STET.

While a tax structured as just outlined would be theoretically preferable, such a structure does raise a number of issues that would have to be resolved to implement the tax. These international considerations can be dealt with in several ways. First, any transfer made through a U.S. broker, regardless of the identity of the principal or the nature of the asset, could be collected in the normal course, as described in the following section. This method would not, however, pick up transfers effected through foreign affiliates of U.S. brokers. Second, the tax on any transfer of equity recorded on a register kept in the United States (whether the principal register or a duplicate) could be enforced by prohibiting the transfer agent from effecting a change in registration without evidence of payment of the tax.

The transfer of beneficial interests on behalf of U.S. persons by non-U.S. brokers, agents, or clearance services without transfer of registration of legal title to the actual assets does raise significant enforcement problems. These transactions would probably have to be subject to voluntary reporting. Capital gains realized by U.S. persons on transactions occurring outside the United States is required now in the income tax context. It is no less likely that the STET would be reported and paid as that the income tax on such gains would be paid. While a certain amount of avoidance will be inevitable, large institutional investors, in particular, are probably unlikely to fail intentionally to report legally taxable transactions. (Although tax-exempt investors such as pension funds are not now subject to capital gains taxes on these or most other market transactions, pension funds are required to file certain annual reports which could be expanded to include reporting regarding the STET.)

The spectre of offshore mutual funds organized to trade on behalf of U.S. persons in foreign assets raises the prospect of avoidance, since the non-U.S. entity itself would be conducting the trading. A very similar problem was addressed in the income tax area with the 1986 creation of the so-called "Passive Foreign Investment Company" (or "PFIC") rules. These rules alone may have been enough to restrict the use of such offshore funds by U.S. investors who are aware of them. However, a similar system of rules in the case of the STET could be used. Such a scheme would impose a very high tax on the investor upon the receipt of distributions from the fund or on liquidation of his interest, which would serve as a proxy for the foregone STET which should have been incurred by the U.S. investor during the period in which he held the fund. In order to avoid this penalty tax, the investor would have to make current periodic payments in lieu of a direct STET, based upon accounting by the fund to the investors regarding the volume of its trading on world markets.

2.7. Nature of the domestic transfers and persons to which the STET should apply

There are several obvious possibilities for exemption from the STET, including transfers of taxable assets by gift, bequest or inheritance, charitable donations, transfers in transactions that are free from federal income tax, and transfers by tax-exempt entities.

It could be argued that an exemption for transfers by gift or bequest would probably create little distortion and that the taxation of gifts and bequests would in any event likely do little to reduce speculative trading. The administration of the tax would be rendered more complicated by the creation of such an exemption, however. Furthermore, there seems to be little reason to exempt such transfers in a tax environment that has seen the simultaneous creation of record federal budget deficits and the virtual evisceration of the federal estate and gift tax.

An exemption for charitable donations could be included as a policy matter. Such an exemption would probably be best implemented through a system under which the donor claimed a credit on its federal income tax return.

An argument may be made that where stock or securities are issued or transferred on a tax-free basis in a nontaxable corporate acquisition or merger, the transfer tax should not apply. However, the logic of the income tax exemption does not necessarily apply to the STET. The tax-free reorganization provisions are premised upon the view that the beneficial interest of the participants in the corporate enterprise has merely changed form in such a transaction, and that the transaction is not, therefore, an appropriate moment to impose a tax upon the increase in value of the beneficial interests in the enterprise. The argument for the imposition of the STET is different, however. In that case the acquisition of interests, and not merely the disposition of interests, is the event giving rise to imposition of the tax. In a tax-free transaction, the shareholders may have retained a requisite interest in their former assets, but they have typically obtained as well a beneficial interest in a different enterprise. Thus, such corporate reorganizations would be an appropriate time for the imposition of the STET.

Exemptions should be provided, however, for the transfer of securities in certain transactions that constitute mere changes in place of organization, identity, or form, and for corporate recapitalizations to the extent that the value of the entity after the recapitalization does not exceed that preceding it. These specific exemptions were included in the old U.S. documentary stamp tax. Exemptions should also be made for certain other transfers, including, for example: (1) transfers of title only, in which the beneficial ownership of the asset remains the same (for example, in the case of a transfer to a grantor trust); (2) transfers through fiduciaries or nominees where a single beneficial transfer occurs, but using multiple steps, for example, to a broker for sale or to the executor of a decedent's estate for subsequent (taxable) transfer to the beneficiaries; and (3) transfers of title or possession only where the asset is transferred for security for a loan. In many cases, these exemptions, like those for charitable donations, would be most easily administered through a credit system, rather than forcing the collecting agents, discussed below, to make distinctions in each case.

One of the key questions raised by a STET is its application to tax-exempt participants in the market. The general rule should be that the tax-exempt status of the transferor or transferee is of no consequence for the imposition of the STET. It might well be argued that the discouragement of short-term, speculative trading is most important for these very investors, since tax-exempt pension funds and other institutions account for a tremendous portion of the volume of trading in the market and thus contribute significantly (on the theory expressed here) to excess volatility. Second, such a tax could serve as an additional regulatory mechanism in the fiduciary context, analogous to the long-standing "short-short rule." This is a provision designed to protect small investors from speculation, which limits certain tax benefits for mutual funds that churn their portfolios too rapidly. If this rule is a sensible one for the protection of the small investor, then imposing the less draconian disincentive of the STET in the case of the retirement funds of workers should likewise be viewed as beneficial. While certain common law and statutory doctrines already govern the investment decisions of pension fund managers, the STET would create additional incentives in the appropriate direction.

Finally, the application of the tax in the case of mutual funds must be addressed. As noted, such entities are already subject to certain tax restrictions that depend upon the frequency of their trades. We conclude that transactions by mutual funds should be subject to the STET in the normal manner. A reduced rate of tax could be applied to transfers of the stock of domestic mutual funds in order to reduce the double taxation effect.

2.8. Collection of and liability for the STET

The two keys to effectively implementing and enforcing a STET are simplicity of record keeping and centralized collection. In the current electronic age, a collection mechanism that relied on documentary stamps would be hopelessly unwieldy. Instead, a system like that used for transactions on national exchanges under the old U.S. documentary stamp tax should be utilized for the administration of a new STET. All registered brokers effecting transactions subject to the tax would serve as the agents of collection of the tax. This would also apply in the case of transfers by brokerage houses of stock held in street name from one account to another. The proper implementation of the tax in these cases could be enforced, in part, through the mechanism of Securities and Exchange Commission (SEC) audits. Brokers now collect a small SEC transaction tax on every sale of shares, so that the requirement of accounting for and withholding an additional more significant tax should not prove unduly burdensome, as long as the tax is imposed upon transactions that are well defined by law, with values that are easily discernible by the brokers.

Further, exemptions from the tax, as outlined above, should as a general rule be implemented by a means of system under which the principal in the transaction would be responsible for claiming a credit on its federal tax return (or by means of a form filed with its information reporting return or separately, in the case of tax-exempt entities), rather than requiring the agent to determine whether an exemption applied.

In order to centralize further the administration of the tax, the tax on transfers taking place on a national or regional exchange should be collected through the exchange itself. This system has been followed in the administration of the British SDRT.

The tax on transactions effected directly with the issuer of the transferred instrument should be collected by the issuer itself. Collection of the tax on transactions effecting a change in registered owner between nonissuing persons without the services of a broker could be enforced by requiring the transfer agent to refuse transfer without evidence of payment of the tax, or by the direct collection of the tax by the transfer agent.

Domestic taxable transactions occurring outside the ambit of any of the foregoing situations would be subject to voluntary reporting, but would be relatively small in terms of economic effect. Reporting and remittance could be accomplished in such circumstances by a form accompanying the annual federal income tax return.

2.9. Is it too late?

Although this discussion has only touched on some of the administrative problems and issues raised by a STET, it is clear from the implementation of such taxes in other countries that the imposition of such a tax on at least a significant volume of securities transactions is feasible. However, it must be acknowledged that there is some trend toward the abolition of existing transfer taxes elsewhere.

Britain in 1988 abolished its capital duties on the original issuance of securities, as mentioned above, although not its transfer taxes. In 1986, the rate of its transfer taxes was reduced (simultaneously, however, with the introduction of the broader based SDRT). As previously noted, Japan has recently reduced the rate of its transfer taxes on equity. Perhaps most interestingly, a proposed EEC directive issued in mid-1987 calls for the abolition of all transfer taxes in the European Community in connection with the economic unification of Europe, although the fate of this proposal is as yet unclear. It was made after a decade of discussion and study regarding the harmonization of all of the transfer taxes of the EEC member states, a task ultimately determined to be extremely difficult, if not impossible. Clearly, this conclusion does not bode well for the feasibility of the suggestion that the U.S. STET should be harmonized with other nations' existing taxes.

To some extent, then, the imposition of a transfer tax at this point might be viewed as bucking the world trend. However, it is quite possible that the introduction of such a tax here would have some effect upon the actions of other countries. The forces leading to the support for a STET in the United States—revenue needs and a concern with excessive speculation—are also concerns in other major financial center nations. A harmonized system among these countries would greatly reduce the potential for offshore flight of trading activities and lessen market competition issues, as well as providing a relatively administrable source of revenue. There is at least a prospect that if a STET were imposed in New York, the rush of other financial centers to reduce their taxes would be slowed or reversed.

3. Conclusions

The analysis in this article suggests that some form of securities transactions tax would have the desirable economic effects of curbing speculation and of raising a significant amount of revenue. The revenue potential would depend on just how the STET was designed and administered. But a conservative estimate based on a .5 percent rate, with only a small allowance for revenues collected from assets other than corporate stocks, would suggest that $10 billion could be raised annually.

In considering the desirability of the STET as a revenue source, it is important to recall that most other tax measures are universally agreed among economists to have adverse effects on incentives to work and save. Even if a STET were to have no beneficial effects on the stock market, it would therefore be a more efficient source of revenue than most alternatives. Furthermore, since its ultimate incidence would fall on the holders of corporate stock, it would be highly progressive as well.

Notes

1. For general discussions of the theoretical validity of the efficient markets hypothesis, see Shiller (1984), Kyle (1985), Black (1986), Summers (1986), and De Long, Shleifer, Summers, and Waldmann (1988).

2. This section draws heavily on the "Staff Memorandum on the Imposition of a Security Transactions Tax," Joint Committee on Taxation (1987).

References

A Guide to Japanese Taxes, 1988.

Black, Fischer, "Noise." *Journal of Finance* (1986), 529–543.

Butterworth's UK Tax Guide 1987–88, 6th ed. London, 1987.

Cutler, David M., Poterba, James M. and Summers, Lawrence H. "What Moves Stock Prices?" *Journal of Portfolio Management* (1989, forthcoming).

DeLong, J. Bradford, Shleifer, Andrei, Summers, Lawrence H. and Waldmann, Robert J. "The Economic Consequences of Noise Traders." Harvard mimeo, 1988.

Fama, Eugene and French, Kenneth. "Permanent and Transitory Components of Stock Prices." *Journal of Political Economy* (1988), 246–273.

French, Kenneth and Roll, Richard. "Stock Return Variances: The Arrival of Information and the Reaction of Traders." *Journal of Financial Economics* (1987), 5–26.

Jensen, Michael C. "Symposium on Some Anomalous Evidence Regarding Market Efficiency." *Journal of Financial Economics* 6 (June/September 1978), 95–101.

Joint Committee on Taxation. "Staff Memorandum on the Imposition of Security Transaction Taxes." Washington, D.C.: U.S. Government Printing Office, 1987.

Keynes, John Maynard. *The General Theory of Employment, Interest, and Money.* New York: Harcourt Brace, 1936.

Kyle, Pete. "Continuous Auctions and Insider Trading." *Econometrica* (1985), 1315–1336.

New York Stock Exchange. *Fact Book.* 1988.

Roll, Richard. "Orange Juice and Weather." *American Economic Review* (1984), 861–880.

——————. "R-Squared." *Journal of Finance* (1988).

Poterba, James M. and Summers, Lawrence H. "Mean Reversion in Stock Prices: Evidence and Implications." *Journal of Financial Economics* (1988).

Scott, Thomas and Mehta, Nik. "The U.K.'s New Tax on Securities." *International Financial Law Review*(December 1986).

Shiller, Robert. "Do Stock Prices Move Too Much to be Justified by Subsequent Dividends?" *American Economic Review* (1981), 421–436.

——————. "Stock Prices and Social Dynamics." *Brookings Papers on Economic Activity* 2 (1984), 457–498.

Summers, Lawrence H. "Does the Stock Market Rationally Reflect Fundamental Values?" *Journal of Finance*(1986), 591–601.

Tobin, James. "On the Efficiency of the Financial System." *Lloyds Bank Review* (July 1984).

——————. "A Proposal for International Monetary Reform." *Eastern Economic Review* (1978), 153–159.

Journal of Financial Services Research, 3: 287–301 (1989)
© 1989 Kluwer Academic Publishers

Initial Margin Requirements and Stock Returns Volatility: Another Look

PAUL H. KUPIEC
Board of Governors of the Federal Reserve System
Division of Research and Statistics
Capital Markets Section
Stop 92
Washington, D.C. 20551

Abstract

This article investigates the relationship between initial margin requirements and stock return volatility. Volatility is measured using a GARCH in Mean model. We find no evidence of an empirical relationship between margin requirements and the volatility of the S&P 500 index portfolio's excess returns. Evidence from short-sale data, and model sensitivity analysis are presented which support the hypothesis of no margin-volatility relationship. The results are consistent with the intertemporal CAPM model of Merton (1973) with an aggregate relative risk aversion measure of 4.1. In addition, we find evidence of long-term memory in conditional return distributions' volatility.

Since the October 1987 market break, the adequacy of initial margin requirements in cash and derivative markets has been studied intensively. To date, the consensus view is that, for prudential concerns, "margin requirements provide an adequate level of protection to the financial system, although they do not cover all possible price movements."[1] Although there is some consensus on the issue of prudential adequacy, researchers disagree about the effects of margins on the demand for, and return characteristics of, risky financial assets. In particular, recent studies by Hardouvelis (1988a, 1988b) purport to show that an economically and statistically significant negative relationship exists between the level of initial margin requirements and the volatility of NYSE stock returns. This result is new and controversial.

The economic intuition behind the hypothesized negative relationship is that initial margin requirements constrain the trading of so-called "de-stabilizing speculators," whose trading activity creates excess volatility. These agents behave like the "noise traders" of Delong, Schleifer, Summers, and Waldman (1987). They form expectations based on nonfundamental information, and these nonfundamental factors affect equilibrium prices.

The analysis and conclusions of this article are those of the author and do not indicate concurrence by other members of the research staff, by the Board of Governors, or by the Federal Reserve Banks.

I am indebted to Pat White, Mark Warshawsky, Martha Scanlon, Pat Parkinson, Doug Pearce, Jim Nason, Jean Helwege, Matt Gelfand, Mark French, Dietrich Earnhart, Frank Diebold, Lee Crabbe, and especially Jim O'Brien for their insights and criticism. Thanks to Gikas Hardouvelis for making available his data.

The influence of the noise traders increases the average return variance on risky assets, causing risky assets to exhibit excess volatility over that which is justified by economic factors.[2] The lower are initial margins, the greater are noise traders' abilities to leverage their positions and create "non-fundamental" volatility. This trading behavior will be evidenced by "pyramiding" and "depyramiding." Pyramiding occurs as noise traders' demands cause a stock's price to rise. These gains allow noise traders to borrow and invest even more in these stocks as the equity in their accounts increases. "Depyramiding," the converse or downside of the this process, is initiated when noise traders' preferences switch to different securities. The higher initial margins are, the smaller the leverage is in noise traders' positions and the smaller the excess volatility they may generate.

Counter to the noise trader argument, theoretical models exist that predict a positive relationship between margin requirements and stock returns volatility. For example, Goldberg (1985) uses Miller's (1977) "Debt and Taxes" model to establish such a relationship. If the Federal Reserve increases margin requirements, firms have the incentive to increase financial leverage to offset investors' decreased leverage abilities. Tax incentives encourage a new equilibrium where firms have higher debt, individuals have lower margin debt, and aggregate stock returns exhibit higher volatility due to increased corporate leverage. Similarly, decreases in margin requirements lead to lower corporate leverage and stock return volatility.

Aside from the Hardouvelis study, little empirical evidence supports the hypothesis of an important relationship between the level of margin requirements and stock prices or returns volatility. Moore (1966) finds a negative correlation between total margin credit and the level of stock prices. This evidence is counter to the hypothesis that low margins encourage destabilizing speculation and is consistent with the predictions of Goldberg's model. Because initial margin levels and margin credit are negatively correlated, the Moore results suggest that increasing margins may increase volatility by damping the demands of traders who are, on average, a stabilizing force.[3] Moore also directly examines the margin-volatility relationship. He finds no measurable effect of initial margins on return volatility.

Largay and West (1973) study the effects of initial margin requirement changes on stock prices. Using an event test methodology, they examine S&P 500 daily returns for abnormal performance around 19 margin change announcement dates. They find that announcements of margin increases are associated with only slightly negative abnormal returns, whereas announcements of margin decreases are not associated with any measurable abnormal performance. They conclude " . . . that although our findings, in contrast with Moore's, indicate that margin policy appears to have an identifiable effect on the behavior of the stock market, this effect is so modest that it can hardly be regarded as more than trivial!"[4]

Ferris and Chance (1988) study the effects of the 19 initial margin changes enacted by the Federal Reserve Board since 1945 on S&P 500 returns' volatility. Their findings do not support the existence of a negative margin-volatility relationship. In fact, Ferris and Chance find weak evidence of a positive relationship between initial margin changes and cash market volatility.

Hartzmark (1986) studies the effects of margins on volatility in the futures market. In the Hartzmark model, margins can affect volatility by changing the composition of traders in the market. If traders have different information sets, different abilities to filter and interpret information, and prices are noisy signals of private information, then the volatility of futures prices depends on the composition of traders transacting in the market. If changes in margin requirements impose disparate costs on traders, margin requirement changes can alter volatility. The magnitude and sign of the volatility effects are not determined by the theoretical model since the effects depend on which trader groups enter and exit the market as margins are changed. Empirically, Hartzmark finds no relationship between margin changes and price volatility.

Largay (1973) and Eckardt and Rogoff (1976) study the effects of special exchanged-imposed margins on individual issues.[5] They find evidence that trading volume and the rate of price appreciation are moderated by the imposition of the special margin requirements (typically at 100 percent).

Despite the mixed evidence of earlier studies, based on his results, Hardouvelis makes far-reaching conclusions:

> At a minimum, the evidence shows that the presence of margins contributes to a more stable market ... The evidence from the cash market experience with different margin requirements over the last 50 years should be taken into account in assessing the adequacy of margins in derivative equity instruments (Hardouvelis, 1988a, p. 89).

This article re-examines the evidence on the existence of a margin volatility relationship. Our critical result is that when volatility is more appropriately measured, there is no statistically significant relationship between initial margin requirements and S&P 500 returns volatility.

The hypothesized margin-volatility relationship is investigated using the GARCH[6] in Mean (GARCH-M) specification of Bollerslev, Engle, and Wooldridge (1988). Our volatility specification and empirical approach are substantially different from that used in Hardouvelis and earlier studies. The GARCH-M specification is consistent with the equilibrium asset pricing model of Merton (1973) and capable of mimicking observed statistical characteristics of stock returns data.[7] The GARCH-M model allows for a time-varying risk premium and long-term memory in the variance of the conditional return distributions. To strengthen support for our conclusions, we present further evidence—derived using both the Hardouvelis volatility measure and data, and data on NYSE customer odd-lot short sales—that indicates that no margin-volatility relationship exists.

An outline of the article follows. After reviewing the approach in Hardouvelis, we discuss the potential sample biases inherit in the data and their impact on the statistical results. We present the GARCH in Mean alternative specification and estimation results. Following the GARCH analysis, we use the Hardouvelis volatility specification and data to provide further evidence against the existence of a measurable margin-volatility relationship. We also analyze short sale data for empirical support of the hypothesis. A final section concludes the article.

1. The Hardouvelis model

To test the margin-volatility hypothesis, Hardouvelis regresses a measure of volatility on lagged volatility, initial margins and some exogenous variables used to capture fundamental risk, financial leverage, and any statistical relationship generated by Federal Reserve policy. The measure of volatility used is a simple 12-month moving sample standard deviation of monthly stock returns. As a result of this measure, all independent variables are measured in 12-month moving average form.[8] Hardouvelis reports results from two sample periods, December 1931 to December 1987, and October 1935 to December 1987.

The study's specification is not consistent with any equilibrium asset return model. It assumes that expected stock returns are constant while concurrently measuring and "explaining" a time-varying variance. Despite the model's deficiencies, the Hardouvelis findings are important because they represent the most extensive (to date) empirical analysis of the margin-volatility relationship.

1.1. Importance of the sample period

The sample time period over which the model is estimated is critically important. Initial margins were not regulated by the Federal Reserve until November 15, 1934. Before that time, initial margins were set independently by the brokerage industry. Concurrent with the introduction of margin regulation in the Securities Exchange Act of 1934 were other major institutional changes, including the establishment of the Securities and Exchange Commission to provide federal oversight over securities trading. Other aspects of the Securities Exchange Act complicate the analysis because their introduction may have had independent effects on the markets' return volatility. To overcome this problem, the model should be estimated over a time period after the Securities Exchange Act of 1934 was introduced.

In addition to the complications associated with the Securities and Exchange Act of 1934, the entire decade of the 1930s exhibits return volatility characteristics that may be influential in determining the reported margin results. Officer (1973) and Schwert (1988) have shown that stock returns exhibit uncharacteristicly large return volatility in the 1930s. Because margin requirements were historically low during this period (less than 55 percent), the significance of the negative margin-volatility relationship may be partially a result of this period.[9]

A second issue we consider is the influence of the October 1987 market break period. The extreme stock market volatility associated with this period is not characteristic of the earlier sample period in the 1980s. It is possible that the market break period alone could be influential in determining the size and significance of the margin effect reported by Hardouvelis. Because the market break itself is not associated with any immediate regulatory change in initial margin requirements on stocks or index futures, nor is it readily explainable by the economic factors related to volatility in earlier periods, the extreme volatility of this period is reasonably considered an "outlier" from the model.

Other issues concerning model stability more directly involve financial market structural change. The introduction of index futures on the Kansas City Board of trade in February 1982 is a structural change that complicates the analysis of the volatility impacts of initial margins in the cash equity market. By trading index futures, investors can establish leveraged positions with far lower initial margin requirements than in the cash market. This innovation in financial markets almost certainly had some impact on any relationship that existed between initial margins and volatility in the cash market.

2. An alternative model of volatility

Although the simplicity of measuring volatility by a 12-month moving standard deviation estimate is appealing, it is not appropriate. It is well known that spurious correlations can be created by measuring variables in moving average form.[10] In addition, stock returns exhibit high kurtosis and conditional variances that are time dependent with autocorrelated and moving average components. Under these conditions, a simple 12-month moving standard deviation is not an appropriate measure of return volatility.

In addition to statistical considerations, an empirical model of market volatility should include the salient features of an equilibrium model of asset returns. The statistical model of returns should allow the conditional expected excess-return (in excess of the risk free rate) to be linearly related to conditional nondiversifiable risk.

Both the statistical and the economic considerations can be addressed in the framework of the Generalized Autoregressive Conditional Heteroskedasticity in Mean model (GARCH-M) of Bollerslev, Engle, and Wooldridge (1988). This specification allows the conditional variance to be a time-dependent process and, in addition, allows the conditional variance to affect the mean of the series. The GARCH variance specification allows the variance estimate to adapt to the extreme volatility of the 1930s and to the effects of the introduction of index futures. Although it is possible that the GARCH variance parameter estimates are sensitive to these sample considerations, because the conditional variance is dynamic, this model is less likely to estimate a margin-volatility relationship that is spurious.[11] The GARCH in Mean model specification follows:

$$r_t = E(r_t/\Omega_t) + e_t$$
$$E(r_t/\Omega_t) = \alpha_0 + H_t\gamma$$
$$E(e_t/\Omega_t) = 0$$
$$E(e_t^2/\Omega_t) = H_t$$
$$H_t = v_0 + \sum_{i=1}^{P} \zeta_i \, e_{t-i}^2 + \sum_{j=1}^{Q} \zeta_j H_{t-j} + \sum_{k=1}^{K} \beta_k X_{kt}$$

Where, $E(r_t/I_t)$ denotes the expectation of r_t conditional on the information I_t.

r_t is the excess return (market return less the risk free rate) over period t (time t to $t+1$).

Ω_t is the information set available at time t.

H_t is the conditional variance of the excess return at time t.

γ is the risk premium per unit of H_t risk.

X_{kt} is the kth exogenous source of volatility at time t.

P is the order of the ARCH lag and Q is the maximum number of lagged conditional variance terms included in the GARCH-M (P, Q) model.

In the GARCH-M model, although the conditional distribution of r_t is normal, the unconditional distribution is not. The unconditional distribution of r_t can exhibit high kurtosis, and its conditional variance can exhibit long-term memory depending on the parameters values of the conditional variance function, H_t.[12] If $\alpha_0 = 0$, this specification is consistent with the equilibrium asset pricing model of Merton (1973, 1980).[13] In the Merton model, the expected market risk premium is proportional to the conditional variance of the market return. The constant of proportionality, γ, can be interpreted as a measure of the aggregate relative risk aversion.

3. GARCH in Mean estimation results

The data are the monthly returns on the S&P 500 index less the return on one-month T-Bills. The models are estimated over the sample period of January 1935 to September 1987. The exogenous sources of volatility considered are the lagged level of the S&P 500 index and the level of required initial margins.[14] The lagged level of the S&P 500 is included to capture the leverage effects on volatility (Christie, 1982) and any spurious correlation that may be generated by Federal Reserve margin policy.[15]

To determine the appropriate GARCH structure for the variance function, H_t, three specifications were compared. Table 1 reports the maximum likelihood estimation results and model selection criterion for an GARCH-M(12,0) model, a GARCH-M(1,1) model, and a GARCH-M(2,1) model.[16,17] A restricted version of the GARCH-M(12,0) model corresponds to the model of volatility used by Hardouvelis.[18] The results uniformly indicate that the GARCH-M(1,1) model is the preferred specification.[19] The likelihood ratio test statistic for the GARCH-M(1,1) restriction is 2.16 which is not significant at any conventional level.[20,21]

The GARCH-M(1,1) maximum likelihood parameter estimates appear in table 2. The test restriction $\alpha_0 = 0$ produces an asymptotic t-statistic value of .0002. Because the restriction

Table 1. Model selection criterion, S&P 500 excess returns; January 1935 to September 1987

Conditional Variance Specification	GARCH-M(12,0)	GARCH-M(1,1)	GARCH-M(2,1)
Log Likelihood	1075.72	1081.72	1082.80
AIC Criterion	−3.35	−3.44	−3.40
Schwartz Criterion	1024.13	1062.38	1057.01

Note: GARCH-M(P,Q): P is the number of ARCH lags, Q the number of lagged variance terms.

Table 2. GARCH (1,1) in MEAN estimation results, S&P 500 excess returns: January 1935 to September 1987

	Mean	Variance
Constant	---	.0141
$\{v\}$		(2.399)
Market Price		
of Conditional	4.163	
Variance Risk	(4.678)	
$\{\gamma\}$		
ARCH (1)		.346
$\{\zeta_1\}$		(8.465)
GARCH(1)		.910
$\{\xi_1\}$		(49.667)
Lagged Level		−.00000039
S&P 500		(.709)
$\{\beta_1\}$		
Margins		−.000051
$\{\beta_2\}$		(.260)

Note: Asymptotic *t*-statistics are in parentheses.

is consistent with the data for any reasonable critical value of the test, table 2 reports the model estimates imposing the equilibrium restriction $\alpha_0 = 0$.

The GARCH-M(1,1) model estimates show that there is no statistically significant relationship between conditional excess return volatility and the level of initial margin requirements.[22] Although the coefficient for the lagged level of the S&P 500 has a sign consistent with leverage effects, it is not significantly different from zero. The results are consistent with the findings of Schwert (1988) and do not show the existence of strong leverage effects as found by Christie (1982).

The GARCH-M(1,1) estimates show strong evidence that the conditional variance function is integrated; that is, that the time series is not covariance stationary. The condition for a covariance stationary process is that the ζ_i and ξ_i coefficients sum to less than unity.[23] Hong (1987) has shown that standard asymptotic results for maximum likelihood estimates hold in the presence of integration in the variance function, and so a *z*-test that the sum of the these coefficients is different from unity is asymptotically normally distributed.[24] The sample test statistic for integration has a value of 8.4608. The model estimates show strong evidence of long-term memory in S&P 500 conditional return variances. The evidence of long-term memory in stock return volatility is consistent with the findings of Chou (1987) and is counter to evidence presented by Poterba and Summers (1986).

The market price per unit of variance risk, γ, has an estimated value of 4.16. Its estimated value is consistent with the work of Pindyck (1988) who finds an aggregate measure of relative risk aversion of 3.4 (with a standard error estimate of 1), and Chou (1987) who estimates this parameter at 4.5.

Figure 1 contains plots of the GARCH-M(1,1) conditional standard deviation estimates,

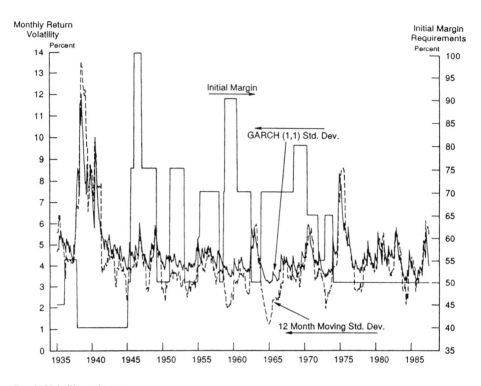

Fig. 1. Volatility estimates

the moving simple 12-month standard deviation estimates, and the level of the Federal Reserve Board's initial margin requirements. There are substantial differences in the alternative time series estimates. Table 3 reports summary statistical measures of the alternative volatility series. These results show that although the volatility estimates are highly correlated (correlation coefficient of .9), the 12-month moving standard deviation estimate of volatility is a substantially more volatile series. This series has a standard deviation about 20 percent larger than the GARCH-M(1,1) volatility series. A particularly interesting characteristic of the GARCH-M(1,1) series is that the conditional volatility estimates do not exhibit the intermittent periods of extremely low volatility that are characteristic of the moving standard deviation volatility time series. Because of the memory in the GARCH variance function, conditional volatility estimates are not sharply reduced by short periods of tranquility in the market. This characteristic is the primary visual difference in the volatility estimates. An examination of the plots in figure 1 suggests that the extremely low volatility estimates produced by the misspecified measure of volatility may be an important cause of the negative margin-volatility relationship estimated by Hardouvelis.

In a following section of this article we document the instability of the margin coefficient

Table 3. Alternative volatility estimates sample characteristics

	Average	Standard Deviation	Correlation
12-month moving sample standard deviation	4.29%	1.80%	.90
GARCH-M standard deviation estimate	4.69%	1.23%	.90

estimate in the Hardouvelis model. To anticipate these results partially, it is shown that the magnitude and statistical significance of the margin coefficient in the Hardouvelis model is extremely sensitive to the sample estimation period. Table 4 reports estimation results that indicate that the GARCH-M(1,1) model estimates are not sensitive to the specific sample period selected for estimation.

Table 4 reports the GARCH-M(1,1) model parameter estimates over an alternative sample period, January 1929 to December 1987. This sample includes two periods of extreme market volatility, the October 1929 crash and the 1987 market break. For this estimation, initial margins were assumed to be 0 before November 1934. This assumption is not correct because industry members voluntarily set non-zero initial margins before federal margin regulation. However, this extreme assumption is sufficient for the sensitivity analysis. Because of the extreme volatility in the pre-1934 period, if there is a relationship between initial margins and return volatility, the initial margin measurement error should result in a stronger estimated negative margin-volatility relationship.

The GARCH-M(1,1) model estimates from the alternative sample suggest that the parameter estimates are stable over alternative sample time periods. Expanding the sample to include two episodes of extreme return volatility has little effect on the parameter estimates of the GARCH-M model. The margin coefficient estimate remains insignificant in the expanded sample. The estimates of the variance parameters are little changed in the expanded sample. The stability of the GARCH-M(1,1) model parameter estimates is in sharp contrast to the extreme parameter instability which is characteristic of the Hardouvelis model.

4. Further evidence on the (lack of a) margin-volatility relationship

The introduction of index futures market trading has implications for the hypothesized margin-volatility relationship. Because of the lower initial margins in this market and the strong arbitrage links to the cash market, the introduction of index futures should increase volatility in the cash market.[25] We analyze the impact of the introduction of index futures trading in 1982 using comparative estimates of the Hardouvelis model over different sample periods.

Table 4. GARCH (1,1) in Mean estimation results, alternative sample,
S&P 500 excess returns: January 1929 to December 1987

	Mean	Variance
Constant	---	.0156
$\{\nu_0\}$		(3.662)
Market Price		
of Conditional	4.037	
Variance Risk	(7.411)	
$\{\gamma\}$		
ARCH(1)		.351
$\{\zeta_1\}$		(10.565)
GARCH(1)		.907
$\{\xi_1\}$		(57.126)
Lagged Level		−.00000044
S&P 500		(−1.518)
$\{\beta_1\}$		
Margins		−.000107
$\{\beta_2\}$		(.673)
Log Likelihood		1110.477

Note: Asymptotic *t*-statistics are in parentheses.

Because the initial margins on index futures are effectively much lower than equity initial margins (at current price levels, roughly 15 percent versus 50 percent), if a negative relationship existed between initial margins and volatility, then volatility should be much larger after the introduction of index futures, other things being equal. Because cash market initial margin requirements were historically low during this period (50 percent), the hypothesized increase in volatility that would accompany the introduction of index futures would cause the estimated margin effect to be a larger negative number.

Table 5 contains parameter estimates of the Hardouvelis model for alternative sample periods. The sensitivity of the model's estimates with respect to sample period are both striking and informative. By excluding both the pre-1934 and the post-1981 data from the estimation period, the size of the initial margin effect is reduced to a third of the value estimated and reported in Hardouvelis.[26] Extending this sample to include data after futures index trading but, excluding the October 1987 break (January 1935 to August 1987), does not materially change the estimated margin effect. The latter result is strong evidence against the hypothesized negative margin-volatility. In fact, the lack of change in the margin coefficient in this comparison is strong evidence that no relationship exists between initial margin requirements and volatility in modern financial markets.[27]

The final results shown in table 5 indicate that the period of the 1930s has a significant influence on the magnitude of the Hardouvelis model margin coefficient estimate. Dropping this highly volatile period (January 1935 to December 1939) reduces the magnitude of the margin coefficient estimate to about a sixth of its orginally reported value.

Table 5. Excess return volatility and initial margin requirements: Sensitivity of Hardouvelis results to sample period*

Sample Period	Intercept	σ_{t-12}	$\bar{P}_t$	IND	BND	Average Margin
			S&P 500 Stocks			
12/31-	.094	−.040	−.021	1.024	.331	−.060**
12/87	(.020)	(.146)	(.010)	(.258)	(.200)	(.021)
1/35-	.054	.111	−.012	.841	.295	−.023
12/81	(.017)	(.126)	(.008)	(.213)	(.183)	(.017)
1/35-	.055	.098	−.011	.812	.230	−.026
8/87	(.017)	(.122)	(.008)	(.207)	(.173)	(.017)
1/40-	.049	.154	−.014	.531	.315	−.010
12/81	(.012)	(.098)	(.006)	(.161)	(.113)	(.011)

*Newey-West (1987) consistent standard errors estimates in parentheses.
**Significantly different from zero at the 5 percent level of the test.
Definitions:
σ_t is the measure of volatility used by Hardouvelis. It is a 12-month rolling sample standard deviation calculated using the current and past 11 months of data.
σ_{t-12} is the standard deviation measure of volatility lagged 12 months.
P_t is the S&P 500 price relative variable. It is constructed by calculating a 12-month moving average of the S&P 500 level and normalizing by a five-year (monthly frequency) moving average calculated over the five years preceding the numerator time period.
IND is the sample standard deviation of the industrial production index calculated over the current and 11 preceding months.
BND is the sample standard deviation of the returns on a corporate bond index calculated over the current and 11 prior months.
Average margin is the average of the required initial margin requirements over the current and previous 11 months.

5. Short sales

If the level of initial margin requirements affects the trading activity of so-called "destabilizing speculators," then these effects should be manifest in trading volume data. Total volume data include the activity of all traders, "destabilizing" or otherwise. Many of these traders are not subject to initial margin requirements[28] and many trades are cash transactions. The aggregation of all trading activity may mask or distort any relationship that exists between initial margin requirements and "destabilizing volume." Customer odd-lot short-sale volume data are largely void of these problems. Although these trades are not exclusively those of destabilizing agents, they all are subject to initial margin requirements. NYSE customer odd-lot short-sales volume is available on a monthly frequency beginning in October 1939.

Table 6 reports the results of the short-sales-margin estimations. The natural logarithm of short sales was regressed on a constant, its own lagged value, initial margin requirements, and the level of the S&P 500 relative to trend ($\bar{P}_t$).[29] The model was estimated for the entire sample period, a subsample truncated at the introduction of index futures (November 1939 to December 1981), and a subsample truncated at the introduction of exchange traded

Table 6. Customer odd-lot short-sales volume

Sample Period	Intercept	Lagged Short Sales	Margin	$\bar{P}_t$	R^2
Nov. 1939-Dec. 1987	1.484 (.293)	.856 (.025)	.169 (.144)	−1.255 (5.34)	.74
Nov. 1939-Dec. 1981	1.495 (.322)	.857 (.023)	.262 (.143)	−6.036 (5.625)	.77
Nov. 1939-Dec. 1972	1.513 (.293)	.853 (.025)	.155 (.143)	−.645 (5.316)	.73

Note: Short-sales volume is measured in natural logarithms. Newey-West consistent standard error estimates appear in parentheses.

options (November 1939 to December 1972).[30] The results do not support the hypothesis that initial required margin levels affect trading activity. Not only are required margin levels statistically insignificant but the coefficient sign is opposite that predicted by the hypothesis that high margins reduce speculative trading activity.

6. Conclusions

The results of this article strongly support the hypothesis that initial margin requirements have no effect on the volatility of stock market returns. If destabilizing traders create excess volatility, there is no evidence to suggest that initial margin regulation can be used to limit their destabilizing effects.

Tangential results of interest arise from the estimates of the GARCH in Mean model. The estimates of the variance function are consistent with the hypothesis of long-term memory in the conditional return variance of the market. The estimate of the market coefficient of relative risk aversion from the Merton intertemporal capital asset pricing model is 4.1. Contrary to Christie, we do not find strong evidence of financial leverage sources of market return volatility.

Notes

1. *Interim Report of the Working Group on Financial Markets,* May 1988, p. 5. (Washington, D.C., U.S. Government Printing Office). For an excellent discussion of margin regulations, margin adequacy, and consistency see, Mark Warshawsky, "The Adequacy and Consistency of Margin Requirements: The Cash, Futures, and Options Segments of the Equity Markets." Capital Markets discussion paper, Federal Reserve Board, 1989.

2. For a more complete description of these noise traders and their equilibrium effects, see DeLong, Schleifer, Summers, and Waldman (1987).

3. The pyramiding and depyramiding of destabilizing speculators would produce a positive correlation between total margin credit and the level of stock prices.

4. See Largay and West (1973, p. 329).

5. Under Rule 431 of the NYSE and Rule 462 of the AMEX the exchanges may impose special initial margin requirements in excess of the Federal Reserve Board's Regulation T margins. The objective of these exchange-imposed margins is to curb potentially speculative trading in individual issues. For a further discussion see Largay (1973, p. 975).

6. Generalized Autoregressive Conditional Heteroskedasticity.

7. For example, stock returns are known to exhibit leptokurtosis and memory in the variance of their conditional return distribution. See, for example, Fama (1965), Blattberg and Gonedes (1974), Bollerslev, Engle, and Wooldridge (1988), or Chou (1987).

8. Exact definitions of the explanatory variables and a replication of Hardouvelis's results appears in table 4 of this article. In Hardouvelis (1988b), the analysis is expanded to include an alternative approach to measuring volatility. This alternative uses the absolute value of a regression standard error as a measure of volatility. The results from this analysis are virtually identical to those obtained from the moving standard deviation model.

9. Although this period (January 1935 to December 1939) may be influential in determining the significance of the margin-volatility relationship, this fact alone is not a sufficient reason to exclude these data from the sample. The model proposed by Hardouvelis includes macroeconomic sources of risk which may partially explain some of this excess volatility. If these macroeconomic variables adequately explain the excess volatility of this period, then this period should be included in the estimation sample. Whether these macroeconomic variables are adequate is the subject of much debate. Schwert (1988) investigates these issues.

10. For example, the works of Brewer (1973), Tiao (1972), and Working (1960) analyze the bias induced by temporal aggregation of time series. For an excellent discussion of these issues, see Diebold (1988, section 3.2).

11. In fact, the bias considerations discussed earlier apply. Including the entire 1930s and the post-index futures data in the estimation sample will, if anything, cause the margin coefficient estimate to be a larger negative number.

12. See Bollerslev (1986) or Engle and Bollerslev (1986) for a discussion of these issues.

13. The model is consistent with the restricted form of the Intertemporal Capital Asset Pricing Model. This approach is taken in Merton (1980).

14. Measures of real-side volatility derived from the industrial production index were not statistically significant or important factors in the model. Consistent with the Merton model, margin requirements were not significant exogenous explanatory factors in the conditional mean specification.

15. Hardouvelis finds that there is a statistically significant relationship between the level of the market and required initial margins. Historically, Hardouvelis finds that, on average, the Federal Reserve Board has increased margins when the S&P index was high relative to its trend value and conversely.

16. An additional specification, GARCH-M(2,2), was also investigated. After extensive computation time and initial parameter value searches, the GARCH-M(2,2) was unable to improve upon the likelihood values of the GARCH-M(2,1). Consequently, this model is excluded from consideration.

17. The estimating results reported in this article are from the Berndt, Hall, and Hausman (1974) algorithm iterated until convergence using numerical first-order derivatives of the likelihood function. Special thanks to Ken Kroner for making available his software.

18. The Hardouvelis model's restrictions significantly reduce the log likelihood values from the GARCH-M(12,0) model reported in table 1.

19. Model selection under the AIC criterion involves selecting the model with the smallest AIC measure. Under the Schwartz criterion, the preferred model exhibits the largest Schwartz information measure.

20. This statistic is asymptotically distributed χ^2 with 1 degree of freedom. The 5 percent critical value is 3.841.

21. The selection of the GARCH-M(1,1) specification for stock returns is consistent with the findings of Chou (1987) and Bollerslev, Engle, and Wooldridge (1988).

22. Although the parameter estimates for the other models are not included, the margin coefficient estimates in these models were not significantly different from zero.

23. If the coefficients sum is one or larger, the conditional variance is stationary but without finite moments. See Nelson (1988).

24. The standard error of the sum of the ζ_i and ξ_i coefficients is computed from the last iteration's estimate of the information matrix. Although the Hong result has been frequently cited (e.g., Bollerslev, September 1988), it is controversial and apparently not universally accepted.

25. Margin requirements on index futures are set by the futures exchanges. The Commodities Futures Trading Commission must approve major changes in margin systems, but it does not set margins otherwise. In futures,

initial margin takes the form of a performance bond, or a fixed minimum cash amount that depends on the type of trader initiating the trade. On a percentage of contract value basis, initial margin requirements have been set at much lower levels in the index futures market than in the corresponding cash market. For a discussion see Warshawsky (1989).

26. See Hardouvelis (1988a, table 4, p. 86). These estimates are reproduced in table 3, sample period of December 1931 to December 1987.

27. If a positive relationship between margins and volatility existed, as suggested by Ferris and Chance (1988), then including post-index futures data into the sample should have increased the estimated margin coefficient.

28. For example, specialists, market-makers and arbitragers.

29. The short-sale series is stationary in logarithms. $\tilde{P}_t$ is the measure of S&P 500 level relative to trend used in Hardouvelis. It is defined formally in table 3.

30. A fourth subsample excluding the 1987 October break period was also used. The margin coefficient results were almost identical to those for the total sample.

References

Berndt, E., Hall, B., Hall, R. and Hausman, J. "Estimation Inference in Nonlinear Structural Models." *Annals of Economic and Social Measurement* 4 (1974).

Blattberg, R. and Gonedes, N. "A Comparison of Stable and Student Distributions as Statistical Models for Stock Prices." *Journal of Business* 47 (1974).

Bollerslev, T. P. "Generalized Autoregressive Conditional Heteroscedasticity." *Journal of Econometrics* (1986).

Bollerslev, T. P. "Integrated Arch and Cointegration in Variance." Northwestern University Department of Financing Working Paper, September 1988.

Bollerslev, T. P., Engle, R. and Wooldridge, J. "A Capital Asset Pricing Model with Time Varying Covariances." *Journal of Political Economy* (1988).

Brewer, K. R. "Some Consequences of Temporal Aggregation and Systematic Sampling for ARIMA and ARMAX Models." *Journal of Econometrics* 1 (1973).

Chou, R. Y. "Volatility Persistence and Stock Valuations: Some Empirical Evidence Using GARCH." UCSD mimeo, December 1987.

Christie, A. "The Stochastic Behavior of Common Stock Variances: Value Leverage and Interest Rate Effects." *Journal of Financial Economics* (December 1982).

DeLong, B., Shleifer, A., Summers, L. and Waldman, R. "The Economic Consequences of Noise Traders." NBER Working Paper 2395, October 1987.

Diebold, F. X. *Empirical Modeling of Exchange Rate Dynamics.* New York: Springer-Verlag, 1988.

Eckardt, W. and Rogoff, D. "100% Margins Revisited." *The Journal of Finance* (June 1976).

Engle, R., and Bollerslev, T. "Modeling the Persistence of Conditional Variances." *Econometric Reviews* 5(1, 1986), 1–50.

Engle, R., Lilien, D. and Robins, R. "Estimating Time Varying Risk Premia in the Term Structure: The ARCH-M Model." *Econometrica* (1987).

Fama, E. "The Behavior of Stock Market Prices." *Journal of Business* 38 (1965).

Ferris, S. and Chance, D. "Margin Requirements and Stock Market Volatility." *Economic Letters* 28 (1988).

Goldberg, M. A. "The Relevance of Margin Regulations." *Journal of Money, Credit, and Banking* 17 (4, November 1985).

Hardouvelis, Gikas. "Margin Requirements and Stock Market Volatility." *FRBNY Quarterly Review* (Summer 1988a).

——————. "Margin Requirements, Volatility, and the Transitory Component of Stock Prices." First Boston Working Paper Series, FB 88-38, November 1988b.

Hartzmark, M. "The Effects of Changing Margin Levels on Futures Markets Activity, the Composition of Traders in the Market, and Price Performance." *Journal of Business* 59 (1986).

Hong, C.H. "The IGARCH Model: The Process, Estimation and Some Monte Carlo Experiments." UCSD discussion paper 87-32, 1987.

Largay, J. "100% Margins: Combating Speculation in Individual Security Issues." *Journal of Finance* (September 1973).

Largay, J. and West, R. "Margin Changes and Stock Price Behavior." *Journal of Political Economy* 81 (March 1973).

Merton, R., "An Intertemporal Capital Asset Pricing Model." *Econometrica* (1973).

————. "On Estimating the Expected Return on the Market." *Journal of Financial Economics* (1980).

Miller, M. "Debt and Taxes." *Journal of Finance* 32 (May 1977).

Moore, T. "Stock Market Margin Requirements." *The Journal of Political Economy* 74 (April 1966).

Nelson, D. "Stationarity and Persistence in the GARCH (1,1) Model." University of Chicago GSB Working Paper, 1988.

Newey, W. and West, K. "A Simple, Positive Semi-Definite, Heteroskedasticity and Autocorrelation Consistent Covariance Matrix." *Econometrica* 55 (May 1987).

Officer, R. "The Variability of the Market Factor of the New York Stock Exchange." *Journal of Business* 46 (1973).

Pindyck, Robert. "Risk Aversion and Determinants of Stock Market Behavior." *The Review of Economics and Statistics* (May 1988).

Schwert, G. W. "Why Does Stock Market Volatility Change Over Time?" University of Rochester Working Paper, May 1988.

Tiao, G. C. "Asymptotic Behavior of Temporal Aggregates of Time Series." *Biometrica* 59 (1972).

Warshawsky, M. "The Adequacy and Consistency of Margin Requirements: The Cash, Futures, and Options Segments of the Equity Markets." Mimeo, Capital Markets Section, Board of Governors of the Federal Reserve System, 1989.

Weiss, A. "ARMA Models with ARCH Errors." *Journal of Time Series Analysis* (1984).

Working Group on Financial Markets. *Interim Report of the Working Group on Financial Markets.* Washington, D.C.: U.S. Government Printing Office, May 1988.

Working, H. "A Note on the Correlation of First Differences of Averages in a Random Chain." *Econometrica* 28 (1960).